INHUMAN RELATIONS

Quality Circles and Anti-Unionism in American Industry

LABOR AND SOCIAL CHANGE
a series edited by Paula Rayman and Carmen Sirianni

INHUMAN RELATIONS

Quality Circles and Anti-Unionism in American Industry

GUILLERMO J. GRENIER

 Temple University Press | Philadelphia

Temple University Press, Philadelphia 19122
Copyright © 1988 by Temple University. All rights reserved
Published 1988
Printed in the United States of America

The paper used in this publication meets the minimum
requirements of American National Standard for Information
Sciences—Permanence of Paper for Printed Library Materials,
ANSI Z39.48-1984

Library of Congress Cataloging-in-Publication Data
Grenier, Guillermo J.
    Inhuman relations.
    (Labor and social change)
    Bibliography: p.
    Includes index.
    1. Trade-unions—United States—Organizing—Case
studies.   2. Quality circles—United States—Case studies.
3. Quality of work life—United States—Case studies.
4. Industrial relations—United States—Case studies.
5. Industrial management—United States—Employee
participation—Case studies.   I. Title.   II. Series.
HD6490.072U645   1988   331.25   87-10116.
ISBN 0-87722-502-8

For my wife Stephanie
and my children Carlos and Alexandra

Many whips are inside men, who do not know how they got there, or indeed that they are there. In the movement from authority to manipulation, power shifts from the visible to the invisible, from the known to the anonymous. And with rising material standards, exploitation becomes less material and more psychological.
—C. WRIGHT MILLS, *White Collar*

The quality of work . . . is determined by, and in turn determines, the nature of society. Thus, for any society, if we understand the essential quality of its work, we will better understand the essential nature and purpose of its social organization; and if we understand the essential nature and purpose of its social organization we will better understand the essential quality of its work.
—RICHARD PFEFFER, *Working for Capitalism*

What men learn as they work for a living reaches far beyond their occupational interests: they learn a style of life, a manner of dealing with others, a habit of subordination or assertiveness.
—ROBERT E. LANE, *Political Ideology*

Acknowledgments

M any people have contributed, through criticism, ideas, and support, to the formulation of the arguments in these pages. I thank Tomas Atencio, of the Southwest Hispanic Research Institute, for serving as an untiring backboard for my ideas and for contributing more than anyone else to my understanding of the relationship between culture and the problems of work in the Southwest. I also thank Susan Tiano and George Huaco for encouraging me to develop the exploratory dimensions of this exploratory study. I also thank Bob Kern, Phil May, and Ray Hogler for reading and re-reading drafts and lending their trained eyes to the project. Richard Bensinger, the head organizer of the Ethicon campaign, opened the files of the campaign to me and tried hard not to interfere with my interpretations of a year of his life. Charlie McDonald, of the AFL-CIO Department of Organization and Field Service, contributed to my understanding of how quality circles can impede or contribute to the work of labor organizers in this country. The three anonymous readers contributed to making this a better work. Special thanks go to Louise Lamphere for helping me develop many of the ideas here presented and allowing me the opportunity to work with her to expand these ideas. My special thanks also to Farrel Brody, Diana Deo, Andy

Banks, Nelson Valdes, and David Bensman for encouraging me to think deeply and analytically about the problems of working people in this country.

I owe my deepest appreciation to the Labor Policy Institute of the AFL-CIO for providing funds for the completion of this work. Without this help, the book would have taken an eternity to complete. The Rutgers University Labor Education Center–Institute of Management and Labor Relations provided me the opportunity to teach and learn about quality circles from unionists in the New Jersey/New York area. For this, and for the use of their resource center to track down obscure sources, I thank Norm Eiger, the director of the LEC.

There are three people whose advice and encouragement have made this book possible. Michael Ames, editor-in-chief of Temple University Press has been a faithful reader and critic from the very beginning. Jennifer French, the tireless production editor, led me through the last painful portions of the process, doing everything a writer would want a complete stranger to do. And special thanks goes to Stephanie Loomis whose clarity of mind helped bridge the gaps in logic I was so fond of creating.

Finally, I would like to thank the workers of Ethicon-Albuquerque who shared with me their experiences and helped me understand them. I also thank the managers, personnel director, and team developer of Ethicon for also helping me understand. All individuals' names used in the book are fictitious.

Contents

Preface

Y ou are part of an elite movement. . . .

We are an important company. . . . We will hire active, interested employees. . . . We will provide an opportunity to make work interesting and for employees to grow. . . . We will have good pay and benefits, job security. . . . We will provide for the dignity of the individual.

Our workers can present themselves and receive fair and responsive treatment from this company without the need or intervention of a third party such as a union.

The above were some of the first statements to be read by employees at the Ethicon-Albuquerque plant upon their being hired. The words were designed, as was every management creation at Ethicon, to support the image of Ethicon as a nontraditional, innovative, new-design employer. The designers of the Ethicon work environment were trying to present a new vision of work in contemporary America, a vision of unity, cooperation, purpose, and inspiration, of managerial wisdom operating unfettered in an expanding union-free utopia.

In recent years, mass distribution of the managerial ideology expounding this "new humanism" has reached a climax. Such best sellers as *In Search of Excellence, The 100 Best Companies to Work for in America*, and *Theory Z* outline the key elements of a new American managerial consciousness supposedly characterized by a renewed respect for the worker, a new and needed commitment to quality, and a new-design philosophy for organizing the work environment. Convincingly, and with profitable results for themselves, consultants expound the virtues of new human relations techniques that will improve the attitudes and performance of workers and thus help the United States regain its industrial superiority.

Conflict between the interests of managers and workers is seen as an aberration in a new-design corporation, and so is the idea that workers shall organize into independent labor organizations to protect their interests. Conflict is a type of sickness that individuals bring into the work environment from outside, from their home lives or from union organizers. Conflict, in other words, is an individual's problem. It does not grow normally inside the organizational structures of an innovative organization; and when it does appear, as it always does, solutions are similarly focused on the problems of individuals. It is the individual that has to be treated, not the organization.

To a great degree, the new vision of work depends on the ability of managers to psychologize work-related problems and treat the worker as a patient. The critical issues of power and power sharing are ignored, trivialized, or glossed over as too conflictive and outmoded. The new-design solution for the future involves a simple and comprehensive idea: harmony between the interests of workers and managers. Indeed, only one interest exists—the efficient production of quality goods at a competitive cost. Once this is understood, any hostility between management and worker becomes superficial, a matter of human relations, not class conflict. This simple, seductive message is expounded by personnel directors and anti-union consultants everywhere. It is the dominant message shaping the way we look at work and what we expect from it.

For the guiding principles of the new humanism, managers have turned to the rigid, highly controlled, society of Japan. A growing literature describes what the Japanese can allegedly teach American managers about resource allocation, plant operations, and more importantly, human relations. The Japanese are viewed as leaders in modernization strategies, and top American executives are eagerly borrowing methods of control from Japanese society hoping for a pacification of the American work force, a characteristic of Japanese labor relations they perceive to be admirable. By following the lead of the Japanese we are, by all accounts, in the wake of a new managerial revolution; a revolution that attempts to combine managerial humanism with anti-unionism.

This book is about how the new humanized management "manages" power and how workers yield to it, not from lack of courage but from lack of choice. It is about how the new managerial humanism can disguise union busting and employee manipulation. It is about events that sometimes occur inside the modern corporation but are seldom reported. Far from being "new," the concepts of control, human relations, and anti-unionism are very old in American industry, and this book discusses how these concepts are being recycled.

In comparison with other current books on managers and their philosophies, this book goes beyond discussing the social environment of a firm as a purely economic variable to be manipulated by managers to increase profits and efficiency. It differs from other books in its concern with how people are affected in their daily work lives by this manipulation. It is about the control and manipulation of workers by company managers and consultants during a union campaign at one of America's most respected companies—Johnson & Johnson. It describes how new methods for controlling workers are veiled by the benevolent work-reform rhetoric of the new managers. It is about what management said to the public and what it did to the workers to bust their attempt to organize and how the rhetoric did not compare positively with the reality.

What is presented in this book is a case study, an exploratory one. The type of participative program described may not be the usual cornerstone of anti-union practices, but I present the argument that it was used in this fashion at Johnson & Johnson. I gathered the information during seven months of research at Ethicon-Albuquerque, a suture-making subsidiary of the Professional Products Division of Johnson & Johnson's family of companies. The case study was conducted between August 1982 and April 1983. During this time I was under the direct supervision of the social psychologist, who also served as internal consultant in charge of team development at Ethicon.

The team is the name given by Johnson & Johnson to the quality-circle technique of organizing workers by production operation and assigning them to small groups that discuss problems on a regular basis. The team concept was the primary method of organizing the work force at Ethicon. I became involved as graduate researcher working with the social psychologist, who was also the team developer. He instructed me, as he did the front line supervisors, in "the art of industrial manipulation," as he put it. In total, I attended thirteen team meetings during my research. Using a nondirective format, I interviewed four team facilitators (supervisors) and had contact with eight more, during their team meetings and on the production floor. I also interviewed the personnel director regarding the role of teams at the plant. These contacts supplemented my primary involvement as the unpaid graduate research assistant of the social psychologist.

My goal was to gather enough data on teams to write my graduate thesis. My ideas about the new managerial revolution, like those of most people, had been shaped by the media. I entered the project convinced that quality circles and their derivatives were essentially pro-worker techniques designed by managers out of a conviction that a happy worker is a better and more productive worker. In the case of Ethicon-Albuquerque, I certainly shared with the public a sense of anticipation and gratitude that such a forward-looking employer had settled in the area. Although during our first meeting the social psychologist mentioned that the team represented an employee organization that was an alternative to unionization, I was unaware of the union drive that had recently been initiated by the Amalgamated

Clothing and Textile Workers Union (ACTWU), a campaign that lasted from May 1982 until the election in May 1983, when the company won.

The ensuing mass of unfair labor practice charges (over fifty) issued by the National Labor Relations Board (NLRB) were not settled until February of 1984. At that time, the company settled out of court, paying back pay to four fired union supporters and a token allotment to workers found by the NLRB to have been discriminated against in hiring procedures because of pro-union sentiments. The agreed settlement was in a very real sense an agreement between the NLRB and the company. At least one worker had to be "convinced" by the NLRB that back pay was the best she could expect. The union never signed the agreement. The company paid nearly $50,000 and posted a "cease and desist" order from the NLRB, which ignores the issue of guilt. As far as our labor law is concerned, all has been forgotten.

During one November meeting, the social psychologist suggested that I investigate the role the team played in the anti-union campaign and said jokingly that this might open some doors to a lucrative career as a "union buster." From that point until February 1983, when the company's Phoenix-based legal consultant became concerned that my extensive notes might be subpoenaed at an expected NLRB hearing, I focused exclusively on the use of teams in an anti-union strategy. At the request of the lawyer, I then "officially" submitted to the company a proposal that requested permission to do research on small-group dynamics in an industrial setting. This, reported the social psychologist, would make me a less "credible" witness at the expected hearing. From that point on, information about Ethicon's anti-union strategy was made available to me, with the understanding that it would be a secondary focus of my research.

From the data I collected piece by piece, I reached the conclusion that there is nothing inherently pro-worker about the new-design work environment. Rather, work innovations first and foremost are intended to exert efficient control over the workers of a specific work site. This control is exerted not only over their behavior while on the job but also, when the design works well, over their attitudes about their work and how they feel about what they do all day and their inability to change it. How the new-design techniques are applied depends on which group has the power to exert control. At Ethicon-Albuquerque, as in all nonunionized industry, management controls. In this case, management controls in order to remain nonunion. To that end, the quality circle was used. It created the perpetual captive audience needed by management to socialize the work force into accepting the anti-union message. This situation had repercussions at all levels of life at the plant during the campaign, and it was a form of terror for workers.[1]

Gathering information during the heat of the anti-union campaign made me question my role as researcher. I concluded that while research must be objective to be valid, it cannot be neutral when it uncovers orchestrated deceit and intentional manipulation of human beings. I did not reach this conclusion easily, but when I did, I spoke out against the tactics of the company. This opened me and my family to considerable harassment, but the threats and surveillance we experienced were dwarfed in significance when compared with the daily sacrifices made by union activists at the plant. After speaking out against the activities of the company at a public forum in April 1983, I was barred from entering the plant. My picture hung like a "wanted" poster inside the guard post at the entrance to the plant. I continued to gather information on the anti-union campaign by interviewing union activists. In total, I interviewed twenty workers (all pro-union) about their experiences during the campaign.[2]

Not everything I observed during my research is included in this book, nor should it be. The focus is on the methods management used to control information and to control interaction, attitudes, and ultimately, the workers in its successful campaign to defeat a union and to create a well-controlled plant culture that would be impervious to unionism. The use of teams, human relations, and the general organization of work—which management tried to present as new and unique—are interpreted primarily as being highly sophisticated control mechanisms in the service of the anti-union campaign.

While claiming to dispell the conflictive relationship between management and workers, the new-design worker-participation program used by Ethicon in fact increased conflict, not only between management and worker but between workers. With calculated precision, the work force was divided and eventually conquered because management controlled formal and informal interactions at the workplace. Management defined the substance and the methods of workers' participation and by so doing controlled the information received by workers about the union and the company. Perhaps more importantly, management used its customary control over the hiring and firing processes to create a special work culture antipathetic to unionism; a work culture held together by fear of unionism.

Because of its emphasis, this book only briefly explores the prevalent and generally positive ideas coming from management schools concerning the new humanism in management. Similarly, it does not deal with the function of new human relations techniques in unionized environments, partly because of skepticism created by my experience but mainly because the subject of my observations and analysis was not a unionized company. Some of the union quality of work life literature is reviewed, and I acknowledge its contribution to the increased understanding of worker participation in America. My experience, however, cautions against accepting new human relations schemes at face value.

Based on my previous presentations of the events and ideas in this book (Grenier 1984, 1985), I anticipate a major question: If the company's tactics were so distasteful, why did I continue my work for seven months? Simply, I was committed to the very end to the subject of my research—the use of quality circles in an anti-union strategy. I had established a research design, and I followed it as closely as possible. Its qualitative nature required that I plan for a long project, which I did. There is nothing unusual about researchers' gathering data they find objectionable. What is unusual is for the researcher to step out of his role and attempt to exert an influence over the subject of his research. I did this only after much introspection and evaluation of what I consider the role of sociology and social planning in changing existing institutions and in translating analysis into socially relevant action. In contacting the union to report what I had learned, and in my willingness to talk to hostile workers about my knowledge, I broke away from the apathy often cloaked in scientific objectivity.[3] At least, that is how I see it.

INHUMAN RELATIONS

Quality Circles and Anti-Unionism in American Industry

1

Old Wine in New Bottles

It is difficult to find anyone associated with the labor or business community who does not know some of the basic history of quality circles. Started in Japan in the early 1960s by the Japanese Union of Scientists and Engineers, quality circles spread quickly throughout the nation's economy, signaling an end of one era and the beginning of another for industry. At the end of World War II, MacArthur's program of rebuilding Japanese industry introduced Dr. Edward W. Deming and the techniques of statistical quality control to the country. The obsession with quality control eventually reached enormous proportions, and throughout the 1950s, the development of a "science" of quality control dominated a large portion of Japan's national agenda.

Thanks to their government's incentives to industry and periodic educational campaigns designed to develop a consciousness of quality in the general population (November has been National Quality Month since 1960), Japanese industry laboriously crawled out from under the stigma of the Made-in-Japan label. This set the stage for the organized development of quality circles in 1962 and for a series of support structures, such as magazines and conferences, to promote the concept. Witnessing this concerted, massive effort at all levels of society, Joseph Juran, another consultant

3

involved in helping Japanese industry, stated in 1967: "Japan is engaged in an all-out effort to seize world leadership in quality by 1980." Few anticipated that these words would become prophetic (Dewar 1980; Dewar and Beardsley 1977; Ingle 1982a).

The spread of the quality circle (QC) in the United States did not occur overnight. In 1967 an article by Juran diffused information about the quality-control circle "phenomenon" occurring in Japan. Japanese leaders in the use of quality circles toured selected industries in the United States in 1968, and in 1973 a team of six Lockheed managers, among them Don Dewar, traveled to Japan to learn more. This resulted in the formation of the first quality circles at Lockheed in 1974. Industry in the United States remained sufficiently unimpressed by the Lockheed effort, so that by 1977 only five additional companies were users of quality circles, but after Don Dewar's formation in that same year of the International Association of Quality Circles, the popularity of QCs spread dynamically. In 1980, 230 companies were using quality circles, and a conservative estimate is that the figure increased twenty-one fold by 1981. Something made QCs attractive to a vast sector of American business.

The definition of a quality circle is simplicity itself: a small group of workers, usually led by a foreman, who "shares with management the responsibility for locating and solving problems of coordination and productivity" (Ouchi 1981: 223).[1] Ingle (1982a: 4) made a list of the key elements of quality circles:

1. It's a people building philosophy
2. It's voluntary
3. Everyone [in a group] participates
4. Members help others develop
5. Projects are circle efforts, not individual efforts
6. Training is provided to workers and management
7. Creativity is encouraged
8. Projects are related to members' work
9. Management has to be supportive
10. Quality and improvement consciousness develop
11. Reduction of the "we" and "they" mentality occurs

Given these general elements, QCs are found in a wide variety of industries under a similarly wide variety of names. General Electric's can-do teams, Honeywell's production-team program and participative-quality teams, and Johnson & Johnson's various applications of the team concept are all considered quality circles.[2] When unions arc involved in the development of quality circles, such as is the case with the General Electric teams, union participation is added to the list of elements. No one gives QCs much of a chance of succeeding in a unionized environment when organized labor does not participate. Most writers agree that labor participation in implementation of QCs is necessary not only for the technique's success in increasing productivity and democratizing the job, but also for the political survival of unions.

The assumption is that most workers, union as well as non-union, are attracted to the QC concept both intuitively and from the practical standpoint of making work more bearable, and unless labor encourages their development, it will find itself in the untenable position of opposing worker participation while management supports it. Even when management takes the initiative in developing the QC program, unions must take the lead in its development. One study pointed out (Wall Street Journal 1984) that if unions do not participate in the design and administration of the programs, not only will QCs not work, but management will benefit from the failure. The attempt to increase employee input into decision making will be associated with managerial prerogatives and will discourage employees from identifying with the union or its leadership. Glenn Watts, president of the Communication Workers of America, voiced the opinion of many union leaders: "The only real risk is if the union does not participate" (Burck 1981: 92).

Although quality circles and quality of work life (QWL) programs are still experimental, they now have attained the status of socially approved experiments. When a company expresses its "bias for action" in this socially approved way, it is certain to gain respect among employees as well as in the community at large.

This is especially true if it asserts that the intent of such action is to increase productivity and democratize the work environment. The proponents of the QC movement make just such an assertion.[3]

Claims that higher quality and quantity in production can be attributed to quality circles are legendary. Robert Cole stated to a Honeywell quality-circle conference (*Training/HRD* 1980: 94) that the primary purpose of QCs is to increase productivity and that any other benefits are peripheral.

Quality Circles do contribute to improved QWL but their primary purpose is to improve quality and productivity. The further the focus moves from there, the further you get from the technological base, the quality control tools that make them work. Hardnosed line people—managerial and labor—respond better to the technical core. They know how to make it fly. The QWL is a side effect, not a reason for being.

While the Japanese downplay productivity increases that result from QCs, executives in the United States embrace the QC technique as though it were the savior for sagging American production. Thomas J. Murrin, president of Westinghouse Electric's Public Systems Company, thinks the use of QCs is "the single most significant explanation for the truly outstanding quality of goods and services" produced in Japan (Zucker et al. 1982: 95). Dewar and Beardsley (1977), authors and consultants on QCs, boldly state in the foreword of their book: "Quality Circles can be the most effective tool with which to effect genuine productivity and work quality improvement in any industry, business, institution, or government agency in any culture or country." Such elan for QCs has appeared in the many reports of dollar savings attributed to increased efficiency motivated by QC programs (American Center for the Quality of Worklife 1981; American Productivity Center 1980, 1981, 1982). Lockheed, the first company in the United States to experiment with QCs, claimed that savings of over $3 million from 1974 to 1977 resulted from ideas for improvement suggested by QC members (Lynch 1981). The government reported savings of $215,000 with costs of $40,000 from using 44 circles at the Norfolk Shipyard (Bryant and Kearns 1981). Clyde H. Molde, an operations vice president at Honeywell, said his division attributed savings in excess of $1 million to the installation of quality circles. Monsanto claimed savings in the tens of thousands from 85 QCs in its 12 southern plants. Dan River Inc., in the same region, attributed an increase of 50 percent in quality to the implementation of QC programs. North Carolina State Offices identified ideas for improvements worth $151,000 in net savings in the first year after the implementation of 39 QCs. Tektronix claimed their adaptation of QCs accounted for 2,500 improvements and savings of $2.6 million, an average of $1,443 per idea in one fiscal year.

Hughes Aircraft reported saving $6 for every dollar spent in developing the QC program. They even reported (Courtright 1981) that some circles returned $200 for every dollar!—impressive figures by any standard. Less spectacular is the general assumption among managers that QCs result in cost savings from $2.00 to $8.00 for each dollar invested. In addition to such accolades, various activities also attest to the enthusiasm for QCs. Westinghouse Electrical Corporation, for example, has over 2,000 quality circles in operation, and it runs a college that trains people from other corporations in how to organize QCs. Quality circles as productivity tools are also the topic of countless seminars held by major consultant firms (Productivity Inc., for example) and the subject for how-to articles in a variety of publications (*Small Business* 1980; Hutchins 1983; *Employee Gazette* 1983).

In this thicket of praise, however, words to the wise have been heard. The idea of QCs as a quick fix for productivity problems has been contradicted by cautious consultants. Don Dewar (1979) said that companies thinking about implementing QC programs must make a long-term commitment to the technique and realize that start-up costs are not cheap (at least $50,000 for materials development alone) and that paybacks are not always forthcoming. Similarly, Robert Cole (*Training/HRD* 1980: 94) warned management that measuring return on investment from QCs can be a red herring: "The Japanese don't even try. Anybody can make a pilot study look successful for six months or a year." Cole did not mean to discourage QC implementation; he meant to discourage management from trying to measure productivity gains resulting directly from it. The point was well taken.

Short-term productivity increases can be achieved easily, but unless some long-term measurements are used, any productivity increase attributed to QC implementation needs to be examined critically. (This was a lesson learned in the Hawthorne experiments; see Chapters 3 and 8.) The longitudinal data to support success claims are hard to come by. In fact, very few American or Japanese data have demonstrated the effectiveness of QCs as productivity tools. Evaluating the literature on QCs, Wood, Hull, and Azumi (1983: 50) found that "there has not been a single published study on the effects of QCs in U.S. industry in which data were collected before and after the QC intervention and comparisons made with a control group." They said that "such an evaluation is obviously needed," and they suggested that success stories as evidence of QC benefits need to be treated with skepticism because the storytellers are either plant managers who are responsible for the programs or consultants selling programs.

Views even differ on how extensively and effectively QCs have been used in Japan. Most consultants have claimed that use is pervasive and includes millions of workers and that QCs are responsible for the high quality of Japanese exports (Dewar 1980; Hoyt 1984); but contrary evidence exists. Ellenberger (1982) reported that only 12.5 percent of the Japanese labor force was involved, even peripherally, in QCs. Robert Cole (1981) admitted that "the circles do not work very well in Japanese companies." He said, "Even in those plants recognized as having the best operating programs, management knows that perhaps only one-third of the circles are working well."

Similarly, Robert Hayes (1981), writing in the *Harvard Business Review* during the initial boom of QCs in this country, was surprised to find on his business visit to Japan that the famed quality circles did not appear as influential as he expected.

Most of the plants I visited, in fact, had experienced problems with QCs for three or four years after their introduction. Moreover, most of the companies I talked to already had enviable reputations for high quality products by the time they adopted QCs. One company treated Quality Circles as secondary, peripheral activities. Another had eliminated them altogether. . . . But the Quality levels at the plant were just as high as at others where QCs were active (1981: 58).[4]

When a quality circle program fails to produce the expected results, it dies quietly. Failures are seldom reported, although they occur frequently. As reported in *Management Review* (1982), Goodfellow studied QCs in twenty-nine companies and found only eight successes among them, as measured by savings-to-cost ratio. The failures reported a savings-to-cost ratio of less than one. Woodruff Imberman, a management consultant, investigated the other twenty-one companies in this sample and found four major causes for QC failure:[*]

1. Employee dislike of management. Many employees saw the QC as another management ploy to reduce overtime and cut the workforce by increasing productivity.
2. Employers did not "sell" the QC concept to their employees. The use of flip charts, booklets, and formal presentations left the workers wondering what benefit the program would have for them.
3. Group leaders did not apply human relation skills effectively in their circles.
4. Most companies regarded the QC as merely a way of improving productivity without having to change managerial hierarchical structures.

The production benefits of introducing quality circles into the organizational structure of a company, then, are debatable. If claims of higher efficiency and productivity are true, QCs are unquestionably worthwhile investments for the cost-conscious entrepreneur. Still, their high start-up costs along with the lack of longitudinal studies make implementation a gamble, especially for small firms. The gamble would be worth taking if other benefits accrued.

The second most commonly mentioned benefit of QCs is that a more humane working environment is created through the increase in worker participation in shop-floor decision making. The resulting democratization of the work environment, which supposedly radiates advantages into all folds of the organization, has been the rallying cry of many personnel administrators in the age of managerial humanism. Just how effective are QCs in actually democratizing the work environment? According to the ideal model for participation presented in most program descriptions, satisfaction is supposed to increase because workers' ideas will presumably be heard, evaluated, and if found worthy, implemented. In addition, with their knowledge of the production process, workers will help management overcome problems that get in the way of greater efficiency. Rather than opposing management, the QC worker will be working with management toward common goals. The conflict between laborer and manager will thus be erased, and in its place we will have participation, cooperation, democracy.

Empirical research on QCs and democratization is almost totally lacking. The few studies that do exist have been conducted either in unionized plants (Kochan et al. 1984) or by research departments in nonunionized companies.[5] It appears that once again the business community is guilty of idealizing the Japanese experience with QCs. Even Robert Cole asserted that QCs in Japan very often have a coercive aspect, with control from the top down continuing to dominate the small-group environment. They are viewed as direct control mechanisms intended to improve the efficiency of the worker as a producer. However harsh this might appear, it is a much more realistic and truthful approach than evidenced in current American industry.

Employee reactions to QC implementations certainly convey a feeling of democracy in action. A Hughes circle participant stated (Courtright 1981: 34): "Several positive circle results include the opportunity to voice my gripes concerning work problems, the chance to be heard on solving problems, more awareness of other problems within my group, and the application of quality circle techniques in finding solutions to problems in my private life." Reactions from Union Carbide (*Productivity Digest* 1982a) included that of one employee who said, "Being a member has been an inspiration to me." Another succinctly expressed the spirit of the ideal QC concept from the perspective of management: "We have learned a new appreciation of management by our being able to participate."

The ease with which this attitude develops makes managers wax lyrical on the people-building philosophy of QCs. Said the Monsanto quality coordinator at the Decatur, Alabama, facility (Lloyd 1982): "I love to see people develop, and I've seen people who have gone from being shy and who would jump if you said 'boo!' to being assertive people."

Although Robert Cole (1979a, 1981) said quality circles are developed not for "people-building" but for increased productivity, some managers have disagreed about the primary reason QCs are implemented (Lloyd 1982): "We hope for quality and cost improvements along the way, too, but the main thing is people building. . . . We already have a good esprit de corps developing. . . . It's a team spirit." By developing this new spirit workers learn to respect management's responsibilities, thereby reducing their resistance to the commands of management, and managers, in turn, get a glimpse of what makes employees tick. Discovering that workers actually know a great deal about the production process sometimes takes managers by surprise. Bill Van Horn, a productivity manager for Honeywell, considered his involvement with quality circles a "profound life experience" (Soyka 1981: 66):

When you sit down with these hourly people and really listen, you realize that they're as smart as you are and have as good ideas as you do. That can scare you at first. But when you get over that and learn to trust what the hourly people are contributing, you're free to do what you were hired to do—manage.

If all this talk of people-building sounds mechanical and impersonal, as if workers were being treated like the machines they operate, it is because part of the QC concept is to "work" on the personality of an employee until it conforms to the requirements of the plant culture. Many of the democratic concepts associated with freedom do not extend into private industry. In private industry, the company defines freedom within the design of its work culture. At Ethicon-Albuquerque, for example, the documented ideals of the Ethicon philosophy outlined the parameters of freedom. Certain behavior and attitudes were accepted; others, notably pro-union sentiments, were ostracized, termed "deviant," and labeled as needing a change. So a worker is "built" through the QC program. Characteristics that do not contribute to the production process must be controlled, if not eliminated.

Allowing participation in limited decision making is a way of keeping workers apprised of the requirements of the job and keeping management apprised of what decisions workers are making. The QC is the ideal structure for controlling decision making while management's power to implement decisions is maintained. As March and Simon (1958: 54) observed, participative management "can be viewed as a device for permitting management to participate more fully in the making of decisions as well as a means for expanding the influence of lower echelons in the organization." People-building is thus seen as being synonymous with developing a cooperative team spirit such that workers are in tune with managerial priorities. Quality circles can then be used as an effective and safe (pseudo)democratizing agent for involving employees in the managerial decision-making process without fear of disruptive conflict. Before participation is allowed, homogeneity of attitudes must be developed.

In situations where workers feel that QCs do not address their problems, the most they can do is become uncooperative and cause the circle to fail, that is, to prevent it from fulfilling management's objectives. This, of course, gives management the opportunity to say, "We tried, but they just didn't cooperate"; and this, in turn, reinforces the opinion, often thought to reign supreme in management circles, that workers prefer an authoritarian rule at the workplace.

Studies debunked this idea a long time ago. The assumption that workers want a more democratic workplace and that QCs are a way of achieving it is based on the commonsense proposition that alienation is reduced by increased control over the immediate environment (Shepard 1971). Unionism is arguably as efficient a way for workers to attain this control (Lipset et al. 1962), yet no enthusiastic attempt has been made by managers to introduce unionism into the workplace. The real issue is one of managerial power and control.

Quality circles are promoted heavily by management consultants and implemented almost unilaterally by managers. This allows management to maintain control over both the work force and a larger portion of total plant operations simply by creating the impression that a democratic workplace can exist without unionization. If the most important functions of managers are to plan, organize, direct, coordinate, and control the labor process (Miner 1975), then the function of a union, as a formal organization, is to demand a say in this process. Quality circles that are initiated, implemented, and controlled by management, demand nothing that management is unwilling to give to the worker.

Freeman and Medoff (1984), in the most complete study ever published on the role and effects of unions in American society, signaled the overriding importance of managerial behavior as a cause in the declining success of unions' organizing efforts. In firms attempting to avoid unionization they identified techniques that use (1) a positive human relations approach, (2) lengthy legal battles, and (3) illegal firings. From the supporting data for their argument, it is clear that we know the least about the first strategy. How do positive human relations techniques help management avoid unionization? By detailing the role of one human relations technique, the quality circle, in a corporate anti-union strategy, we may arrive at a clearer understanding of the strategy of human relations vis-à-vis anti-unionism—what the social psychologist at Ethicon called "the battle of the '80s."

Before the anti-union strategy of the company is detailed, several points need to be made regarding the general nature of union busting and its specific use in the new design participative organization, which relies on more than a positive human relations approach to avert the threat of unionism. Consultants who specialize in directing the legal and illegal behavior of a firm very often utilize the new-design environment to implement their well-honed anti-union strategies. The National Organizing Committee of the AFL-CIO (American Federation of Labor and Congress of Industrial Organizations) publishes an annual list of firms or individuals known to have assisted businesses in either busting or avoiding unions. The 1984 list contained over 600 names of lawyers, legal firms, and human behavior specialists. The National Organizing Committee of the AFL-CIO estimates that three-fourths of all anti-union campaigns waged in the United States are led by these consultants.

Companies that hire labor-management consultants are over three times as likely to avoid unionization as companies that do not (Lawler 1981; Allied Industrial Workers 1981). The techniques used by these consultants were disclosed in a U.S. House of Representatives subcommittee investigation (AFL-CIO 1983). They are tailor-made for the small-group environment of the quality circle. The congressional panel found that "the frontline supervisor is probably the most important aspect of the consultant-led campaign" (AFL-CIO 1983: 3–4).

In day-to-day contact with employees, the supervisor pushes the campaign while ferreting out employee sentiments to relay to top management and the personnel department. Under the guiding hand of the consultant, the supervisor controls workplace communications, spreading management's message while keeping employees from hearing the union's side. Behind the scenes, the consultants manipulate the campaign through delays and discharges to keep workers from exercising their rights through representation elections or collective bargaining agreements, despite the fact that the federal law encourages these processes.

Using short lecture types of workshops, many consultants emphasize the need to control the work force at various levels. Dr. Charles Hughes is one of the top union busters in the country and billed as "an alumnus of two of the most successful nonunion companies," IBM and Texas Instruments. He has run workshops on "How to Handle the Chronic Complainer" and "Shaping Employee Thinking," in order to "assure that your employees have positive attitudes toward the company" (Bailey 1984). This strategy, sometimes called the happy worker program, socializes employees by giving them "symbolic input" and by using an open-door policy. One of the often stated goals of this approach is to enable the employer to do what he wants to do while convincing employees that it was their input that influenced management's decision (Bernstein 1980).

Industrial psychologists, like the one involved with quality circles at Ethicon, frequently develop employee attitude surveys to determine a worker's likelihood of joining a union. The employer can use this information to develop strategies that minimize organizing potential among workers. According to the Washington-based social scientist Steven Lagerfeld (1981b: 18), a manual developed by West Coast Industrial Relations Association "cautions management on the necessity of properly indoctrinating" the worker. "It is important to shape their attitudes," say the consultants.

Another favorite tactic of the anti-union consultant is to produce statements and letters that come from the employer and are designed to convince employees that it is not in their best interest to join a union. These stress the evils of unionism and often link unions to left-wing activity or corruption and describe organizers as "outsiders." The standard letter to employees describes the company as "one big happy family" with no need for "outsider interference." Workers are often told that union membership may pose a threat to their benefits. Ethicon's management was fond of reading such letters aloud at QC meetings, emphasizing that "everything is negotiable if the union gets in."

Even in approaching companies of the traditional type, many consultants favor meetings led by a supervisor where anti-union information is passed on. The bombardment with anti-union sentiments often frightens and intimidates workers (Bailey 1984). When weekly meetings are institutionalized in the form of quality circles, the mechanism for potential intimidation awaits the consultant. One study shows that as management's face-to-face communications with employees about a union increase, the chances of the union winning the election decrease. When only written communications are used by management, unions win about 85 percent of the elections; when both written communications and workers' meetings are used, unions win only 39 percent of the elections (Curtin 1970).

Consultants encourage management to isolate union members to make them look like "deviants." The internal consultant at Ethicon (trained as a social psychologist) emphasized the importance of labeling pro-union people as "losers" and anti-union people as "winners" by depriving the former group of status-enhancing opportunities. Management established a system of rewards and punishments, creating what Lagerfeld (1981b), in another context, referred to as "routinized anxiety" designed to convince workers that union membership would lead to insecurity, endangered job security, hostility by supervisors, and possible loss of jobs.

Analysts of how participation can be used as a form of control assert that there are three interrelated methods. These should also be kept in mind in considering the case-study data that follow. First, workers can be co-opted, that is, made to see the work environment from the perspective of management (a point of view expressed by the Union Carbide worker quoted earlier who felt a renewed empathy for management thanks to the quality circle experience). Secondly, management can limit worker participation to the most meaningless aspects of plant operations. Thirdly, management can employ a variety of "intimidation rituals" (Moch and Huff 1984) to get workers in a participative environment to submit to managerial interpretations of the problems of work. Intimidation tactics are particularly effective when abusive or dominating language is used during the face-to-face interaction made possible in the small-group environment. The ultimate goal of those searching to control by using participation depends on maintaining the distinction between implementing decisions and decision making.

Certain characteristics of quality circles make them an extremely attractive form of worker control and union busting. These characteristics should also be kept in mind in approaching the Ethicon case.

Personal Involvement: QCs are attractive control mechanisms because of their apparent humanizing effect on the bureaucratized work environment. In a sense, they help to de-bureaucratize the cold and impersonal work environment by getting people personally involved with each other and with the process of production. Rules and regulations become less formal; they are not directly associated with management, and they appear to be more the workers' responsibilities. This de-bureaucratization of control was the cornerstone of the new-design plant at Ethicon.

Peer Pressure: In the de-bureaucratized environment at Ethicon, peer pressure was institutionalized as the dominant control mechanism. Under the guise of participation, workers were told that they would have increased responsibilities over the hiring, disciplining, and firing of fellow workers. Although this responsibility was largely illusory, it was an effective means of making most workers feel some degree of supervisory responsibility over their peers. Management, as if by magic, became more democratic, more innovative, more responsive to workers because workers were given more responsibility in enforcing the rules. With such a strategy, the identity of those who actually make the rules is forgotten or obscured.

Work Force Fragmentation: QCs fragment the labor force, and this results in three related phenomena. First, employees get a satisfying sense of belonging to a group, something that might be impossible on the shop floor. Second is the flip side of belonging to a small group: workers are prevented from feeling a sense of community with other workers in the plant. The segmentation into small groups engenders an us-them view of work relations among the employees themselves, and this detracts from the already difficult task of recognizing that the common interests of workers are distinct from the interests of managers. Thirdly, the small group allows management the opportunity to monitor employee behavior more closely and obtain conformity to organizational norms (Ouchi 1977). This is especially the case if the authoritarian structure of the firm is transposed on the QC structure; that is, if a supervisor, representing management, directs and controls the meeting. Because what is normal is defined to a great degree by the team leader, controlling the leadership of the team helps management define deviance and identify deviants. An Ethicon employee reported to me, "They made us understand that they were keeping an eye on us. It is easier to keep an eye on 10 people than 200 people."

Individualized Confrontation: The QC creates an arena for confrontation between an individual worker and seemingly individual managers. It diffuses the power of the collective workers by presenting problem solving and conflict resolution as tasks for individuals to perform.

Humanized Power: While the work force is fragmented, the power structure remains intact. The supervisor is still the supervisor; the powers he (and sometimes she) wields have not changed, only his methods of communication. Rather than communicating with workers through bureaucratic procedures such as memos and postings, he now wields a humanized power. By exposing himself as a "human being" through frequent, seemingly informal interactions in the QC, revealing the same ups and downs and the same problems to solve as all human beings have, and drawing from the same choices of solutions to those problems, the supervisor deftly becomes "one of the workers," embedded in the same organizational structure as his subordinates. Drawing the lines of commonality along the human level rather than the class level, the QC gives authority a human face. Workers and managers are ostensibly part of the same family, working toward the same goals, worshiping, in effect, the same god of higher productivity and two-car garages. This was the message encouraged at Ethicon during seemingly informal QC interactions made possible by the proximity of the small-group environment. Such personalized authority figures wield power previously known only at the higher levels of the organization, where bureaucratization often yields to the influence of the personality cult (Wright 1979).

Managerial Language: The QC is a perfect conduit for using the power of language and managerial knowledge to influence workers, many of whom are put at a disadvantage when dealing with areas of knowledge usually considered the property of management. William Wipinsinger states (1984 personal conversation with author). "Workers often have a 'leave it to the experts' attitude when it comes to many issues of management. This puts them at a disadvantage when talking with managers 'equally' about problems." The quality-control manager of General Electric's Columbia, Tennessee plant puts it plainly: "This is the first time that we managers have had to train the workers to speak management's language." It is this issue of whose language is spoken that very often places workers at a disadvantage in QCs.[6]

Elitism: The QC structure of the social relations of production at Ethicon allowed management to design equally sophisticated screening procedures for newly hired people in an attempt to exclude those who might prefer another type of employee organization, such as a union. By presenting the QC as the most innovative approach to an employee organization and QC participants as members of an elite group of workers, such traditional approaches to work relations as unions were rejected as ineffective and undesirable.

Susceptibility to Strategies: Ethicon designed three strategies to fight the union—the traditional approach, the proactive approach, and the individual-conflict approach. Each utilized the QC as the primary structure for identification of union sympathizers and implementation of the anti-union strategy. The small-group environment also magnified the tensions of the union campaign. In response to the conflict that was engendered around the union issue at QC meetings, only the strongest individuals managed to express themselves. Management controlled such conflict as part of the proactive strategy, effectively silencing the work force.

The QC was utilized as the main forum for the identification of pro- and anti-union sentiments. Based on interactions at QC meetings, facilitators charted their "people" on a union rating scale that identified pro-union people and helped management gauge union strength and design company strategy. Facilitators were trained in subtle ways of controlling the attitudes of QC members regarding unions. The social psychologist attempted to develop in the facilitators the "art of industrial manipulation."

While some analysts refer to QCs and other structures related to quality of work life (QWL) as "antidotes to Taylorism" (Simmons and Mares 1983), this study shows otherwise. Taylorism was much more than a mere engineering phenomenon concerned with time and motion measures of efficiency. In a broader and more significant sociohistorical context, Taylorism presented to the captains of industry the first cogent argument for effectively controlling the work force by careful study of the social dynamics of production. It is no overstatement to assert that the questions posed by Taylorism made possible the famous Hawthorne studies, arguably the first controlled use of QCs in American industry (see Chapter 3). Combining small-group dynamics with controlled participation greatly increases the power of the powerful and the disorganization of disorganized (and unorganized) workers.

In relation to Ouchi's work (1981), which relies heavily on the use of quality circles, Robbins (1983: 67) succinctly addresses the issue of control in the new-design organization: "The attractiveness of the Theory Z organization is not due to any inherent improvement it offers in organizational effectiveness. Top management will be attracted to the Theory Z concept because it increases their control while giving the impression of lessening it."

The evidence that QCs might be an effective tool in the antiunion arsenal of consultants and corporate designers is, on the face of it, compelling. The Council on Union-Free Environment of the National Association of Manufacturers acknowledges this by publishing a pamphlet detailing how to use quality circles in staving off unionization (Parker and Hansen 1983; Parker 1985).

Academics and union leaders have expressed concern that the boom in work innovations, participation programs for employees, QWL programs, and QCs represents a new wave of management initiated anti-union control mechanisms. Union organizers tell war stories about employers who implement QC programs overnight after hearing rumblings of an approaching organizing drive or who use QCs to stave off signing a contract after the union has won. Many unionists see the QC as yet another strategy of management for effecting the withdrawal of worker support from labor organizations (Parker 1985), and some have gone on the record as opposing QCs in unionized as well as nonunionized plants.[7] Some workers have written accounts of their own or other workers' experiences in QCs, and theirs is the voice of opposition (Parker 1985; Hansen 1981; Glaberman 1981).

But the opposition is weak. The U.S. Chamber of Commerce conducted a major survey of industrial plants and found that most workers would be more excited about work and would produce more if they had a voice in decision making. They recommended that more companies implement quality circles to give workers that "feeling" of participation. Good feelings, after all, go a long way in making work more tolerable in any society.

As is made clearer in Chapter 8, the QC and most other innovative human relations techniques can be understood only by looking at the social dynamics in the larger sphere of unionism and anti-unionism during particular periods in industrial history. A company's "bias for action" (Peters and Waterman 1983) and for innovation in workplace organization must be seen as a reflection of the broader social values that accompany contemporary political dynamics.

To human relations experts, one basic conflict in managerial thought is whether to treat the worker as an individual or as a member of a group (Scott 1962). The social environment of an epoch often helps determine which view dominates. The use of small groups of workers as an organizational control technique offers managers the best of both worlds. A worker can be made to feel unique while management maintains tight control over group processes. For this reason, the study of small-group dynamics under the general headings of human relations and worker-participation programs has a long tradition in American industry, and it is often related to periods in history when avoiding unions played an important part in the business of managing. Today, perhaps more than ever, workers are being encouraged to view themselves in the same boat as managers, a sinking boat, frequently portrayed as being union made. As a method of creating commonality of purpose and derision for unionism, the use of the small group is resurging as management's preferred method of worker control.

2

The Company, the Work

The first shift at Ethicon-Albuquerque begins at 6:30 A.M.—earlier than the fall and winter sun rises over the Sandia Mountains east of the city. It is dark when the more than 100 workers on the first shift fold out of their cars in the large communal parking lot in front of the plant. "We all park in the same lot, management and workers," one worker told an interviewer. After giving this example, she proudly concluded, "We are all equals here."

It usually takes Judy an hour and a half to get herself and her six-year-old daughter ready for the day. She is one of the many single parents who work at Ethicon, a group that represents approximately 52 percent of the predominantly female work force. This might suggest that what goes on at Ethicon is somewhat special, and the plant is indeed unique in many ways. But the work, including Judy's work, is anything but unique. It is machine work, similar to the other manufacturing work in the employment landscape of the Southwest. Smokestack-free, new, clean, low-paying nonunion industry has been drawn by state and city incentives to areas rich in unskilled labor and poor in knowledge about the manufacturing process. Judy, however, doesn't care why Ethicon is there. She just needs the paycheck.

23

At the entrance of the plant, she passes the guard post. If the guard is new and doesn't recognize her by sight, she flashes her identity card. She does the same thing when she works the night shift, a change in schedule she does not like to make at the required two-week intervals. In the dressing room, she changes from her street clothes to the whites that identify her as a production worker at Ethicon. Management people and supervisors wear white lab coats over their street clothes, but Judy and her co-workers strip off all their street identity to put on the Ethicon uniform. If she decides to go out to eat lunch at a nearby fast food place rather than eat at the machine-stocked cafeteria down the hall, the uniform comes off, the street clothes go on, and the ritual is repeated again before she resumes her production duties after lunch.

She scrubs and dons her white cap in the co-ed washroom before entering, through an electric-eye door, the "clean-room" environment of the production floor. Near her work station is a computer where workers line up to clock in. Aida, one of the other fourteen workers on Judy's team, is at the front of the line, so Judy asks her to clock her in. She calls out her I.D. number, and her friend does her the favor. Anyone who knows this number has access to Judy's file. She heads straight for her machine and begins the laborious process of setting up the needles, the dyes, the suture materials. She checks again to make sure her hands are clean enough to handle the product. Her hat keeps her long hair out of the machine and the product. She is ready to work. Working at Ethicon is a clean business.

Except for the fifty minutes alloted for breaks, she will touch nothing for the next eight hours but her machines and the needles and suture materials necessary for manufacturing medical supplies for Johnson & Johnson, Ethicon's parent corporation. Her clothes, the only things that belong to her within the plant walls, are locked up beyond the electric-eye door. At her work on the machines, she has supervisors and "peers." Ethicon does not have employees—"We have peers," she remembers a manager telling her. She has her team and the goal of making her production quota for the next eight hours. As she controls her machines by means of foot pedals and hand motion, she is likewise controlled by the supervisor and by her peers, by rules and regulations, by meetings and consultations, and also by the machines. For these eight hours, her time belongs to someone else, her interactions are used for someone else's purposes. Even at team meetings, where the quality-circle concept has been designed to make her feel less alienated, more part of a family in this heart of the heartless work environment, she lives by someone else's agenda. At 3:30 P.M., when she's back in her car, in her own clothes, on her own time, she regains control until the next day. It's a grind and there's no way out.

Most workers who began working at Ethicon soon after it opened had seen the plant rising from the mesa at the south edge of Albuquerque and had investigated the employment picture almost immediately. Some heard from friends or employment agencies that it was a J&J plant and that hiring would start in December of 1981. The local CETA office (Comprehensive Employment and Training Act services) supplied most of the first cohort of workers, and Kelly Services was the official employer of trainees until individuals in the work force successfully completed the training sessions and were put on the Ethicon payroll. Judy is one of the workers who began at the beginning. She heard from a friend at CETA that Ethicon was hiring. She filled out an application and was eventually called to participate in "selection Saturday" at the local convention center. She remembers the tests of skills as being totally unrelated to production but very important to the social character of the plant.

All day on that Saturday in December she and fifty other applicants for fifteen production jobs took a series of tests designed to measure how well each of them could work with others in a small group. Consultants from the University of Southern California divided the participants into groups of about eight each. Each group was confronted with a problem and commanded to solve it. Judy's group was told to build a bridge out of sticks. Another group was given the scenario of being on a raft with certain objects, all of which had to be thrown overboard except one. They were asked which one they would keep to make the voyage successful. As the groups attacked the problems, the consultants observed with a quiet omnipotence, taking notes. The trick, said one worker looking back at those days when he didn't even know what a suture looked like, was to talk and be assertive.

It mattered less that the problem was solved than whether the group found a leader and was controlled by the leader's ideas. In this selection process, the consultants were looking for leaders and followers, looking for the most perfectly cohesive team with which to develop the plant's team concept. Applicants who heard the personnel manager's description of the team concept walked away impressed. The idea of the quality circle, a group of working peers who had control over vital decisions that governed the working lives of the members of the team, was an exciting, innovative idea unheard of in New Mexico.

The concept was likened to a sports team, where all participants worked together for a common goal and had a voice in how that goal would be reached. Coaches of the company team, the supervisors, would be there simply to facilitate communication between team members. As facilitators, their task would be, in effect, to make their jobs obsolete because workers would eventually have complete control over the operations of the teams. Workers, not management, would control the hiring and firing processes of the plant. Workers would have power, and the selection process through which applicants were led was management's way of selecting workers who would handle such power wisely. Judy remembers feeling apprehension at the thought of having to fire a fellow worker but prudently deciding to worry about that when the occasion arose.

On "selection Saturday" Judy concentrated on taking all the tests, filling out all the forms, answering all the questions. It was difficult to judge, but her performance did not seem very good. She was a reserved person by nature, and her contributions to the team exercises were minimal. Mostly she listened and agreed with what sounded like good suggestions. When decisions were made, she implemented them to the best of her ability in spite of the nervousness she felt at the consultant's judgmental stare. She did her best, but she walked away that day feeling sad because she thought she would not be hired by this new and exciting company.

Judy was hired for the second team to start work at the plant. After working in drill swaging for over a year, Judy has forgotten how strange the needle looked the first time she saw it. Drill swaging is a specialized process of attaching the needle to the suture. It requires a series of complicated and delicate steps. With a bundle of gut material on one side and needles on the other, in front of a machine that looks a great deal like a sewing machine, Judy attaches the gut material to the needle by means of the pressure supplied by the foot pedal. Sometimes she uses silk, other times nylon. The movements, the functioning of the machine, the elaborate setting-up process, which includes adjusting dyes and testing for the destruction level of the string, all are tediously repetitive.

Judy once considered transferring to channel swaging, another production department, but she decided it was not worth the retraining because the pay would remain the same and the channel swaging process was more difficult. It required three steps with the machine in place of the one-step pedal-pressure release of drill swaging. In channel swaging the needles are not pre-curved as they are in drill swaging, and the last step is to curve the needle. In both swaging procedures workers are expected to shift every one or two weeks from their swaging machines to the tables directly behind them, where the winding of the suturing material takes place. The winding involves working the suture material onto a cardboard-like casing in a figure-eight pattern, thus readying it for the quality inspectors and for shipment. Alternating between the two jobs makes each job less monotonous. The less monotonous a job is, the fewer mistakes are made, and quality is the most important consideration at Ethicon.

After a batch is produced and twenty sutures are tested randomly for defects, Judy takes the box to the quality-control person, a worker who uses a magnifying eyepiece and looks for defects and imperfections in the size, diameter, and length of the suture and in the size and construction of the needle. Usually, the defects are found in the swaging process because the needles themselves have already been inspected at other Ethicon plants. Yet, defects occur, and it is important to detect them. Drill-needle defects are considered more crucial. Minor defects in the stem of the channel needle are tolerated because the needle cuts the tissue as it enters. Drill needles, on the other hand, have the tapered point used for sewing up incisions, and defects on the drill needles could cause them to hang up on the skin and tear it, a problem no surgeon wants.

The quality-control person's job is very important. If a defect is found and cannot be corrected by a simple adjustment of the suture, the quality-control person returns the suture to the production worker who is responsible. She, in turn, "100 percents it," as they say, redoing the job she did before. This type of "rejection" can occur at the QC-team level or at the quality-assurance level, the next level of workers that inspect the suture. Each time a defect is found, the production worker is held responsible, and it is her job to correct the problem. Rejections are not taken lightly at Ethicon. Too many rejections make it impossible to meet the required production numbers for the day and also leave workers open to disciplinary action by team members and supervisors.

A simple reprimand can be followed by a full-fledged discussion of any problems a worker might have, personal or otherwise, that might be causing the poor production results. If production does not improve, the team, under the guidance of the facilitator, can vote to terminate a worker. This was what Judy had dreaded, and one time it occurred in a very messy fashion. The worker, a nice fellow by all accounts, simply could not pull his weight. The facilitator was under pressure to increase production in his team, and having this person around did not help matters. He discussed the issue with some team members before one of their meetings and suggested that the issue of the worker's poor production be brought up from the floor during the meeting.

As the team picked the man apart, Judy remained her usual quiet self. When asked directly for her opinion, she said they should give him another chance. She was in the minority. The team voted to terminate. He left a few days later, after upper management approved the team action, although he was allowed to quit rather than have the termination on his record. Judy said the team had just done its job, but since neither teams nor individuals received incentives when they produced more than their share, she thought dishing out punishment for low production didn't seem fair. By incentives she meant money. She didn't feel she was being paid enough to be a supervisor.

Like almost all other aspects of the plant culture at Ethicon, the way workers get raises is also considered "innovative." Sixty days after being hired, an employee receives a raise of $.20 per hour on top of the $4.20 base pay. This raise signals the successful completion of the probationary period, during which facilitator and team members have carefully monitored and evaluated the new employee's performance. In fact, each employee must undergo a formal evaluation process by the team members before the raise is approved. Questions to be answered are: Do your peers approve of the job you're doing? Are you making your quotas, and are you making them regularly? Do you fit in with the team members and the team system, meaning managers? To Judy the entire evaluation process boiled down to one question: Do we like you? If the team members didn't like you, they would try to torpedo your raise. If management didn't like you, they could torpedo you directly.

Except for the yearly salary increases in July, employees receive raises only by demonstrating an improvement in their personal performance or by mastering additional skills. When a worker feels she has mastered the production process, she petitions her facilitator to allow her to "demonstrate" to management that she deserves to make more money. For thirteen weeks after the start of her demonstration, she is required to maintain an average of 100 percent in her daily production quota, for example, in swaging and winding. (With a good day, above 100 percent is possible.) A successful demonstration increases a worker's paycheck by $.35 an hour. But there's a catch. After a successful "demonstration," the worker enters the pay-back period. During this time, she pays the company back for the time it took her to learn to produce at a 100 percent daily clip. If it took her a year before she could demonstrate, she pays back the company by averaging 100 percent in daily production for a year. In effect, she pays the company back for allowing her to perfect machinelike behavior.

Until a worker has paid the company back, she cannot move on to other skill blocks, such as quality assurance or another production area. It is by moving to other skill blocks that workers receive another $.20 raise. Positions are at a premium, however, and openings are rare. When they do occur, management often encourages selected employees to apply. Quality-assurance workers do not have the pressure of quotas, and they have more control over their time. The added responsibility gives status to the worker, and her opinion on quality issues is valued at team meetings. In fact, since quality-control employees are hand-picked by management, they are not thought of as other workers. At team meetings they seem to think and talk as if they had more in common with managers than with workers.

According to Judy, there isn't much about team meetings to like. Even before the union campaign came into the picture, many workers referred to the team system as the rat system, and she agrees. The meetings don't work the way she was told they would. If a worker is lucky, discussions during meetings will restrict themselves to work-related issues. Judy knows, however, that private matters have a way of becoming very much public at team meetings. This was the case even before the union issue became the dominant topic. One facilitator, no longer with the company, held two-hour meetings in which he apparently enjoyed picking away at people. If it wasn't one thing, it was another; something always managed to drive some poor soul into tears. Lately, ever since a social psychologist was hired to develop the team concept, things have been different—not better, but different. The union issue is the big thing, and it is always raised at team meetings.

Judy's facilitator has a degree in psychology, and Judy feels he enjoys messing around with team members' minds. After the social psychologist started working in the personnel department, the teams became more structured and less cohesive—but still a rat system. Managers seemed intent on creating little cliques, little factions of workers that fight each other over the union issue while managers and facilitators stand back and watch the fireworks. Judy knows how this works, but it still bothers her. Since she is known as a union activist, team meetings are not her favorite part of the week. She doesn't mind fighting management over the union issue, it's fighting her co-workers she can't stand. It's not hard to find workers that will fight management's battle if management makes it clear that it is in the workers' interest to do so.

When comparisons are made, Ethicon rates as one of the most attractive working environments in Albuquerque. It is clean, respected by the local business community, and important to a city that is trying hard to attract its share of the clean industries moving to the Southwest in search of higher profits. The city competes continually with Flagstaff, Phoenix, Tucson, and Austin to entice migrating industry. In the case of Ethicon, Johnson & Johnson had surveyed the Albuquerque area with an interest in establishing a plant there several years before the site was chosen. At that time the incentives offered by San Angelo won out. In 1979, however, thanks to the city's commitment to support an industrial development bond issue for $10 million and a government subsidy of $1.5 million in the form of an Urban Development Action Grant, Albuquerque was selected as the site of the Ethicon plant. It was one of five in the continental United States (one is in Canada) and two hundred in the worldwide network of J&J companies. Since the Albuquerque expansion, two other plants have been built by J&J—one in Singapore and one in Taiwan.

The employee benefits at Ethicon are unsurpassed in the Albuquerque area. Even the local university cannot match the excellent health insurance coverage and maternity care benefits. These are fringe benefits that appeal to the mostly female labor force. And the clean-room working conditions lend a dignity to the monotonous manufacturing process. Most of the workers who seek employment at Ethicon have a tradition of low-paying jobs, sometimes in sweatshop-like conditions, and this makes the work seem all that much better, in spite of its low wages.

People are willing to put up with a great deal for this type of work. They will defend it by attacking fellow workers and by justifying outrageous abuses of power by management. Besides, if sides are clearly drawn and you place yourself on the side of management, then work can be easy, even pleasant, during times of corporate crises. One male worker, a strong union activist, knew why the union had a rough time organizing at Ethicon. He knew why workers fluctuated, to the very end, between voting for or against the union. He knew why management was able to convince the workers that a vote for the union was a vote against the company and that the company, not the union, was the true friend of the workers. "Working at Ethicon," he said, "is the best and the worst you can imagine."

Ethicon is the world's largest producer of sutures and one of the oldest subsidiaries of J&J. It supplies the North American medical profession with a large share of all the sutures and ligatory clips on the market. Going into the 1980s, J&J had a strong position in the surgical instrument and supplies market as well as in hospital supplies, a position made possible by the strong tradition and commitment to the professional and pharmaceutical corporate sectors within the company.

Johnson & Johnson and its products enjoy a good reputation. Even its problems with product sabotage resulted in a negligable reduction in consumer confidence. A 1983 *Fortune Magazine* survey placed J&J as the third most respected company in the United States, behind only IBM and Hewlett-Packard, and in front of a pack led by Kodak. Significantly, it ranked number one in community and environmental responsibility (Makin 1983). The same survey in 1984 found J&J number five among all corporations and second only to Merck in the pharmaceutical field (even though pharmaceuticals contributed only 20 percent of total J&J sales). The 1985 *Fortune* survey showed J&J off the top-ten list for the first time in many years yet still ranking third in community responsibility.[1]

Few companies match the rags to riches story of J&J. From a

relatively humble beginning as the Band-Aid company in New Brunswick, New Jersey, it now operates 94 holdings in the United States and 106 in 46 foreign countries, employing over 79,000 workers worldwide. Browsing through their annual report is like an adventure in Third World industrial development. Their empire stretches from Singapore to Sao Paulo, Brazil, from Paris to Tokyo to New Zealand. For every plant location in the United States, J&J holds over 2 in foreign countries.[2]

The geographical distances of the empire are vast, as is expected in this day of multinationalism, and wage differences for production employees are diverse—less than $2.00 an hour for production workers in the Far East, a $5.30 average at Ethicon-Albuquerque, and a $9.75 average at the (unionized) Ethicon sister plant in Somerville, New Jersey. For every employee receiving union wages at the 24 unionized plants in the United States, over 7 employees work for local wages in less developed countries. Similarly, in the United States and Canada over 27,000 nonunion workers take home lower wages than their unionized counterparts, and this is justified by the company based on differences in local economic conditions.

All this by way of pointing out the obvious—as with all major corporations, J&J is constantly seeking ways to expand geographically as a means to expand financially, and J&J is nothing if not an expanding company. This is what gives it its competitive edge, according to the chief executive officer, who rose to the chairmanship in 1976 and launched the company on an aggressive expansion campaign with an emphasis on consumer products and biotechnology. Analysts wonder whether J&J can maintain the 13 percent average annual growth achieved during the 1970s and early 1980s. It is the expansion into high tech that concerns them the most. Without looking back at the advice of the corporation's founder, and perhaps ignoring it ("never acquire any business that you don't know how to run"), J&J ventured to diversify by the high-tech road; and, for once, the failures outnumbered the successes.

A venture into the sophisticated dialysis equipment business in 1978, for example, resulted in a $38 million write-off in 1983 because J&J could not modernize its production techniques. Other high-tech acquisitions also floundered in mismanagement and red ink. While J&J is involved in biotechnology in at least eleven small high-tech firms, the company's only clear winner in the high-tech scramble has been Eyelab Corp., makers of intra-ocular lenses. The chief executive officer said of the less than distinguished performance, "One of the things we insist on here is that everybody understands part of their job is to fail. You don't move forward unless you make mistakes" (Business Week, 1984:131). If this is the case, J&J has been perched for a great leap forward.

Johnson & Johnson is a very tightly run company. The tradition of a high degree of control over both internal matters and information that is made public comes directly from the founding father of the company, General Robert Wood Johnson still remembered respectfully as the General.[3] The General was well known for his obsession with corporate privacy, a trait that survived in his successors, if not with his pathological fervor, at least in spirit. Not until 1978 did J&J have an outside director, one who wasn't an employee. Such isolation is unheard of among major public corporations (Crawford 1982).

It is perhaps because of this laundering of information that J&J has enjoyed a clean reputation. In the field of labor relations it has an image of being relatively progressive. This image is bolstered by the partly selective and partly accurate portrayal of the General as a far-thinking individual, virtually alone among top executives in encouraging the development of unionism. In his book *Or Forfeit Freedom* (1947:206–7) the General states:

Since unions are here to stay, and since they can be made to function well, it behooves management to find ways of successfully working with them. The first step is to face things with realism, accepting the union for what it is as well as for what it can be. Since the union is an organized community of workers, management must be prepared to accept the political machinery of organization as well as policies, objectives, disciplines and procedures that will make the union effective. Management also must admit that labor leaders are bound to increase the prestige and power of their unions, since this will help them do their job and will reflect honor upon themselves. To accomplish this they must employ recruiting agents and "agitators"; men who will win new members or whoop up enthusiasm for the union, just as political campaigners whoop it up for their party.

. . . Management must make concessions to the political necessity for prestige by negotiating improvements and benefits with the leaders of unions instead of offering them directly to members. This procedure will cost management nothing, even if union leaders take more credit than is due them. It also will dignify union leadership, conferring both honor and responsibility where they should be found. Finally, it will relieve union leaders of the need to adopt indifference, skepticism, or hostility as means of self-preservation.

Evidence shows that the General's concern for the worker was genuine, if paternalistic. He advocated higher wages, shorter hours, and the recognition that workers have their minds as well as their labor to contribute to the corporation. The famous J&J corporate credo (Johnson 1947: 79–81) stated the humanistic ideals of the General as well as the ethical responsibilities of a multinational empire. The credo reflects the keen knowledge of a businessman who realized that America was shifting from a production-dominated society to a consumer-dominated society, that most consumers were also workers, and that if you take care of the consumer, business will take care of itself:

We believe that the First responsibility of business is to its customers: Products must always be good, and manufacturers must strive to make them better at lower prices.
Orders must be promptly and accurately filled.
Dealers must make fair profits in order that they may give good service.
The Second responsibility of business is to those who work with it; to the men and women in factories, stores, offices, as well as in service establishments and on farms:
They must have a sense of security in their jobs.
Wages must be fair and adequate.
Management just, hours short, and working conditions clean and orderly.
Workers should have an organized system for suggestions and complaints.

Foremen and department heads must be competent and fair-minded.
There must be opportunity for those who are qualified to advance as
workers and as people.
Each person must be considered an individual standing on his own
dignity and merit.
The Third responsibility of business is to its management: Our execu-
tives must be persons of talent, education, experience, and ability.
They must be persons of common sense, endowed with full and trained
understanding.
The Fourth responsibility is to owners and stockholders: Business must
make a sound profit, since, in order for it to continue
Reserves must be created,
Research must be carried on,
Adventurous programs developed, and
Mistakes made and paid for.
Bad times must also be provided for;
High taxes paid,
New machines purchased,
New factories built,
New products launched, and
New sales plans developed.

The credo symbolizes all that is good about the multinational
corporation that is J&J. The company and all its subsidiaries find
refuge under the credo's umbrella of enlightenment, benevolence, and respectability. "Fortune 500" surveys aside, and in
light of the present study, we can at least question how well this
reputation is deserved. A curious, subtle, and vehement anti-
unionism seems to be rising as a trend to be explored at J&J. Its
new acquisitions in the high-tech area are without exception
nonunionized. This is a characteristic of the high-tech industry
in general. For a corporation that needs to regain market superiority by increasing surplus value, nonunionism in new acquisitions might easily, if mistakenly, be viewed as a necessity.

But perhaps most important is the fact that in the last twenty
years, whenever J&J has fought an organizing effort, it has
fought it strenuously, and it has won. No J&J enterprise has been
organized in that time span without the "consent" of corporate

strategists.[4] During a 1977 campaign against an organizing effort by the Amalgamated Clothing and Textile Workers Union (ACTWU) at a New Jersey dental product plant, for example, J&J hired a firm of labor consultants from Atlanta, Georgia, to design and conduct the strategy. Employees were bombarded with anti-union information as only a consultant-led campaign can bombard.

Four captive-audience speeches were given by management, two during the last two weeks of the campaign. Four "personal" letters were sent to employees' homes, and at work, anti-union literature was passed out daily during the last three weeks of the campaign. To add that personal touch, personnel-department officers spoke with each individual worker. The dominant themes during these communications were predictable and effective. Employees were threatened with a loss of benefits if the union came in. The scheduled July raise would take place only if the union did not win. If the union did win, any contract gains would have to wait until after the bargaining process, and that might take up to two years.

To add just enough coercion to get the workers' attention, the police were summoned to disperse union supporters who had gathered to distribute leaflets and discuss the campaign on the company's parking lot. These are hardly the actions of a benevolent employer, and the National Labor Relations Board agreed. After reviewing the objections filed by the union, the federal agency invalidated the election, which the union lost, because of threats made by the employer to withdraw benefits and a scheduled salary increase.

During this New Jersey campaign, ACTWU officials wrote letters to J&J officers at various levels of the organization. A letter from the manager of the New Jersey Joint Board went to the chief executive officer himself asking him to intervene in the "broad anti-union action" against ACTWU being waged by management. Another letter, with basically the same message, went to the vice president for labor relations. The company responded that they did not believe unionization was in the best interest of the dental product company or its employees; that after reviewing company campaign literature, they found nothing that warranted retraction; that this did not mean they were anti-union.

In spite of its behavior, J&J continues to paint itself as a company that does not have an anti-union philosophy. In a letter to the director of organizing at ACTWU in 1981, the vice president for labor relations worldwide wrote: "I do not believe I have to defend Johnson & Johnson's record of dealing with organized labor. That record demonstrates that J&J takes its obligations to its employees and to bargaining in good faith in respect of matters affecting those employees very seriously."

The quality-circle technique was introduced into the J&J family of companies in 1979 at the Corporeal Inc. plant in Tampa, Florida, through a pilot project designed in a quality-improvement program. Success figures, as briefly reported in the annual report, followed the standard criteria for QC evaluation and indicated increased employee involvement in plant operations, improved ideas for the production process, and ultimate savings measured in dollars and time. All pointed to a successful trial run for the QC innovation.[5]

In spite of the measurable success of the QC program, J&J put Corporeal on the block in 1983, writing off a $38 million loss. Employees, who had responded superbly to the call for higher productivity and quality, were left wondering what had happened. Changing market conditions and failure to modernize, forces that could not be altered by using a team system to reorganize the labor process, were blamed for the failure.

The corporate interest in teams did not fade. Following the national trend, many unionized plants worked together with J&J to develop some sort of worker-management teams. It was at two nonunionized plants, however, that the most extensive J&J team programs were developed—McNeil–Round Rock Consumer Products and Ethicon-Albuquerque. Both represented the new breed of J&J plants. The Texas plant had a new-design participative system, and managerial structures were condensed, as J&J corporate structure had been for years, to allow more direct control of the production process by upper managers and more access to upper management for production workers. By the second year of operation, the plant was producing at the rate of the long-established plant at Fort Washington, Pennsylvania (*World Wide* 1982).

The Texas project resulted in such impressive increases in production and worker satisfaction that a detailed booklet on the design and implementation of the participative team approach was developed by management in 1981 (McNeil Consumer Products Company 1981: 1–2):

McNeil–Round Rock presents many special design features that distinguish it from "traditional" companies. These design features include the following:

The use of a "team" approach in the production process, whereby the plant's various production functions (processing, packaging, quality assurance, and warehousing) are organized into flexible work groups that function as teams sharing with, and supporting, each other in the completion of the teams' operational responsibilities.

The implementation of a participative management philosophy, ensuring that employees have a voice in matters such as job assignment, job design and evaluations, scheduling work and breaks, and other organizational policies and procedures that affect the employees' lives in the company.

The design of broad, challenging, and "enriched" jobs, where employees have the opportunity to learn and use many different skills, and where teams have responsibility for completing one whole phase of the operation.

The development of a skill-based compensation system that rewards employees for acquiring, retaining, and demonstrating mastery in the different skills necessary for effective plant operation, rather than rewarding employees for job assignment and seniority exclusively.

A relatively "flat" organizational structure, with few managerial levels existing between the plant manager and the production workers. Innovative employee selection procedures, which emphasize the participation of all managerial echelons in the selection of production employees, and which familiarize potential employees with the nature of the jobs and the managerial philosophy used at McNeil–Round Rock.

A heavy emphasis on training and development among employees at all levels of the organizational hierarchy.

The use of many "sensing" mechanisms (such as quarterly employee attitude surveys and plant-wide meetings, organizational health meetings, and open-door policy for all managerial personnel, a direct line that permits employee access to all managers, etc.) that help keep management in touch with the pulse of the organization.

An evolutionary managerial style that enables the development of structures and policies as necessary rather than a managerial style that imposes many structures and policies from the time of plant start-up.

The Round Rock experiment was a direct antecedent of, and served as a blueprint for, the Ethicon-Albuquerque experiment. As McNeil–Round Rock was starting operations in 1979, the Ethicon plant was being designed, and the team system was inserted into Ethicon's organizational structure. All the new-design features so thoughtfully recorded by the Round Rock managers were duplicated at the Ethicon facility. A special feature at Round Rock, "selection weekend," screened candidates for production jobs that were necessary for the plant's start-up by measuring their technical and interpersonal skills. This feature resurfaced at Ethicon-Albuquerque over three years later in the form of "selection Saturday." After reading the Round Rock report about the elaborate screening processes that were set up, it was difficult to discern a difference between the two organizations.

To ensure the success of the participative approach at Round Rock, managers emphasized the importance of screening for "misfits"—applicants who would not fit into the new-design structure of the plant. Admitting that their screen was not bugproof, management nevertheless reported that once misfits were identified inside the plant they were on the whole "counseled/reassigned satisfactorily" (McNeil Consumer Products Company 1981: 33). Unlike the Ethicon plant, however, Round Rock has not been threatened by a union-organizing campaign. The test of the team system as a union-avoidance tool was reserved for Ethicon-Albuquerque.

3

Team Work

In August 1982 my supervisor at the Health Systems Agency suggested that I contact a woman who was the director of New Mexico Employee Assistance (NMEA), a private firm that handled the employee assistance program (EAP) for various plants in the Albuquerque area. We were in the process of designing an agency project related to the ways private industry in our area was handling health planning, given the shrinking programs and resources. The approach at NMEA seemed innovative; employees' rights to a safe and healthy environment were linked with the cost concerns of employers. The director of NMEA gave me a brief description of the functions of employee assistance in local industry and praised a local firm for its progressive "experiment" with employee programs. The firm that she could not say enough about was Ethicon.

Referrals from Ethicon to her organization were based on productivity measures. It was by measuring production that management judged whether an employee was suffering from some physical, behavioral, or mental difficulty. This meant that if workers' productivity did not suffer, they were considered "healthy" and not in need of EAP services. When a disturbed employee was identified, the person was given the option of going to EAP for as many as five free sessions with the appropriate specialist. Employees who refused to go for assistance were expected to improve their performance without the intervention of a third party. The EAP director was understandably interested in the Ethicon experiment. She explained that the team concept, a quality-circle approach to organizing the work force, facilitated the identification of employees with problems.

She also suggested that I contact the plant's Chicano social psychologist, who was in charge of the teams. His credentials, including his Ph.D., had impressed her, as had his commitment to the team's progressive approach to workplace organization. Although corporate headquarters frequently sent in consultants to help in the development of the teams, the social psychologist was the internal consultant in charge of the process. The employee assistance function was performed in-house at the Ethicon sister plant in Somerville, New Jersey, and the director of EAP felt that the team system at Ethicon had encouraged the strategy of contracting out with a local agency. The employee assistance director from the sister plant had visited the Albuquerque site frequently to make sure all was working according to plan.

The reputation the plant had for being progressive was fostered by management's apparent concern for employees. The director of NMEA said there was talk of starting a single-parent group in the plant and also a child-care cooperative, which would be a great asset to the work force because about 74 percent were female and approximately 46 percent of the females were working mothers. For this area of the country, the plant was clearly in a league by itself.

While teaching at the Valencia County campus of the University of New Mexico, I would pass the plant several times a week in the summer of 1982. It had gone up almost imperceptibly at the edge of the poorest section of town, up on a hill next to the university golf course. It had opened in December 1981, and during the time of my involvement it employed approximately 288 workers, around 220 of whom worked on the assembly line, in maintenance, or in shipping and receiving. (Tables 1 and 2 show

TABLE 1
Gender and Ethnicity of 221 Production Employees

		Hispanic		Non-Hispanic		Total (Workers)
Gender	No.	(Row %/ Col. %)	No.	(Row %/ Col. %)	No.	(Row %/ Col. %)
Male	24	(52/ 17)	22	(48/ 29)	46	(100/ 21)
Female	119	(68/ 83)	55	(32/ 71)	174	(100/ 79)
Total	143	(65/100)	77	(35/100)	220	(100/100)

the characteristics of the labor force.) The turnover was less than 5 percent a year. Estimates varied, but plant sources reported the ultimate projected size of the work force to be around 600. Politicians involved in locating the plant in New Mexico said the company projected a maximum employment figure of between 1,000 and 1,200 within five years. Two shifts were already operating, and a third planned.

The team system was the organizational foundation of the plant, and the job of the social psychologist was to develop it to its "full potential" as an alternative to other forms of manage-

TABLE 2
Salary-Range Distribution of 288 Employees

Salary Range	No. of Employees	Job Category
Under $10,000	104	Production
$11,000–$15,000	131	Production maintenance support staff
$16,000–$20,000	15	Secretaries, mid management
$21,000–$25,000	26	Mid management
$26,000–$30,000	3	Mid management
Over $30,000	9	Upper management
Total	288	

ment-employee organizations, such as unions. Very few places were utilizing the concept of the quality circle as fully as Ethicon, and what was happening was being watched closely by the area's work force, by J&J top brass, and by other manufacturing industries. The social psychologist saw the team as a quality-control mechanism for helping workers develop the "same criteria as surgeons" when producing sutures. The high quality requirement for the product almost demanded that some sort of quality circle format be used.

One day as we toured the production area outside the glass encircling the production room, he related company plans for making the plant a showcase in the community, for inviting hospital administrators to tour the facility, and for identifying and using local talent for contract work, such as technical writing and research. Albuquerque seemed lucky to have landed such a progressive firm.

I looked through the glass. The facilitators, or frontline supervisors, wore white lab coats and white billed caps. So did the area supervisors, whose jobs were one level above facilitator. The workers kept their hair covered also and dressed in white pants and shirts—no sweaty brows or callused hands. The machines were clean and almost silent, at least through the glass. It was all very antiseptic and professional.

Essentially the plant was designed as a shell, with enclosures restricting free access only between the production floor and the remainder of the plant. The production room, especially, gave me a feeling of emptiness at first glance because there were no separating walls—only the machines at which workers wrapped, pressed, wound, or otherwise manipulated the materials necessary to produce sutures and ligatory clips. The heart of the production process took place in this large, clean-air environment, where five of the seven production procedures were handled.

Each department had its own area within the production room and was in charge of a specific aspect of the production process. Each individual had her own work station and brought materials to it on trays from a nearby area.

The machines were close enough to allow limited interaction

among the workers, but because great concentration was required for the maneuvering of needles and devices among high-powered presses, little interaction actually took place. Each department was broken down into subareas, and each area was supervised by the department supervisor. For example, swaging, or attaching the needle to the suture material, was subdivided into areas A and B. Each area comprised a team, and the supervisors were the team leaders. Supervisors had desks on the production floor next to their areas. In the social organization of the plant, the company implemented a new-design philosophy of managerial control. The philosophy, set out in an employee handout, claimed to "maintain flexibility," "to keep communications open," and to "be flexible to change."

The team approach was part of the participative management method, and the Ethicon experiment was considered an example of a highly participative management style because it offered several methods of communication between employees and management: (1) the suggestion box, for immediate problems to which management tried to respond immediately; (2) the open-door policy, which allowed for direct communication of more long-term and difficult problems to the plant manager, who formulated an answer and posted it for everyone to read; (3) the open line, which dealt with long-term problems that were communicated in written form; and (4) various committees for including hourly workers in policy development, such as the compensation committee. The purpose of the design was clearly stated in the company philosophy document: "Our workers can present themselves and receive fair and responsive treatment from this company without the need or intervention of a third party such as a union."

The two basic types of teams at the plant were production teams and nonproduction teams. Production teams consisted of teams of workers and teams of supervisors and managers. Each QC production team met once a week to discuss production issues related to its particular area. Nonproduction teams, which met regularly but on a less frequent basis, were made up of accountants, computer people, etc.—people whose jobs were not strategic in the control of the labor process. The team at Ethicon was the basic vehicle for soliciting worker input and questions concerning working conditions, working environment, and other related issues. This information was passed on to upper management by the facilitators. On management rested the responsibility for implementing company policies and clearly conveying information to facilitators, who passed it on to workers at the team level. The workers, it was hoped, would then use the information to make wise, work-related decisions.

Although further divisions were planned, the production areas during my research were divided into two subareas, each of which formed a team of from seven to fifteen people representing day and night shifts. The team leader was the supervisor of the entire production area. Weekly meetings occurred at shift change, on company time, and on a specified day. One peculiarity of the Ethicon system was that attendance at team meetings was required—which is in direct contradiction to statements in the QC literature emphasizing that voluntarism is the requirement in any type of quality-circle program. In fact, attendance at team meetings and participation in discussions were part of employees' evaluations, which determined raises and promotions. Although the meeting agenda was controlled by the facilitator, theoretically the team was encouraged to discuss openly any type of problem or concern.[1]

The importance of the team concept to overall plant organization was exemplified by official management rationale for the rotating shift. In relation to this, one employee asked the following "open-line" question: "How did you ever decide on this rotating shift?" The plant manager responded:

As I've said before . . . in response to a similar question, I believe rotating shifts are essential to make the team successful. If we allowed shift selections based on seniority, we would lose a lot of people who do not want to work nights permanently, and this would break up our teams. Without stability, the teams will not be able to function as well as a unit.

Another peculiar characteristic of these teams was their eval-

uation of members. After the completion of a member's probationary period and when pay increases were scheduled, the per-
formances of individual members became a topic on the agenda
of the meeting. Team members rated their peers on forms passed
out by the facilitator. Various aspects of performance were evaluated according to four performance criteria: quality of production, quantity of production, absenteeism, and support of the
team. Quality was checked by randomly sampling an individual's
work; quantity was based on work output; absenteeism was calculated as a percentage of total work days; support of the team
was measured by one's participation in team issues and one's
attitude toward team members and company policy.

On the evaluation form, workers indicated whether they felt a
fellow team member's performance was satisfactory, unsatisfactory, or poor. Most of the evaluation items on the sheet seemed
like standard measures for a high-quality operation like Ethicon,
but some stood out as unique in their attempt to measure attitudes toward the team system and toward the company philosophy in general. For example, whether a co-worker wore clean
uniforms daily or wiped her feet at the clean-room entrance or
washed her hands frequently appeared to be legitimate produc-
tion-related concerns to team members. Other items were more
questionable, considering that evaluation results determined
whether a worker got a raise or not and that an unsatisfactory
evaluation by one's peers supposedly destroyed one's chances.
Included in these items were "maintains positive attitude towards self and others," "commitment to company philosophy,"
and "understanding of quality-of-work-life philosophy."

According to the social psychologist, using the team as the primary focus of employee evaluations was considered by Ethicon
management to be a step forward in the evaluation procedure.
"The true individual comes out and fully develops," I was told. As
was written on a handout, the team offers an "opportunity for
Personal Growth . . . [to] learn about yourself through team
meetings" (*Our Plant Philosophy: Maximize Productivity and
Worker Satisfaction*).

Team identification of employees' problems was also an

important innovation. If an employee had a problem, one or two sessions were spent discussing it at the team level in the hope that airing it would help solve it. If further help was needed, the employee was referred to the EAP for one or more of the five free sessions. The director at NMEA referred employees to other helping agencies when necessary. Whether the problem was one of physical health or mental health or attitude, all were lumped, together with union sympathies, under the general category of "counterproductive behavior," the elimination of which was mandatory for an employee's continuation with the firm. In a confidential (September 1982) memo on the subject of "confronting counterproductive behavior," the personnel director wrote:

With any counterproductive employee, two approaches must be used by the Facilitator:

1. The individual must be reminded that our success as a plant depends upon mutual commitment to achieve our goals of productivity and worker satisfaction. The person needs to decide if they can commit to upholding team norms, productivity expectations or common sense rules. If not, they would be better off pursuing other employment.

2. As managers, we are able to discern performance problems but not underlying causes contributing to that behavior. An employee who wishes to stay should be confidentially referred to New Mexico Employee Assistance Program (NMEA). . . . If there are underlying marital, emotional, alcohol, drug, legal, or financial problems, the NMEA will spend up to five hours of evaluation with the employee to see if there is professional help needed. (In the meantime, this does not relieve their performance responsibilities. Their improvement must be acceptable regardless of their accepting NMEA or not.) . . .

When NMEA is utilized in these circumstances, a contract between the supervisor, employee, and NMEA should be developed where the supervisor is kept informed of adherence to the program, progress, and any non-confidental information pertinent to the employee's work ability. The supervisor should feel the NMEA is working through the problem with them.

As I compiled information on why teams were being used at Ethicon and what their function was in the organization of the labor process, what I felt was no doubt much the same as employees must have felt when they first heard of the team concept and the company philosophy—that this employer actually cared about the quality of work life, that the company was bending over backwards to satisfy the "need to belong" for individuals involved in the production process. A series of structural avenues for employee participation clearly supported Ethicon's claim of being concerned about the welfare of its employees. The team system struck me as peculiar in its domination of plant organization, but it was a peculiarity to which I was willing to give the benefit of the doubt.

For researchers studying alienation and worker dissatisfaction in manufacturing environments, the work itself usually serves as the experimental setting. Most types of work subject workers to a hierarchical structure that is a bastion of authoritarianism, and they have no say or control over the environment that affects them for over a third of their waking lives. Ethicon seemed different. The employees were confronted with responsibility and a measure of control over their work environment. Here, I thought, they were using a pro-worker technique.[2]

On the day of my first observation of a team meeting, the social psychologist reviewed the typical agenda with me. By following this agenda, facilitators could maintain control of their teams at all times. What was also important was that although facilitators were always talking, building their agenda, dominating the team by asking key questions—although always in control—they had to be perceived by team members as having an open attitude. This was a skill, I was told, that few facilitators ever mastered. First on the typical agenda were memos, explicitly designed for employee consumption, that management sent to facilitators to read at meetings. Employees could comment on any points, and facilitators could clarify them.

The second agenda item was discussion that focused on output numbers, quality, absenteeism, and team support—issues that related directly to production and to employee's performance evaluations. Records of the previous week's statistics for each individual would be passed out, and workers would see their own performance records as well as those of all other team members.

After this, facilitators sometimes introduced a disciplinary issue for the entire team to address or a general question regarding team interaction or any other issue they felt was the team's business to discuss and resolve. At this time team members could raise questions related to their work environment, working conditions, and shift responsibilities and to any problems they might be having with management or other employees. Clearly, this portion of the agenda might get difficult, and it was up to the facilitator to see that complaints did not get out of hand.

External and internal issues came next, and as examples of external issues that I might encounter in my observations, the social psychologist mentioned union issues, cardio-pulmonary resuscitation (CPR) training, and safety classes. Internal issues were more sensitive and concerned relations between management and the individual—situations not tied directly to the team. Not all meetings discussed this type of issue, but problems such as an employee's negative behavior or attitude might come under scrutiny and be discussed.

As part of my research agenda, the social psychologist wanted me to observe and quantify aspects of team dynamics. He was trying to develop a general measure of cohesiveness in teams so he could measure a cohesive team against a noncohesive team. He did not yet know what the optimal team size was—the largest had twenty-seven people, the smallest, a lab team, had five. He told me to observe and quantify everything I could—seating patterns, number and quality of comments made by team members and facilitator, demeanor of the facilitator, whether he elicited comments from team members or dominated the interactions entirely, what his tone was, and how he represented management to the workers. He said I should keep a record of all this and report back to him after any meetings I observed.

He also suggested that I tape team meetings for later review as part of a strategy to help him "keep an eye" on teams and their development more extensively.[3] On our way to the meeting room, which was adjacent to the production area in the clean-room environment, we were required to scrub up and put on white surgeon-style hats. This was my first time in the production area, and it felt good walking in white among the machines, which were as quiet as I had suspected. The workers glanced at us between procedures. Only managers and supervisors had freedom to walk around, and immediately I realized I was allied with the group not tied to the machines. The workers seemed to identify me as "one of them," meaning managers and supervisors, whatever their opinion of "them" might have been.

As we walked across the width of the production area to a small room at the back, the social psychologist reminded me to keep the tape recorder hidden. He introduced me to Jack, the regular facilitator of the team, and to Cathy, a woman who was training to run a team of her own. He mentioned that I was going to tape the meeting, and Cathy asked if I would tell the workers. I said no. She seemed relieved and pleased. It served as a form of reassurance that we were both on the same side.

I was apprehensive about attending my first team meeting. Although I had reviewed the proper methods for conducting non-participant observation in small groups, I felt anxious about how these working people would react to being the subjects of an outsider's research. Some of this apprehension was erased because before the social psychologist left, he introduced me as an assistant, working with him on team development. Other concerns remained because I wanted to document everything, even processes that cannot be so easily quantified. The power plays, the resistance of the workers to having to be there at all, all those between-the-lines concerns that I had run across in social scientific literature on work-related issues—I wanted to write it all down as it happened and use the tape recording only as a backup.

The small rectangular room was full, and workers were seated on chairs along three sides. The facilitator, Jack, introduced me as "someone helping with teams" and motioned for me to sit next to him on the only other chair at the front of the group. Cathy, the facilitator trainee, sat along the wall with the workers. Jack started the meeting by asking a question: What is the policy on name tags? Four team members answered almost simultaneously after quickly raising their hands but without waiting to be recognized. He seemed satisfied and asked another question: What is the policy on uniforms? This question seemed to stump the workers. I didn't know there was a policy, said one. Keep them clean, said another. Jack partly agreed with this last comment and added that, more importantly, nothing should interfere with the appearance of the uniform, including what is worn underneath. He suggested that women either dispense with underwear altogether or wear light colored undergarments so that "it won't detract from the uniform."

Understandably, this set off a series of comments and laughs from the mostly female group. The only two males (I later discovered they were union supporters) sat quietly throughout the whole meeting. Jack tried to explain that some colors show through the white uniform in a very tacky fashion, but no one really listened. Some workers took advantage of the opportunity offered by the apparent breakdown in the agenda and began to talk freely with each other. I noted on my pad: Facilitator out of control. When things settled down, Jack informed the workers of a meeting to take place on the topic of the company credit union. A discussion ensued on the best time to hold it and where. During this discussion, as in most of the others, only three or four workers actively participated. The rest sat by, patiently waiting.

Next came the topic of production numbers. Jack gave out the weekly figures and emphasized the issue of rejections. Quality was deteriorating significantly, he told them. The numbers were there, but with too many rejections. This was true not only for this team, but for the entire channel department. In reaction to this topic the group became animated. Workers turned to each other and made comments about the rejection rate. Some of the comments were critical of another team in channel, Frank's team. One worker made a charge placing most of the blame for the high number of rejections on that group. They're sloppy, she said, it's not our fault. Addressing the question to no one in particular, Jack asked whether Frank's team was bad on swages. Some answered yes. Another worker agreed that Frank's team was somehow responsible for the high rejection rate. Jack acknowledged that this could be a problem because Frank's team was not as good as it should be. As if this final word explained everything, the subject was changed to what to do about shift rotation.

Who wanted what working hours was the major question, and workers voiced their preferences. Typically those who had been working nights for the last two weeks would shift to days for the next two, but in this case the issue of preferential treatment for pregnant women came up. One of the women was about six months pregnant, and she asked whether she could stay on the day shift. A joke about having to get pregnant to get a break around here and similar comments were made, and this, in turn, encouraged a general chaotic outbreak of remarks on a variety of issues. Until order restored itself, Jack was satisfied to talk quietly with Cathy, the facilitator trainee, laugh at a joke, and wait. Again I noted: Facilitator loses it.

Eventually, someone suggested that the pregnant worker go and talk to Evelyn, the clerk in charge of benefits. By the face she made, I could tell that the pregnant woman did not care for Evelyn. This suggestion cooled down the topic enough for Jack to regain control. A new work schedule was set, excluding the pregnant worker, and Jack continued taking up items on the agenda. He returned to the topic of production, not so much to discuss it, since he had done that before, but to use it to stroke the team. He liked the effort put out last week, he said, and felt good about everyone's numbers. Someone said it was nice to hear this from Jack because his mood had been a real "bitch" lately. Jack recognized this and apologized for being in a bad mood. The pressure, he said, got to him too. He felt better now and back to business as usual. After thirty minutes, and on this hopeful note, the meeting adjourned.

As the workers filed out and I tried to finish the notes I had been furiously taking, Jack asked me what I thought of the group, which he referred to as "my team." I made some remark about the casual atmosphere and informal meeting procedures being nothing out of *Robert's Rules of Order*, and he laughed nervously. They are not an easy group, he told me, but they are okay. I thanked him for letting me observe, and as I left, I made a general comment to reassure him—"It was good."

On the way back to the social psychologist's desk I realized that as a supervisor Jack also saw me as "one of them," this division being between supervisor and upper management. He was obviously concerned with what I was going to report about the team meeting and, more importantly, about his handling of the team. As an ally of the social psychologist, I was removed from both production workers and facilitators. The first group saw me as an authority figure with an unknown amount of power over their lives. Jack and other facilitators saw me as an evaluator, someone who came from the top office with the specific mandate of judging teams and those who run them. It felt good to be perceived as wielding power, and this reassured me concerning my ability to act like a manager.

When the social psychologist debriefed me, which became the practice after meetings I observed, I emphasized the informal atmosphere fostered by the facilitator and said the agenda had been covered but not in the order I expected. I described the dynamics as good because Jack knew when to convey information and when to hold back, when to talk and when to let the spontaneous outbursts run their course. To my surprise the social psychologist shook his head and said that Jack's teams were moving away from him, that he was losing control and not functioning as a "solid" facilitator. I was embarrassed to show disunity, but I said the team seemed to get things done, albeit not in textbook fashion. He was quick to point out that I would see better facilitators in future observations.

He wondered about the apparent dislike for Evelyn, whether the information discussed about Evelyn was important or "bitchy." I said it must have been important because it persuaded the pregnant woman not to go and talk to Evelyn. He did not seem very concerned about this, and quickly moved on to the subject of my coding scheme, reemphasizing the importance of quantifying everything. He was interested in who initiated discussions, whether it was the facilitator or a worker; who continued the discussion; whether it was related to production or nonproduction issues; whether it was positive or negative. I asked him to clarify the use of his terms, and he drew a graph on my pad as an example of a coding scheme he might use for quantifying observations. The graph's horizontal axis was for charting the types of remarks made by team members. All comments related to production would be charted to the right, those not related to production to the left. Every comment would fall somewhere on the graph.

The vertical axis of the graph was for the behavioral component of the comment and the team member who made it. Was the person proactive in her interactions with other team members, or was she quiet and subdued? Did she remain disinterested while others discussed quotas and expectations but suddenly spring to life when talking about nonproduction issues? Charting comments in this way would give him a good idea of the nature of the social groupings within the QC, and he suggested that I try using this scheme the next time I observed a team. I was to review my notes and focus my thinking more on the issues of cohesion and dynamics. It seemed that studying the workers, analyzing their behavior, and deducing their attitudes about work and about each other were subjects that completely occupied his time.

I told him soon afterwards about research I had done on the famous Hawthorne studies. These experiments, in my opinion, described the first large-scale operations of quality circles in American industry. He seemed genuinely pleased that I had discovered some of the traditions associated with the types of controls Ethicon was trying to implement. The Hawthorne studies were perhaps the most far-reaching sociological experiments ever conducted. They took place at the Western Electric plant in Hawthorne, Illinois, starting in 1924 and continuing into the 1930s. Employees were subjected to the most comprehensive testing ever undertaken of workers' social skills. With what they found out, almost by accident, the group of Harvard social scientists revolutionized relationships between managers and workers in American industry.

Many volumes were written describing and analyzing the many findings (Mayo 1933, 1945; Roethslisberger and Dickson 1939; Roethslisberger 1942; Whitehead 1938; Landsberger 1958). What interested me for the development of my own argument were the findings regarding apparent changes in workers' behavior resulting from managerial manipulation of the social environment of the workplace. Particularly significant, if not for their scientific validity then for the subsequent development of a method of control based on human relations, were findings that resulted from experiments in April 1927 in the relay assembly room. A small group of women in this production process were observed in order to determine factors in their work environment that most affected their productivity.

Improved lighting, reduced lighting, longer breaks, shorter breaks, incentive pay, and other factors were introduced to detect what would make workers produce more. To the surprise of those involved in the experiment, productivity increases seemed unrelated to managerial intervention. To virtually all the researchers involved, the increase in productivity was seen instead as a result of the social organization that the experiment itself had imposed on the production process. Separating groups of women from other workers and identifying them as a source of specific interest had developed in them a sense of belonging that they had not experienced out on the floor with the mass of employees. The experimental situation had created the necessary environment and individual producers had become a group. In addition, management had involved the women in making decisions about changes that might be introduced into the experimental situation, which also developed a sense of belonging and sharing among them.

Elton Mayo wrote (1933: 69):

At first shy and uneasy, silent and perhaps somewhat suspicious of the company's intention, later their attitude is marked by confidence and candor. Before every change of program the group is consulted. Their comments are listened to and discussed; sometimes their objections are allowed to negate a suggestion. The group unquestionably develops a sense of participation in the critical determinations and becomes something of a social unit.

The importance of the group as a major influence in individual behavior so impressed Mayo that he became one of the most ardent promoters of using the human relations approach in solving industrial problems.[4]

For a phase of the experiments that involved the bank wiring room, W. Lloyd Warner, an anthropologist, designed a study to obtain information about the nature of relationships that developed in informal social groups within the plant. Specifically, he wanted to discover the impact of the group on the behavior and attitudes of the individual worker. Sixteen male production workers were observed for six and a half months without managerial interference, and researchers discovered that they developed an elaborate social organization. The relationship each individual had with the other men in the group helped determine much of his behavior in the group, with respect to production as well as nonproduction issues. The group had its own standards to define what was deviant and what was normal. Sanctions based on peer pressure and imposed by the informal group were much more effective in controlling behavior than sanctions imposed by the formal organization, the company.

This was clear because the small group, not management, became the primary determinant of production levels achieved by the men. The standards and control mechanisms of the informal small group protected it from outside interference or control. These findings were puzzling to management, as was the discovery that an individual's ability and performance were not related. The most able men in the group were often the leaders in restricting output. This posed the problem of how to motivate the work force and also raised serious questions about whether testing for potential ability and fitting the person with the job was a sure way to assemble a more efficient and more highly motivated work force. The Hawthorne studies raised the new managerial problem of how to get small, informal groups of workers to accept the formal goals of management.

At a subsequent team meeting I attended, another "management" type in addition to myself was present, a personnel administrator in charge of screening applicants. John, the facilitator, opened the meeting, which began on time and lasted about thirty minutes, by highlighting the team's great productivity, praising the team's effort, and saying it should continue. He then related some comments made by team members in their evaluations of two employees who were not present. He said it was unfortunate that one of them, who was pregnant, was sick today since she was doing so well, and that the other, as all agreed, had to improve her attitude toward work so her numbers would improve. He didn't know why she was absent today. He said she was probably home watching TV, and a couple of workers chuckled.

He then asked the group a specific question: "Speaking of TV, did anyone see the '60 Minutes' spot last night on Coors beer?" Several of the workers and the personnel administrator, Pam, raised their hands and answered that they had. He asked Pam to describe the story, which she related at some length. "It showed how the union keeps trying to get in at the Coors plant in Colorado even when the workers don't want anything to do with it. It was real funny because they showed how they got all the employees in a great big room asking them what they thought of the company, and every single one of them said how much they liked working for the company, how much the company was trying to help them, and all that stuff.

"One man said he was proud to have a job for such a good company. The union was saying that the company broke all kinds of laws. They said, the union said, that the company discriminates against Hispanics, lies about polygraph tests, and all this stuff, and this guy was saying that he thought the company was great—and he was Hispanic. The AFL-CIO is sponsoring this boycott against Coors, and it's hurting them. They've had to lay off about 2,000 people because of the union trying to get in there.

"Then they showed the head organizer or something from the union, and Mike Wallace told him that the union steward himself had said to him that the company did not do all the things that the union accused them of doing. He said that the treatment was great, and this guy said 'well, he's lying.' I couldn't believe it. He called his own union guy a liar because he had said the company did not break the law.

"They showed all the stuff the company was doing for the workers. The gym they had set up, the benefits and all that. And I know people here, one of the husbands of a worker here, who works for Coors here, and she says the benefits are great. Not as good as ours, but great anyway. And it was a really good show. . . ."

When she finished speaking, John said, "Thank you, Pam. I wanted you to tell it so I could see if someone else thought the same things about it that I did. Yeah, it was good, and what got me was that it was a perfect example of how the union would not leave the workers alone even after they had said no to it. The union was voted out, and they still won't leave the employees alone. It was a real good example of that." When he paused, a woman said, "I don't know why the union wants to get in here. The union is only good when there are problems. We have no problems here. You guys are doing real good things." Another person said, "Only the people in channel want the union."

John said, "Yeah, the people in channel complain too much. If you would get this group over there, we would do a much better job at their jobs. They are not trying hard enough." A male worker said, "I don't know. You know, this is my opinion, and I don't want anyone to think management put me up to it, but I don't know why this deal with the union is such a big thing. We have good jobs and the economy is real bad. We should be lucky to have good jobs. I know a lot of people that don't have good jobs." After a number of such remarks, he ended by saying, "Remember the economy. That's all I wanted to say." John thanked him, and since there were no other comments, said, "Okay, that's it." As everyone walked out the worker said again, "Remember the economy."

This meeting had a great impact on me. It was the first time the union issue had surfaced in a discussion, and what caught my attention was how it all seemed so well planned, so well orchestrated. After the meeting, when I asked the social psychologist whether the union issue was a "big deal" at the plant, I discovered I had underestimated its importance. He told me about the company's anti-union strategy. They had committed themselves a long time ago to keeping the plant nonunion. "we're fighting it tooth and nail," he said. To that end, three basic strategies were being used against the organizing effort and its supporters.

"We are using the traditional management approach [against unionization]," he said, "where management gives the workers information not necessarily solicited by them but nevertheless important in informing them about the anti-union stance of the company. Another approach [we are using] is the proactive approach. The facilitator sort of orchestrates and initiates the discussion of the union at the QC meetings, and in that way gets across certain ideas about the union to employees."

He informed me that John, one of the best facilitators, was using the proactive approach and that I had just witnessed it. Only the very best facilitators were successful at it, however, and John's degree in psychology made him particularly adept at orchestrating discussions. I mentioned that the episode of the Coors piece on "60 Minutes" had appeared premeditated. The social psychologist laughed. The entire scene had been discussed at a morning facilitators' meeting. It had been set up. I kept quiet about my suspicions that the worker's comments on the economy had also been scripted.

He went on to explain the third anti-union strategy. "The third approach is the individual-conflict approach where individuals already known to be pro-union are isolated at the team level and individual level. We try to keep them isolated from other team members and at the same time confront them individually concerning the union issue."

Clearly there was much more to this team concept than I had been led to believe.[5]

4

Union Organizing and Company Strategy

Mike Galiano had been active for a couple of months in trying to get the Textile Workers Union (TWU) into the Ethicon-Albuquerque plant, but he was frustrated by the TWU organizer's apparent lack of commitment to the unionizing effort. Mike expected the organizer to be more interested in the Albuquerque plant because of the TWU's presence at the other western plant of the corporation in San Angelo, Texas. When, after a quick leafleting and one signed card (Mike's) the organizer left town, Mike thought of contacting the Amalgamated Clothing and Textile Workers Union (ACTWU), which had a longer commitment to Ethicon. The Somerville plant in New Jersey, the headquarters, was organized in 1944, the Chicago plant in the 1960s. In total, ACTWU represented approximately 3,039 J&J workers at ten plants. In May 1982 ACTWU came to Albuquerque.

The chief organizer for the ACTWU district was aware of the TWU's attempts and did not want to raid another union's turf, so he contacted the TWU organizer. Certain that the TWU had no intentions of waging an aggressive organizing campaign, he began the long, laborious process of contacting Ethicon workers to gauge their need and desire for organizing a union. After evaluating the job requirements, the wage scale, the social organization of the plant, and the worker's satisfaction with the work environment, he concluded that there was sufficient need and desire to warrant a commitment from the ACTWU. It was obvious that the workers he contacted were not getting from Ethicon-Albuquerque the kind of treatment ACTWU workers and others at unionized plants were getting. The decision was reached, and the ACTWU began to organize. They stayed for more than a year during the campaign to organize the plant.

This campaign started much the same as others. Contacts were made, meetings held, strategy mapped out. Employees were encouraged to become involved in the debate over the union issue. The union supplied its already identified supporters with relevant information on the benefits of unionization. Their mission: get the facts out on the floor, and make the company react. How a union benefits employees, makes the existing work environment better, and increases workers' participation in decision making at the shop-floor level are universal topics in the educational process known as labor organizing, and this campaign was no exception.

Quickly, the employees responded, and the campaign was off on the right foot. On June 30, 1982, the ACTWU signed the first card at Ethicon-Albuquerque. The first official member was Mike Galiano. Two weeks later, six production workers from Mike's team constituted the first union organizing committee in the plant's short history. By July 27th, that number had grown to fifteen, and supporters numbered in the scores. Union strength grew daily. Encouraged by the quick show of support, the committee proposed a debate between union organizers and management. As customary among managers faced with the threat of an open debate, the challenge was summarily dismissed with a letter on July 27th to each of the petitioning employees claiming that a debate would play right into the union's hands, given the one-sided restrictions the NLRB law imposes on management in such debates.

In a litany of regrets, the plant manager bemoaned the law: Management can't promise anything, while the union is unrestricted in its promises. In order for employees to hear both sides of the argument, he said, management would rely on the innovative method of the open line (a method that is company controlled). Additionally, he said, "Debates are known for their appeal basically to emotions, not reason." Emotionally speaking, he said, the issue of higher wages, comparable to those at other unionized plants in the J&J family, would offer the union a great advantage in the debate. Rationally speaking, however, "We would not anticipate paying more than community standards in any event—whether our employees are represented or not."

The union took the opportunity to point out how the predictable refusal to debate manifested not only management's commitment to withhold information from employees, but also the extent of centralized management control. Evidentially, the refusal signaled management's general resistance to a free exchange of ideas among workers and to a free flow of information about the union. A debate would make control by the company impossible. "In a truly free atmosphere," the chief organizer told employees at a meeting, "it would be unacceptable not to debate." Where the issue is management's total control over the work force, however, a debate becomes an unacceptable proposition.

The union's educational campaign during this time concentrated on wages. Because of the higher wages at the New Jersey plant, what the company emphasized at team and plant-wide meetings and in private discussions with employees were the differences between Somerville, New Jersey, and Albuquerque in cost of living and quality of life. The union, in turn, emphasized the similarities. The message was simple and clear: Not only should you get paid the same as your brothers and sisters doing the same work elsewhere for the same company, but you really don't have it better here when it comes to buying what you need. And they had the data to prove it. Committee members were given copies of the minutes of the last J&J-ACTWU negotiations at the Somerville plant, during which the average wage rose to $9.56 per hour. They were given Chamber of Commerce statistics showing the similarity of the cost of living (except for housing) in the two areas.

At the request of an employee, the union also made available information on the Japanese system of quality circles. It was common knowledge that most facilitators were learning about the technique, and some workers wanted similar information. It was also no secret that the union was concerned about the use of teams to discourage union support. Some facilitators used team meetings and shop-floor interactions among team members to identify and harass pro-union people. This practice was clear from the very beginning, weeks before I became involved with the company, and it had negative effects on the organizing drive.

More generally, and more importantly, since the team was clearly designed as an alternative to unionization, the union very early in the campaign encouraged employees to test the team's "participative" function. Although managers claimed that grievances could be handled by the team, team members who tried this out to see how far it would get them found that facilitators gave the most predictable and frustrating answers when faced with grievances. "I'll get back to you on that" was one such answer. "When they say that," said one worker, "you can kiss it good-bye."

The company, on the other hand, insisted that if the union were voted in, it would get rid of the team system, and most workers liked the system, if for no other reason, because of its uniqueness. Some even saw it as a paid break from the monotony of the production process. In any case, the union was sensitive to the appeal of the teams and never considered challenging their integrity, except for questioning their true participative intent and opposing the evaluation procedures. On this last point, they found support among workers. Peer evaluations caused discomfort rather than feelings of participation, and people who really wanted to lower the boom on team members found it a convenient way to express their dislike, which was often unrelated to the job at hand. Although not many people liked the evaluation process, a fact even the personnel director acknowledged to me much later, it was part of the team system because it helped management keep tabs on the pulse of the organization.

The early stages of the campaign were a series of formulaic

jabs and parries in which neither side flexed any muscle but during which both sides presented the face by which they would most like to be identified. The union knew management would refuse to debate, but by getting workers involved in an aggressive campaign that would force management's hand, they became the advocates of workers' right to know. Managers, on the other hand, wanted workers to know that it was managers, not the union, who controlled the plant. They did not want to be seen as unreasonable about it, and their stance was that if a debate would do any good, they would be the first to accept the invitation. However, the facts, which they alone possessed, clearly pointed to the futility of such an event. Therefore, acting reasonably, they would refuse. The logic of management is difficult to debate.

Despite the early quick gains made by the union, most workers accepted the managerial interpretation of the work environment, and even people who later became strong union supporters saw little to criticize about the Ethicon system. Many thought it would be foolish for management to pay them more than the area average if they were not coerced to do so, and support for the teams was widespread even if they were sometimes referred to as a type of cult organization. The team concept was new, and people felt a certain amount of pride in working for an innovative employer like J&J. Those who accepted company philosophy and liked the attention given them by facilitators disliked the prospect of losing benefits if the union came. This prospect was initiated as a topic by supervisors as early as May 1982, and the thought followed many workers into the voting booth.

Many also disliked the fact that the Communist Labor Party, a miniscule faction of the area's leftist community, had distributed a leaflet questioning the integrity of Ethicon and its failure to improve the employment scene for the area's poor. The leaflet, which was answered by management in a skillfully written letter to all employees, inadvertently offered management an opportunity to reaffirm its legitimacy. Posing as the sole possessor of the relevant facts, management quoted from the agreement they had made with the city to hire a certain number of employees from the pocket of poverty and then described how they had, in effect, complied with the agreement. Full of tabulations and percentages, the letter attempted to inspire confidence in the goodwill of the company. The message was: Management is up front with the facts; management can be trusted.

The union increased its educational campaign gradually with house calls and information handouts, and by the beginning of August 1980 the company was countering with ever-increasing numbers of invariably intense anti-union meetings. Their nice guy image began to look a bit worn. Plant-wide meetings (by shifts) soon emerged as an effective weapon in the company's anti-union arsenal because on company time and with the agenda tightly controlled, management had the opportunity to give captive-audience speeches throughout the campaign. The employees asked questions and were answered by a top manager, usually the plant manager or personnel director. The answers, however, were not spontaneous responses to spontaneous questions. They were from a booklet of answers to the most often asked employee questions, compiled by legal consultants. For these theatrics new questions were continually added, and from May to November of 1982 a total of 120 appeared in the document under a series of headings.

The meetings also served to exhaust employees on the union issue and to help management identify shop-floor union leadership. They were held an average of almost one a week, in addition to team meetings, which often served the same purpose. At one mass meeting the plant manager admonished workers: "You can't discuss the union on company time." This restriction would have pleased most people had management followed the same advice. Workers frequently heard facilitators making sly comments about union supporters and about how they would clear them out of the plant.

Facilitators often initiated conversations about the union with their team members, and only the most courageous resisted the harassment. One union supporter was told to remember that she could not discuss the union on company time. "You mean like you're doing with me right now?" she asked. The facilitator quickly answered that he was not discussing the union, he was only commenting on it. She responded, "It's okay to comment about the union on company time?" He promised he would check and get back to her on it.

Throughout the campaign, whatever management did or did not do was attributed to the union. The new light installed to brighten the parking lot would supposedly secure the area in case of union violence. The implementation of a training program for the drill department was supposedly delayed because the union might file an unfair labor practice charge if such a change occurred during the campaign. Why did the channel machines lack lights? Installing them would constitute a change, and that might constitute a violation of labor law. This was all part of a strategy to increase the tension on employees and turn them against the union, against the third party that was making a pleasant work environment inflexible, intolerable.

As far as the union and its supporters were concerned, management was creating the inflexibility and the intolerable working conditions. After all, management still had complete control over the production process, which did not change in the face of the employees' desire to organize. Indeed, the union had only introduced the possibility of change; the potential for organized workers and organized management to share control of the work environment. Management's refusal to entertain such a possibility was manifested in its tightening of the structural controls at its disposal. When its power went unchallenged, management could afford to be flexible. Faced with a threat to its power, however, management declared the shop-floor equivalent of martial law and proceeded to discourage dissent by limiting its expression.

Because of the ACTWU's long tradition of aggressive organizing strategy and even longer tradition of working with J&J, top brass had expected the union to make a strong, determined move that would not be discouraged as easily as the TWU's attempt to organize the plant.

Thanks to their consultants, Ethicon took early action. Immediately, training sessions began for facilitators, instructing these frontline supervisors in how to identify and influence pro-union employees. Encouraged by consultants, the plant manager made an early and anticipatory anti-union speech the third week in May 1982 in an attempt to nip the whole union organizing process in the bud. Even the first letter in July to selected employees refusing the debate offer, however original it might have appeared, was a formulaic response to the union's request, which was also formulaic.

The long relationship between the union and J&J had been a relatively harmonious one. The J&J industrial relations expert, who was to have a great deal to say about the strategy at Ethicon-Albuquerque, had stated in previous negotiations with the union that the two organizations enjoyed a "great friendship" over the years and that a continuation of the relationship was beneficial for both of them. The ACTWU's approach to labor relations with J&J was not regarded as antagonistic, regardless of what campaign propaganda insinuated (only seven strikes totaling 183 days in nearly forty years); but the ACTWU was not regarded as subservient to management either.

Although the union had lost members in recent years—mostly because of shutdowns, the effects of imports, and the flight of industries to areas of cheap labor—it remained one of the most active unions on the organizing trail. This was especially true in the western region and in the South, where in the last decade their organizational machine won a series of impressive victories. The Farah struggle of 1973 and the valiant seventeen-year struggle against J. P. Stevens in South Carolina, finally won in 1980, are but two of the ACTWU's most memorable successes.

In spite of J&J's expectation that the ACTWU would make a move, an overreaction at the local as well as the corporate headquarters followed the union's initial contact with employees. The lawyers and experts in labor relations who journeyed west from New Jersey were anticipating the worst—that great inroads would be made by the union before management was even aware of their presence. Facilitators were told to poll their teams to see how many of their workers had been contacted by union organizers and to begin keeping track of pro- and anti-union attitudes. The numbers reported by the facilitators were treated as estimates and multiplied by four to attain a more accurate appraisal of union contacts. Apparently management underestimated the efficiency of the team system in identifying attitudes and thought supervisors would be easily kept in the dark.

The number they came up with, ninety-five employees contacted by the union as early as May 1982, flabbergasted corporate headquarters and surprised local management. Convinced that this was a ridiculously high estimate, and relying on facilitator reports, the plant manager traveled to New Jersey to assure the worried brass that all was under control. He tried to convince them that union activity was being closely monitored, that employee morale was high, and that workers were against unionization. He tried to convince them that local management had a strategy. The strategy was: hire them anti-union and keep them that way.

Since the onset of psychological testing after World War I, managers have increasingly relied on sophisticated techniques for screening job applicants in an attempt to ensure the tightest possible fit, at the lowest possible cost, between a plant's workers and organizational culture. Industrialists soon discovered that personality traits could not be completely controlled simply by chaining workers to machines. It became important to identify and screen counterproductive traits and undesirable characteristics before hiring to ensure the machinelike efficiency of the ideal plant culture and a homogeneity in the work culture.

Such screening processes are now considered a major component of the structure of control in modern business enterprises (Tosi 1983). By selecting workers with desirable skills, knowledge, and attitudes, managers can make training costs cheaper, production higher, outcomes more predictable, and their jobs easier. So it was at Ethicon-Albuquerque, where screening mechanisms were specifically instituted to develop a work force susceptible to peer pressure controls as institutionalized in the team system. The company, during the anti-union campaign, increased its efforts to identify new employees who were anti-union.

Workers who expressed a negative attitude towards unionism were preferred, and the fine line between screening and discrimination was crossed a number of times until the company became entangled in a web of unfair labor practice charges. As the company attempted to stuff the ballot box by hiring anti-union employees in preparation for an election, the NLRB issued four charges that were directly related to discrimination in hiring.

The personnel department had confidence in the screening mechanisms. A major goal in developing a cohesive plant culture was to hire anti-union employees and keep them that way through internal control mechanisms. The issue of screening for anti-union attitudes surfaced as a dominant theme in the company's strategy during a series of meetings and observations I made in October 1982. The first female facilitator, Cathy, whom I had met as a trainee the previous month, now had her own team. It was a new team composed of new employees who had been hired less than three weeks before. When I arrived at the meeting room, Cathy introduced me as someone helping the social psychologist with the teams. She was visibly nervous as things got started. A discussion of the rotating shift schedule took up most of the meeting. Cathy wanted to get everyone's input for making up the next two-week schedule. She gave out blank schedule sheets and asked the ten members to design their own schedules. Some objected, saying she should decide since it would take forever this way. After much discussion on this, while Cathy tried to solicit input with little effect, her schedule was accepted unseen. She said she would make it up as soon as possible and give out copies before the week's end.

The role of the facilitator in determining who fit and who didn't fit into the team system was brought up during a discussion of the probation period. The topic was of particular interest to this group of recently hired employees. One person asked if the facilitator had any say about which team members would be permanently hired and which would be fired. As this worker understood it, the team as a group decided on the hiring and firing. Cathy responded, "If the facilitator feels you would not fit in, termination is possible. . . . A thirty-day extension is possible if the facilitator wants to do it. It's up to the facilitator." This meant that even if a worker received a good evaluation from her team members, the facilitator could initiate the termination procedure and, conversely, that the facilitator could presumably override a bad evaluation with a grace period of thirty days. One woman turned to a co-worker and whispered that this was not mentioned when they hired her. "I thought we had all the power," she said.

After the meeting, Cathy told me about her nervousness at running her first team, and I reassured her that it was an adequate performance. When I asked whether the union issue was big in this team, she said she usually brought it up at each meeting, but it wasn't really a hot topic since this team was composed of all new people. Then she said something that added considerable focus to my research: "We hire anti-union people by screening for them, and it's my job to see to it that they stay that way."

At my next meeting with the social psychologist, I asked for more information on the anti-union campaign and the hiring strategy. We sat outside on a patio overlooking a green lawn that had somehow been enticed to grow on the desert mesa. I said that unionization seemed the one issue weighing most heavily on plant operations at this time, at least from what I could observe, and that I would like to explore it as much as possible since it probably wouldn't be around again. I asked him why J&J was so adamantly against unionization. His answer was: "The main reason this has to be a nonunion shop is because J&J has to cut back on employee wages and benefits."

He explained that the decision to keep the union out of this plant was made before the plant opened. For each year the company kept the union out, they estimated a profit of $3–5 million while the plant continued to grow. Given this incentive, identifying and hiring anti-union workers had become both a goal of the personnel department and its contribution to company success. This identification process occurred at practically all levels of organizational communication between workers and management personnel. It began before a worker sewed her first suture.

The social psychologist told me: "We have two ways of selecting employees: the psycho-motor skill criteria, can you make this widget with accuracy, quality, all that, that's the easiest to select for. We have a training center . . . where we spot the good trainees and the slobs. The second criteria [sic] is person-environment fit. Here we have to cull out those people that might have a negative impact on the environment of the plant. One of those impacts is unionization. . . . They have to fit the team environment and keep out the union environment. . . . We have to catch them at the door."

When the first hiring announcements appeared in the newspapers in early December 1980, a great deal of thought had already gone into designing the social organization and screening procedures of the Ethicon plant. Employees who filled out applications were required to attend an all day "assessment orientation" (evaluation) at the convention center. In the plush environment of the center's conference rooms, the aspiring workers filled out many forms, underwent many interviews, and under the watchful eyes of consultants, were evaluated as "team players." The first group to apply underwent an all-day testing session, an initial screening session known as selection Saturday. Their aptitudes and attitudes were closely scrutinized by plant personnel and external consultants from the Center for Improved Productivity at the University of Southern California.

The battery of surveys and questionnaires all attempted to shed some light on the motivations and expectations of the future work force. This first group of employees was most impressed by the group dynamics session, when small groups were given a problem and instructed to solve it. The applicants were graded on their contribution to the solution. As one worker said, the important thing was to talk and have ideas, not as if the quality of the ideas were being evaluated, just the personality of the individual and whether a person was able to talk and work in a group. Another worker said that management conveyed the importance of the exercise by introducing the team as the "new way of organizing" workers.

Workers needed to work in groups and take responsibility for group actions. This was the philosophy of the new-design plant, and these initial behavior measurements eliminated applicants who were deemed unwilling or unable to work well in the innovative team environment. In addition, the team concept was reaffirmed as a basic building block of the new plant in the eyes of its new workers. Enough employees were identified as compatible with the new-design philosophy to create the first team, which started operations at the pilot facility on January 12, 1981.

As the number of employees at the plant increased, initial hiring interviews were used to describe the team as a special benefit of the industrial culture, a nontraditional and innovative type of worker organization. Aware that direct questioning about union sentiments violated a NLRB law, the interviewer would bring up the topic of unionization as subtly and as imperceptibly as possible. The idea was to have potential employees express their attitudes without direct questioning. Among managers, the personnel administrator had a reputation for being "pretty good" at having people disclose their union sentiments. The acceptance of the team concept as the organizational strategy of choice to the exclusion of all others was the first step in accepting the "Ethicon identity."

It became clear to me that the influence of the team on the work force began even before an applicant was officially hired, a particularly subtle and powerful force in creating a homogeneous plant culture. If potential employees survived the initial interview with the personnel department, they were referred to the plant manager or a department supervisor for another interview and then for a final interview with two members of the team to which the applicant would be assigned, if accepted. The two peer workers ostensibly had the authority to hire, or veto the hiring of, the applicant.

This procedure was extremely efficient in impressing on future employees the importance of being accepted by fellow workers if they were to be hired. An employee's very real concern about approval from team members was raised here for the first time. Having been "hired" by team members and having been told that team members also have the authority to fire them, employees felt dependent on the continued good will of team members in order to continue their employment. This created enormous pressure on new employees to gain the friendship of co-workers quickly because failure to do so could result in termination or in being denied pay raises. Conformity, normally a question of individual temperament, became at Ethicon-Albuquerque a condition of employment.

As much as possible, the work force had been chosen from individuals who seemed to accept the managerial interpretation of the work environment. Clearly, the selection process and its use of the team gave management a sizable advantage in controlling the labor force. Ethicon philosophy equated traditionalism with archaic and outmoded concepts and plant operations, and if nothing else, employees understood that this plant represented a break with, and maybe an improvement over, past industrial practices. The traditionalism associated with unions was regarded as undesirable and inferior to the team method of organizing the work force.

Some of the workers had been told that over 7,000 applicants were reviewed in filling the first 200 production jobs. In an area known for its traditionalism, the 200 employees hired represented the "nontraditional" vanguard of the area's work force. Being hired was an honor; accepting the company philosophy was a duty. Any screening process, however, can only ensure a limited amount of homogeneity, even on the issue of unionism, and it was in order to dissuade those who might have slipped through the screen like bugs into the clean and anti-union environment that management tried to keep a cap on discussion and information flow at the plant. This was certainly not a new technique, but my own introduction to how efficient the team was in keeping the company nonunion certainly was unique.

I knew Frank was one of the good ones, one of the facilitators who kept a tight rein on team members. Perhaps because he knew he was highly esteemed among upper managers, he was particularly friendly to me. Before my observation of his team meeting he commented on just how tired he was of all the "union stuff" and how he had to get his team in line before it was too late. As though warning me, he mentioned that the team meeting that day would be "intense." It was. The entire meeting was taken up by his incessant attack on counterproductive behavior.

"And another type of counterproductive activity," he told the team, "which is the most blatant . . . and from what I can see, I can see some people losing their job over this real soon, that is, creating an atmosphere [that] in any way harbors failure or excessive frustration for people out there on the floor. And that is someone coming over to you and saying . . . you are being treated unfairly. Now if any of you have ever worked at another plant . . . [you know] you've got it good here. . . . Anyone that is going around telling you over and over that it's not right, they're treating you unfairly, that person is on their way out as far as Jack and I are concerned. . . . And unfortunately I'd hate to see it happen to someone I really like, [who] I think is doing a good job overall."

There was no hiding the fact that he was specifically addressing the pro-union employees in his and other teams. He went on: "That kind of attitude does more to hurt productivity than anything else. And that attitude has gotten to be the norm of [our production unit] and we can't allow that. . . . I think . . . part of the problem is a lot of people in manufacturing have given too much as far as some of the freedom we've gotten. . . . [Now we are back] to this point . . . where this is the alternative. Get your butt in gear and do your work, or get out. . . . If you don't want to do that, there are plenty of places out there that will take you . . . but there won't be too many. . . ."

He continued, saying that he and the other facilitator in chan- nel department had clear orders to fire anyone for counterpro- ductive activity, and although this team was not as bad as his other team, all should be aware that he intended to carry this order out. "Negative attitudes" toward work at Ethicon and to- ward how the work was organized must stop or someone would pay the price. Some of the employees saw how to stop or at least slow down Frank's attacks: point to other teams, other workers.

"There are negative people all over the plant," said one man. "They are hitting us hard all over." Another said, "The negatives are beating the hell out of the positives. I wish the negatives would keep to themselves."

A third worker asked whether he was in trouble personally. Frank softened as if on cue. He said no, and that he knew the worker wanted this job and that he'd try to help him keep it. When another person mentioned that Mike, the most respected of union supporters, often asked him why he was working so hard for so little, Frank jumped. If anyone was willing to document that type of behavior, Mike, or anyone else with that attitude would be on the way out. That attitude verged on insubordination, and the area supervisor had told all his facilitators that "he would get rid of anyone that [said] anything like that." Things were good there [at the plant], he repeated, and people were literally lining up for a job.

"Betina," he turned to a worker huddled in the corner, "you used to work at Pioneer Wear. How was that?" Not surprisingly, given Pioneer Wear's reputation for being the closest thing to a sweatshop in Albuquerque, she reported that it was terrible. "The supervisor was always on your back. Here things are much better." Another chimed in, "The young people are being misled by the union." This gave Frank the opportunity to ask if there were any questions on the union. "They try to trick you," said a worker, "they came to my house and I wouldn't let them in." I discovered later that this worker had not only let the organizer in but had appeared sympathetic. Frank mentioned what he thought was obvious. "We don't need a union here. We have it as good as San Angelo, and they have a union."

During the long meeting, various workers asked how they were doing personally. Frank gave vague answers, suggesting that he didn't know exactly and that he would talk individually with each worker to update their status. This clearly made the employees nervous. Perhaps sensing this, he reiterated it in his closing comments, somewhat out of context. "One last thing. I'll be talking to everyone on an individual basis. Next time I hear someone say that something is unfair or too hard, that person gets days off. If anyone is making your job difficult, let me know. Document it. Only way we can get rid of someone like that is to have documentation. Jack [is] ready to do it. It's not right to make your job difficult. But we can't fire him without documentation." Everyone knew that the "him" Frank referred to was Mike.

For union sympathizers, the possibility of being terrorized at Ethicon was always present. Many facilitators recognized the value of inducing fear to control the expression of pro-union sentiments. Andres's case is illustrative. Andres recounted his story hesitantly. It was not easy for a man like him to admit having cried at a team meeting over what some "crazy women" had said.

At our team meetings the facilitator usually reads some memos from the company and then discusses any changes in policy, or whatever. Then we discuss production. The numbers, quality, stuff like that. John usually asks if there is any other business that needs to be discussed. At one meeting in September, it was either the seventh or the fourteenth, he asked if there was any other business. Josephina, you know Josephina [fervent anti-unionist], asked something about how far the union would go to get in the plant.

It wasn't really a question, or I couldn't figure out what the question was. And it seemed strange because next John pulls out a paper and said something like, "Oh, by the way, I've got something to read you about the union." The thing is that he speaks with Josephina everyday and it seemed to me that he had coached her to raise the questions when she did because he was ready with an answer. Anyway, he read this thing about some union in New York that got its members a 25-cent raise and he laughed. "Is this the kind of union you want representing you?"

That's when I said, hey, why don't you stick to the facts of what the union has done back east and what it can do here and not some other union at another place. Then Elena [another fervent anti-unionist] said, "If you're not happy with the company why don't you resign? If it were up to me I'd fire you." She said, just like that. And I told her that we had different points of view and that I could respect hers and she should respect mine.

She said that the union was just using me and that if it were up to her she'd fire me. She was really yelling and I was getting kind of upset, you know. Nobody was speaking up for me. I asked her why she'd fire me. She said, "I don't like people who mess up a good work environment." I guess she was talking about herself because it sure wasn't good for me. Then she said, "The only thing I respect is trying to get you fired."

All this time John did not say a thing. He was glad all this was going on. He encouraged it by not stopping it. I told him that if he was there to build a team, he wasn't doing his job, allowing the wolf pack to attack me. He just said this was the type of discussion facilitators should stay out of. There was no team concept. No nothing. It was dog eat dog, and workers were the dogs.

According to pro-union workers interviewed, inducing fear was the tactic from the very beginning of the campaign. It was used to coerce union sympathizers into compliance and discourage new employees from entertaining pro-union notions, or at least expressing them. It was fear that kept the workers down: fear of being ridiculed, fear of being fired, fear of the actions of facilitators and fellow workers, fear of the team turning against you like a rabid dog, fear of persecution. "It was like a witch-hunt," one woman later told me.

At Frank's meeting, where he had evoked the evils of counterproductive activity, I had been struck by his coercive authority. He had been angry and no one had dared go against him. Team members had actively sought to placate him, to make him see them as his friends, if for no other reason than to ease the tense atmosphere in the room. By creating an atmosphere of conflict, he had prevented the team members from thinking about the issues—any issues, and encouraged them to seek refuge from the conflict by agreeing with management. Apparently he could do whatever he wanted with that team as long as they perceived him as the person who wielded the power to punish or forgive.

Frank and I talked after that meeting. As we stood on the production floor, he asked me if I thought his team was anti-union, pro-company. After thinking about it for a few minutes I told him that his people seemed to be more pro-authority than pro-company, that they appeared to be very aware of who had the power to control their work environment and seemed very willing to appease the source of power in return for a pleasant eight hours. Although I made these comments off-the-cuff, they must have struck a responsive chord in the facilitator because a couple of months later he thanked me for this advice. It had been a help to him in increasing his control over the team and his influence with upper management

He admitted that he had become hardened and callous. This attitude would take him far. After the union election, he was promoted to personnel administrator, and his career with the company was secured. He had not foreseen this, just as neither of us foresaw the intensification of the campaign that was occurring as we spoke after the meeting. Jack, another facilitator I knew, had come up to us, smiling, shaking his head. Pro-union workers were outside, handing out leaflets. "I bet Mike is out there," Frank said. "Yeah, Mike is out there," Jack had laughed. "A bunch of people are out there." He shook his head again, "You'd be surprised at who is out there." He was expressing surprise at the inability of the work system to suppress dissent, to induce subservience and control the work force for those who controlled the firm.

For a worker whose livelihood depends to a great degree on recognizing the importance of subservience, passing out leaflets in front of the plant is a supremely courageous act. It can only be brought about by experiencing the work process as unjust rather than natural, changeable rather than static. It is the act of a worker who chooses to have a voice on the important issues of work rather than to exit an undesirable situation.[1] It is not surprising, then, that the union's campaign centered on developing in the workers a sense of potency, a need to express themselves, and vitality to combat the powerlessness they faced every day at the plant.

Union organizers conducted a re-education campaign among employees who were willing to listen, emphasizing workers' right to voice their opinions about the way their work life was structured.

Through meetings, house calls, and telephone conversations

the employees built up a committee that one of the organizers called the best he had ever worked with. These few acted confidently at team meetings and brazenly demanded equality by challenging management to debates and calling for a clarification of policy issues. They began to experience the work environment as something personal rather than impersonal, something that was theirs rather than management's. One of the few workers that was pro-union all the way said of her first contact with the organizers: "They made me feel like I was something, and that I was something at work too. It's easy to feel like a machine when you're treated like one."

Probably most of the union committee shared this feeling, but the feeling was not contagious. The number of workers willing to speak out about the need for change grew slowly. The July 27, 1982, letter to the plant manager demanding a debate and signed by fifteen people had marked the height of union strength for several months. After that show of strength and audacity, management had tightened the screening mechanisms, and pro-union workers had begun to feel the heat associated with their attitudes.

In August 1982 the company provided catered buffets for both shifts as a show of thanks for the plant's receiving the Corporate Award of Merit for Safety (twelve months without time lost). At this point they felt that the union's educational campaign would not gather enough support to warrant a full strategic attack. They sensed correctly that the issue of higher wages was not making much of an inroad in the work force. All the talk about what workers made in New Jersey simply did not affect most of these workers. They would not consider working in New Jersey for higher wages, and they accepted as logical management's argument of not paying more than necessary to get a good day's work out of people. A crusty old mechanic spoke to a group of leafletting workers one day: "If you want to make what they make in New Jersey, go live there."

The organizing committee decided to run an in-plant educational campaign using the angle of wages but emphasizing the profits that Ethicon was making in Albuquerque. Mike was a respected and active committee member, and he became an expert on the cost and retail price of sutures. He distributed information describing how much profit nonunionized labor offered J&J. Their estimates of $1 million per year turned out to be far off the projected corporate estimates of $3–5 million, but the angle began to move some people.

The company combined its "nice guy" approach with the tightening up of screening procedures. Employees who later became involved with the union reported a rash of questions regarding union sentiments during the hiring process in September 1982. For example, one woman told the NLRB that she was specifically asked her opinion about unions. Like most people who managed to get hired during the campaign, she had told personnel she knew nothing about unions and cared less. Another worker hired in the same cohort, whose husband was a union member, was asked point blank if she was a member of a union. She had answered truthfully and negatively, and she was working within the week.

It's impossible to estimate how many people during this time were denied jobs because of pro-union sentiments. At a party, I overheard the spouse of a sociology colleague talking about his application to work at Ethicon not having been acknowledged. I asked him if he had mentiond anything about unions in it, and he replied that he had not said anything specific, only that his father was a union steward. I told him not to expect a call any time soon.

Also in September the company began to require the presence of a facilitator at the training centers where employees were screened for psycho-motor skills. Specifically, they were concerned that pro-union people would initiate conversations with new employees and that union organizers would come by to make their appeal. Neither of these two things ever occurred, according to my respondents. One worker who trained frequently because of the time-and-a-half incentive told me that she would never talk about union issues with new workers.

Shoot, they have enough problems trying to figure out those machines, and all the pressure that they have to get hired. I'm not going to bother them there while they are thinking of getting a job. I never did it and none of the other committee people did either. They can't vote if they're not in and they can't get in unless they do a good job in training.

Once hired, a worker could look forward to an orientation meeting within two weeks in which the anti-union stance of the company would be elaborated by the plant manager. The meetings focused, predictably, on the uniqueness of the work environment at the plant, the friendly atmosphere between managers and workers, the open-door policy and other benefits related to quality of work life, and how all this would change if the union came in. A favorite line used by the manager repeatedly at these meetings was, "If the union gets in, we won't be able to talk to each other." The open-door policy would go out the window and "strict work rules" would take the place of the presently flexible work environment. The teams would disappear and so would each worker's ability to "be yourself" in front of management since the union would make all the decisions for the workers.

The way it is now, the personnel director or plant manager would say, each worker is an individual, with valuable and valued opinions. Workers were told that with a union, they would lose their individuality. Certainly, the people hearing these words at the September 20th orientation, as well as others to come, must have wondered why a union would try to disrupt the best working conditions they had ever enjoyed. They might also have been amused at the announcement of overtime for the next Saturday, the day of an important union meeting.

The union committee's most effective organizing angle, at least during the early part of the campaign, seemed to be best worded in the slogan, "We are the union." In a rapidly fragmenting work environment, the idea of unity, of comradery among the workers, struck a harmonious chord. While management pictured the union as a third party, organizers worked hard to convince workers that it was a second party, the workers, trying to break the present one-party system of management. This issue began to move workers, and the company found itself with a rapidly deflating rhetorical arsenal to parade at orientation and team meetings. Workers began to perceive the company's attitude as whistling in the dark. More importantly, they began to see management's approach to fighting the union as unjust and devisive.

Faced with growing union strength, management began to use the job-evaluation process to deprive pro-union people of their raises by increasing the importance of the "attitude" component. Even if a worker produced at 100 percent, I was told, termination based on some attitude interpreted as poor by peers or facilitator was still possible. One worker was denied a raise evaluation by her facilitator because she influenced people the "wrong" way, her supervisor told her. It is hard to imagine how this would not increase feelings of fear and powerlessness.

Facilitators talked openly of how they had "permission to fire anybody" they wanted and of the "union bullshit." Official anti-union meetings were held lasting one and a half to two hours where employees were treated to the usual dosage of anti-union sentiments from management plus a grim view of the future if the union got in. An anti-union meeting on October 22, 1982, introduced the issue of a possible loss of benefits under a union contract. After this, facilitators used this angle frequently and sometimes unethically. A worker reported that a facilitator asked a pregnant woman, "How would you like to lose your maternity benefits because of this union stuff?" Facilitators told workers they would do anything in their power to keep the union out, and they meant it.

By its actions, the company convinced the work force that all was fair in the anti-union strategy, but some workers didn't like it. By the time of the first leaflet in early October 1982, well over twenty people belonged to the committee, and it was growing. Near the end of October the plant manager received a letter, with twenty-one names on it, informing him of the intention of the workers to become organized. The union filed a charge with the NLRB that the company "threatened, restrained, and coerced its employees in their exercise of the rights guaranteed in Sect. 7 of the NLR Act."

October was a good month for the union, and the head organizer reflected on this in a letter to the local union lawyer written during the first days of November. "The last two weeks . . . have gone well, although the company has waged one of the most vicious attacks I have ever seen on any group of employees." The viciousness was carried out most visibly by the frontline supervisors. The ambitions of Ethicon facilitators for moving up in the company (and possibly making J&J their last employer) had an effect on their interactions with workers as well as with upper management. In spite of their attempt to seem working-class and just one of the guys, their aspirations and position of dominance over the workers aligned them with upper management. Most workers knew this, and most distrusted their actions on behalf of workers.

Alfred DeMaria, in his book *How Management Wins Union Organizing Campaigns* (1980: 201), states a union-busting axiom tailor-made for plants that are quality-circle controlled:

The real value of a supervisor during a campaign is utilizing his knowledge of each of the employees who work under him; their predilections, personal characteristics, and attitudes. Supervisors can be told to make individualized arguments that will have the most impact on each individual, taking into account each employee's problems, job attitudes and motivations.

To identify and control pro-union sentiments in "their people," facilitators at Ethicon recorded in a loose-leaf notebook (kept in the personnel department and known as the "Union Rating Scale") the strength of each team member's attitude toward the union. A +2 rating signified a strong anti-union and pro-company attitude; a −2 identified a strong union supporter. A zero was used for undecided workers who were still susceptible to being wooed by management. This technique, which follows age-old anti-union common sense, was designed by the Ethicon social psychologist who was also the team developer. He was confident about evaluating attitudes through scaling methods.

It would be hard to overestimate the importance of this rating scale from the very beginning up to the end of the campaign. It allowed managers to keep a running tally of projected voting returns and also helped upper management evaluate the efficiency of facilitators in controlling pro-union sentiments. To guard against facilitators' giving overly complimentary evaluations of their teams and thereby undercounting real union support, the social psychologist–team developer served as a secondary voice in evaluating the pro-union sentiments of workers. If he disagreed with ratings, explanations were required from the facilitators, one of whom reported: "We don't tell all because we are kind of judged by it. But we keep it in mind. I don't think any facilitator would lie when it came right down to it. Especially if we felt we were losing to the union."

Similarly, those facilitators considered superior in judging attitudes often "overruled" the ratings of others. One facilitator reported her anger when her area supervisor and the personnel director changed some of her ratings: "I told them, 'okay Frank, why don't you and Joe figure out what my people are and let me know. I really don't want to spend the time *really* finding out.'"

During the early stages of the campaign, upper management restricted the possible range of interactions between facilitators and team members. The union issue, or as the personnel director referred to it in a personal memo to the facilitators, "counterproductive activity," had to be brought up by the employees in order to be put on the agenda of the meeting. The late September 1982 memo reflected managerial policy and emphasized control with a human face: "We have been extremely successful in reviewing counterproductive behavior in front of teams. . . . Perception of fairness has resulted in no discrimination charges being filed. . . . Ideally, team members should bring up these non-productive issues. In the absence of this, the facilitator may need to lead the discussion."

The October 1982 push by the union encouraged management to lift this hold they had on facilitators. The social psychologist–team developer said: "Instead of having to depend on employees to bring things up about the union, to try to keep the union out, we are letting facilitators go. They can do what they want on the union issue." If a facilitator failed to control the team, management exerted its control over both the team and the facilitator. An example of this occurred in late September when a heavily pro-union team (the second of Jack's teams) was disbanded because of the facilitator's lack of control over attitudes. Team meetings, according to him, had turned into "bitch sessions" and nothing was getting done. After talking to team members, however, the picture I got was of an extremely cohesive team that solved problems related to production on the shop floor, as they occurred, instead of waiting for the weekly meeting.

While team initiatives undoubtedly reduced managerial control, they increased the productive efficiency and solidarity of team members. One worker says of her experience on that team: "We worked great together. He said nothing got done but it's because we did it all. They told us that a goal of the team concept was to make the facilitator unnecessary and the team self-controlling. Well, we did that, and see where it got us." Another team member related how the team developed its own very efficient network of support: "We've gotten closer, and we look out for each other, like we are supposed to be doing . . . like what they are saying. You know, disciplining each other and stuff like that. But Jack's getting upset, because he doesn't know what is going on."

Most team members did not mind the decision to disband the team. They were getting little satisfaction and thought the facilitator had a lack of concern for the team. This team carried the fiction of the team concept to its ultimate conclusion, and in so doing, exposed the true colors of the company to many workers. The team was cohesive, productive, participative. It was, by objective standards, a nearly perfect team. From the standpoint of management, however, it exhibited counterproductive behavior, and thus it did not conform to the anti-union sentiments required in management's view of a perfect team.

The suspension of the team supported the view many workers had of the team system as a cult or a "rat" system. As long as criticism was restricted to fellow workers and their attitudes and production deficiencies, then the team was working properly. If criticism turned toward the company and its low wages and obsessive anti-unionism, then the team was considered counterproductive and beyond the control of the facilitator, who was considered deficient. Collective action by workers in the team system has to be tightly controlled or it might spawn independent thinking that is at odds with managerial concerns.

To make sure their spontaneity did not lead to a rash of unfair labor practice charges, facilitators attended weekly meetings, led by external legal consultants hired specifically for their knowledge of anti-union strategies. Information about the legality and illegality of certain actions and about techniques that help blur the differences between legal and illegal developed the facilitators' sense of "gray line" areas. "It's my job to make them understand what they can and can't do during the campaign. What they should and shouldn't do," the social psychologist–team developer said. His job became an entanglement of legal points and frustrations. "They have to understand our ass is on the line here."

Lawyers and managers were pleased with the legal training and the facilitators' self control until the union filed its initial charge, ironically on the same day that the "hold" was lifted on the facilitators. This action by the union was greeted with surprise from management, but it was in line with the legalistic orientation of the strategy orchestrated by their legal consultants, and they were confident, as they were throughout the campaign, of their ability to win the legal battle they initiated. The willingness of the union to take the campaign to the NLRB worried local managers, however, and the filing of the first charges prompted a "big anti-union push" in the form of a meeting on November 5th. The meeting signaled a shift of strategy, which intensified the conflict on the shop floor.

I spoke with the social psychologist immediately after the meeting, and he described a subtle but significant split between the lawyers, who had been dominating the strategy until the charges were filed, and the local managers, who were emphasizing, under his influence, the social aspects of the campaign. He appreciated the need to maintain a legal respectability in fighting the union but thought the lawyers were not fully in tune with plant needs. He and the plant manager felt that the legal consultant was looking to perpetuate the legal battle to the detriment of the company's immediate needs. "[What] we're thinking of [is] getting the union out of town," he lamented, "and he is thinking of a Supreme Court case. We have different goals and that is part of the reason why we have a fragmented strategy. . . . Our problem is that we have no real strategy." By this he meant that the strategy tended to be legalistic, removed from the direct social processes affecting daily operations.

The Supreme Court case the legal consultant had his eye on had to do with the function of the team in the organization of the plant. Apparently thinking of the National Labor Relations Act (NLRA), Section 8(a)2, which prohibits management from establishing and controlling a labor organization in the plant, he asked a question that confirmed the social psychologist's conviction that the legal consultant did not understand the dynamics in the plant. He asked whether teams could control supervisors' decisions.

"He asked because hypothetically, the union could say that teams do control decisions on wages, hours, benefits, etc.," the social psychologist told me. "By claiming this, they could argue that the teams are management-controlled labor organizations. But I told [him] that only facilitators have the power to make decisions, and they represent management."

"But then he asked me if facilitators had ever gone against team decisions, and I said never, but they have the power to do so at any time. . . . Then [he] said that . . . the team could [then] be said to control what the union said it controls. I don't agree with that though. The facilitator controls, not the team."

Perhaps the most craftily contrived method of control that veiled the source of power was the infamous Committee Opposing Organized Labor (COOL), organized in November 1982 and active until the end of the campaign. The members of the COOL committee, as it was redundantly called, were production workers and support staff personnel, but it was organized and directed primarily by the support staff. This was expedient in that it allowed management to keep tight control over the activities of the committee; it was also necessary because in the beginning strong anti-union leadership could not be found among production workers.

Most of the leadership for the committee came from white-collar workers, who were eventually excluded from the bargaining unit. One of the most active members was the secretary of the plant manager. Another member, a key link between upper management, the COOL committee, and the shop floor, was the social psychologist's secretary. Although it is illegal for the company to organize workers explicitly for the purpose of fighting the union, it is not illegal for other workers, whether future members of the bargaining unit or not, to organize against the union. By having the support staff intricately involved in the anti-union committee, management could control the committee while avoiding the legal restrictions involved in such control.

The entire personnel department worked closely with the committee, passing information to its members through the support staff. Most, if not all, of the anti-union literature conceived and distributed by management was either typed or copied by the secretaries and clerks who, in the same week, would meet as COOL members. This allowed management to inform and direct the committee while characteristically hiding its controlling hand. The social psychologist once commented on how this was frequently done: "If I happen to leave some information on [my secretary's] desk telling her to copy it, and she takes it to her boyfriend, who works in printing and is on the committee also, there is nothing I can do about it."

The committee's activities included printing and distributing fliers, and distributing anti-union, pro-company buttons. "I'm pro-company," one union supporter pointed out; "they are anti-union." Most significantly, the committee provided role models of workers that management could support. To be a member meant to be a chosen one, to have status based entirely on attitude toward unionization rather than on performance in the production process. Members received privileges ranging from a preferential work schedules to unquestioned freedom of speech during team meetings. Some even managed to blind facilitators to their tardy arrivals and early departures, and pro-union employees charged that selected and vociferous anti-union committee members miraculously made 100 percent of their daily quotas while spending hours roaming the floor proselytizing. The COOL committee provided management with an organizational mechanism that made workers fight each other over the union issue.

This and other tactical manipulations of the social relations of production were designed and developed under the guidance of the social psychologist, who saw the campaign as a social process. He viewed the legalistic approach as a necessary preventive activity but did not think that an election could be won by simply avoiding unfair labor practices. Thanks to the campaign, he told me, the team was developing as a good "union-busting" organization. The team's potential for this continued to be undermined by the dominantly legalistic approach, and since avoiding legal gaffes was not going to win over the workers, something was needed that would directly affect work relations between pro- and anti-union workers. In November 1982, he supported, with the agreement of the plant manager, a psychological campaign against the workers. "We have to deprive the pro-union employees of status and identify them as losers." This approach would increase conflict on the shop floor and continue to pit worker against worker.

Contradictory statements were made about what Ethicon workers wanted by observers on the scene. A lawyer working on union strategy commented during a private meeting with the social psychologist and me that most workers he talked to simply wanted a more "traditional" approach to authority from management and therefore did not support the participative method. Ethicon workers, he said, were used to paternalistic work relations, and they expected to be told what to do by their supervisors. According to an Ethicon facilitator, however, rather than offering direct and viable input into the system, the team veiled

Ethicon's patterns of decision making: "They talk innovation," she told me, "but this plant is really very traditional, very hierarchical, and very authoritarian."

What was told to workers at hiring interviews about their role in the running of the firm was something quite different from what occurred on the shop floor. This uncertainty made most of them, understandably, desire a situation in which they knew where they stood. "One thing is being shit on," said one worker, "another thing is being told those are roses falling on your head." A distrust of the managerial view was the result when evidence showed that the workers' power was illusory and allowed for more managerial participation in a worker's life than worker participation in the process of management.

The uncertainty about participation, which occurred frequently, was exemplified when one of the earliest teams was saddled with the responsibility of evaluating the poor performance of a fellow worker and decided to suggest termination. The decision was not an easy one, and no team member would have suggested firing the individual had not the facilitator brought up the topic. Yet the decision was made, or so thought the workers. The terminated worker returned the next day, and it turned out that upper management had to review and approve all firings and that this one had not been approved yet. (Eventually, the worker quit.)

Such incidents awakened workers to the dichotomy between what management said and what management did and to the true nature of power. Power was granted to those who supported management's anti-unionist policy, and it was used against those who did not. Favoritism, a tried and true method of dividing the working class at the shop-floor level, was rampant, and lines of conflict and distrust were drawn not only between facilitators and workers but also between the workers themselves.

At Ethicon letting the workers fight each other was of overriding importance, whether it was over the union issue or any other issues. The team system fostered conflict among workers, and management encouraged it. Letting the workers slug it out at team meetings, in evaluation reports, at committee meetings of one sort or another, and in their interpersonal relations was supposedly part of "worker participation" and thus had a profound psychological impact on employees.

One woman had recently returned from an operation. Her doctor had written an adamant note excusing her from any heavy lifting, something she would have to do when setting up her device machine. Joaquin, a facilitator trainee, put her in welding, considered a simple, no-strain job. One of the top plant activists, Maria, who uses a wheelchair and is the only handicapped person at the plant, told the woman that she should not have been made to work, even in welding, immediately after her operation. She was concerned enough about this to call other workers' attention to it. Reportedly, one of them went to the plant manager and complained about Maria's interference. This worker also mentioned that she had signed a union card but wanted it back and that the only reason she was friends with Maria was that she was the link that could get her back her card.

Advice on how to handle all this came from the social psychologist, who suggested that it be brought up at the next team meeting. He told Joaquin, the facilitator trainee, to make sure he was not perceived as attacking the union supporter. "Make it so that other employees come down on Maria," he advised. He also suggested that from then on Joaquin should make Maria do "backflips" for him and should ask her to do small and large favors for him. He said Joaquin should work at making her seem like his "little pet" to destroy her credibility as a union activist and increase Joaquin's control over her. This is an example of how management used the team as a stage for anti-union guerrilla theatre. I was told by the social psychologist that the superficial reason for teams those days was to discuss production issues, "but we are officially using them for the primary reason of keeping the union out." In this game plan all was fair, and nothing was excluded.

The hardened and callous approach in controlling pro-union sentiments in the work force, which I had inadvertantly encouraged in Frank, was widespread and devastating. What happened to a worker named Rosa after she was identified as a union supporter is illustrative of the effectiveness of the company's use of certain workers to fight certain other workers.

When I first started working at Ethicon, I thought the team idea was great. They told me that we had the responsibility of hiring and firing team members and that we could evaluate to see if someone deserved a raise or not. I didn't like the firing part, but I figured if that was the way it was, that was the way it was. I was interviewed by two team members when I was hired, and although I haven't seen any team action on my team resulting in a termination, I've heard of it happening on other teams. We're all told that problem employees can get fired if they don't have the support of the team.

I interviewed a prospective employee when I was fairly new, about a month after starting to work there. My facilitator asked me if I would, and I didn't feel like I had a choice. Her name was Teresa and I recommended hiring and she was hired. On October 25 (1982) the union handed out leaflets at the plant entrance. That was the first leaflet we made out. I didn't hand out any leaflets, but my name was on it since I was a member of the organizing committee. I'm, or was, a member of the compensation committee at the plant too. That's a committee of supposedly six production workers and six supervisors designed to set up a compensation plan or pay scale. I say supposedly because I've never seen six production workers at a meeting yet.

The day they handed out the leaflets I was at a meeting of the compensation committee. The next day, about 7:30 at night, my facilitator came up to me on the floor just when I was heading for lunch and said, "Rosa, I'm very shocked. And a few others are shocked too. Are you having problems in this department? Can I help you with them?" It took me a second to figure out what he was talking about, but I told him, "No, I have no problems." He said, "I just want you to be prepared because I'm going to attack the leaflet at the team meeting tomorrow."

I told him okay, and he said that he didn't think the union was the answer to any problem. The next day we had the team meeting at our usual time [2:45]. He went through the leaflet point by point cutting down the ideas in it, saying the union was lying about its promises. The standard stuff, but he really tore it apart. He didn't make any outrageous threats or anything. He just gave us the argument real strongly from the company's side on why he thought we didn't need a union. After he got through with tearing the leaflet apart, he asked if there were any questions or comments. Teresa spoke up.

She said, "I don't feel Rosa should be on the compensation committee because I don't feel she is trustworthy enough now to express what we feel or want." She said my name had been on the union leaflet with other people she thought were not trustworthy enough because we were not for the Ethicon philosophy, compensation plan, or team concept. She said, "I've been doing my homework. I've talked to Evelyn and I've found out that the people in Somerville are very unhappy with their union. And the people are not happy with themselves. I talked to John," she said, "and I feel that Rosa should step down from the compensation committee." She went on and on about how she had attended a union meeting the previous Saturday and that our issues were asinine.

I was at that meeting and she wasn't there. I mean, there wasn't a huge crowd so [that] I wouldn't have been able to see her or anything like that. When she got through, I said that I'd voluntarily step down from the committee. I didn't want to be on it if people felt that way about it. Plus, I suspected that I was being set up. Teresa had always been my friend. People said we were like sisters, that we even looked like sisters. So I said I'd step down. I hadn't wanted to be on it anyway, really.

My facilitator said that that wasn't right because he thought the other teams should have a chance to hear the issues and decide and all that. He asked the team members what they thought. Most of them just shrugged their shoulders or looked at their watches. Rachel said that she thought I was doing a good job on the committee and she didn't see what my being pro-union had to do with it. A couple of other employees agreed with her. The meeting kind of ended like that. Teresa wouldn't look at me as we walked out. I was a mess. We had been very close friends. She never told me she was going to take this position.

The next day at 2:30 we had a mass meeting of all the employees and teams in drill. The purpose of the meeting was to become acquainted with the new employees and new teams and all that. We had had a very rapid expansion, and we didn't know many of the new employees. My facilitator handled the meeting with another facilitator taking the minutes. We talked about operations for a while and the open-door policy and other communication issues, and then he said, "I have one final issue. It is a concern of [a certain] team that the compensation committee representative step down because she is pro-union. Any comments?"

Then Teresa stood up and brought out all the same stuff she had brought up before. She was very loud about it. Almost yelling. She looked at me and said nothing personal as she went on and on about how there were four others on the compensation committee who were pro-union and that we had to get rid of them too because they are against what Ethicon stands for. Another employee called us hypocrites saying we couldn't be for both. He is a quality-control guy in [another] team. Many employees hollered from all parts of the room saying I shouldn't be on the committee. That I was two-faced and many other derogatory things.

The other facilitator taking the minutes then said that since many of the newer employees didn't know who the representative was, that I should stand up. I stood up with my head down and sat down as quick as I could. Rachel then stood up and said that I had tried to voluntarily step down at the team meeting but that my facilitator hadn't let me. The second facilitator then said, "Well let's ask Rosa what her feelings are on this."

I said, "I feel I'm being harassed for my political opinion." I said, "And that is discrimination." Somebody in the back couldn't hear me and asked what I'd said. An employee said, "She said she's being harassed." Teresa then said, "I'm not harassing you. I'm just stating fact." My facilitator asked, "How many of you feel Rosa should step down from the compensation committee?" There were a few "yeses." Then he asked if anyone was opposed. Herrera, a real anti-union guy, stood up and said, "I'm not opposed. I just want to tell Rosa that I hope we're still friends. But fact is fact."

Rachel said I had done a good job for the committee. And Teresa agreed but said that they wanted me off because I was pro-union. Andres said that if I was doing a good job there shouldn't be any differentiation with regard to whether I was pro- or anti-union.

Nobody much listened. That was pretty much the whole meeting. I was really upset and it took me a while before I composed myself. After a while John approached me and asked, "Is there anything I can do to help you?" My mother was with me at the time and she said to him, "haven't you done enough already?"

Later in the shift John came up to me and asked if he could talk with me a few minutes. We went into the team meeting room and he asked, "How are you doing?" I said, "Fine. I'm a basket case, and I'm real confused, but other than that I'm fine." He said, "It's unfortunate that you had to go through all this." He said he felt I was not totally for the union that my mother had probably pushed me into it. He went into this speech as to why he felt we didn't need a union. Then he said, . . . "Talking to John [a friend] and not your facilitator, what are some of the issues and concerns of the union [that is] trying to get in here?" I told him,

"John, not to be disrespectful, but I'm not going to tell you what any of the issues are." He said, "Okay."

I told John, "You know, this reminds me of a preacher's advice I got with regard to my marriage. She told me to put all the good things I felt about my marriage on one piece of paper and all the bad things on another, weigh them and make my decision." John said, "That sounds like a good idea. What did you decide?" "I left him," I said. "Oh, well I guess there's nothing more for us to talk about." That ended the meeting. As we walked out he said, "Things are not going to get better. They're going to get worse. I'm going to do everything I can to fight the union's getting in here."

I told him to do what he had to do. From then on he hardly talked to me. He wouldn't even look at me, where before we had a very easy, talkative relationship. That next Friday my machine broke down and he just said "Move to another machine, and when they get this one fixed move back," and he walked away. And also, I had never ever had a rejection for quality since I'd been working there. The Monday after all this happened I got a winding rejection right after I got on my machine. They found a beard hair in my tray!

The quality people just pulled it out and forgot about it since it could have just gotten into the product from anywhere, but when they kept going through my tray, they found a long hair wound in one of the sutures, which is really impossible to do accidentally the way we make that product. The thing is that the person on that machine before me is a real vociferous anti-union person, and I really feel I was set up and that she could have done it. Of course I have no proof of this. On the second of November, right after I got in [to work], John told me he had discussed it with management and the corporate lawyers, and it was felt I should step down from the compensation committee, and he was going to bring it up at the team meeting that day. He said he figured it would come up as an NLRB charge, but he said "Such is life." I said, "Yes it is."

One last thing. I know Teresa was set up to do what she did to me because she came up to me days later and said, "You know they forced me to do that, don't you." And I said, "Yes I do." And she said, "Do you forgive me?" And I told her that I never would because some people say things against the union because they really feel it is not the best thing, and I can respect that. But what she did was done to hurt me in a real underhanded fashion and . . . I would never forgive her for that.

This abuse of power turned some previously undecided workers into union supporters. They feared that without the protection of a union, what happened to Rosa would eventually happen to them. Unfortunately, just as many workers were scared away from supporting the union for the same reason. These people realized that what happened to Rosa could, and most likely would, happen to any union supporter. Indeed, without a union, they had no real protection. Instead of being outraged at the incident, they were terrified by it. Instead of banding together to resist, most reacted as management hoped they would react—as individuals afraid of torture.

5

Psychological Tactics and Firings

The decision to develop a psychological approach came in November 1982, at a time when managers, perhaps mistakenly, felt a lack of control over daily strategy. They were afraid the union might file for an election, carry the campaign to the public, and open up a full-fledged attack on the company in order to, as the social psychologist said, "force a big company like us to our knees."[1] Generally, local managers showed strong solidarity during the anti-union campaign, and clashes were the result of corporate strategists' attempts to control major decisions. Needing the corporate okay was inefficient and resulted in a managerial position in which the union acted and management reacted.

The vastness of the J&J empire precluded a higher level of involvement by the corporation, and local managers complained of "half-assed" cooperation from industrial relations experts in trying to get the union out of town and "token" concern with daily operations of the campaign. The social psychologist fumed over the apparent willingness of headquarters to make Ethicon-Albuquerque a part of a "package deal" between J&J and the union. After one especially troubling meeting, he expressed his concern that the corporate lawyer was trying to use Ethicon-Albuquerque as a "bargaining chip" with the union at Somerville, New Jersey, and other plants. "He figures that he can tell the union to lay off Albuquerque now, and we'll give this or that at other plants. Then maybe we can talk about Albuquerque in the future. We really don't want that to happen. We don't want this place to ever have a union, not now, not ever."

In the historical conflict between the area people and the "easterners," the social psychologist, being from the region, was sensitive to the "outsider" image of corporate strategists who frequented the plant. According to feedback he received from supervisors and employees, it seemed that J&J's industrial relations expert lacked credibility because of his "style" and personality. Among the concerns about this man, expressed on various occasions in January and February 1983, he stated: "He comes across . . . as a person who is afraid of his job and who sees the coming of the union as a foregone conclusion. . . . I don't know if he's taking things under the table or what. I'm really suspicious of that. . . . He comes across as a Cosa Nostra type."

To local managers, the most accurate information on which to base a strategy was information they gathered day-to-day, and they often resented corporate headquarters' apparent insensitivity to some of the issues. As his human relations approach to the campaign gathered force, the social psychologist wryly remarked that J&J was always surprised at how smart local management was, that corporate consultants who came to town with preset notions usually found local management's own ideas to be effective. This perception of corporate ambivalence frustrated local managers. It was one reason that the plant manager waited until the last week in November 1982 to insist on a full-fledged strategy.

Local managers preferred a six-month strategy, presumably because they would have fewer dealings with the corporate industrial-relations department; but they were told that a three-month strategy could be more easily controlled. After the November meeting on strategy, at our usual debriefing discussion, the social psychologist told me that the anti-union committee would be given greater importance. He had spent a whole day gathering information, copying it, and passing it on to his secretary for distribution to the COOL members. Also, he said, increased pressure would be put on pro-union employees by intensifying the psychological approach. The key here was to withdraw status, during team meetings and other public occasions, from those identified as pro-union.

"We have to separate the 'winners' from the 'losers,' he said, "the pro-company people from the losers. . . . The quality of employees is significant. The pro-company employees are real winners, in my book. . . . That is the general scope of the strategy. And not screwing up on the legal end. Put pressure on the employees and keep our tails covered legally."

Keeping their tails covered became increasingly difficult because at that same strategy meeting it was decided that the firing of pro-union people would be part of the strategy. Brash as he was, even the social psychologist was surprised at the corporation's acceptance of such an approach. It hardly fit the J&J reputation. Perhaps realizing this, it was decided to wait until January 1983 to start any mass firings. "We don't want to come across as Scrooge", he said, "firing people right before the holidays; but the strategy is to do it."

Instead of being a last resort in fighting unions, the firing of union supporters has become a major tactic for many managers. More workers are being fired today than at any time since the 1920s (Freeman and Medoff 1984). Firing shop organizers, or merely threatening to fire them, creates a climate of fear and intimidation that significantly reduces the fairness of a campaign and the possibility of union success. Indeed, Freedman and Medoff (1984: 236) show decisively that the dramatic increase in firings during union organizing drives has had a great negative effect. They estimate that one out of every twenty union supporters are fired during organizing campaigns. When you consider that most supporters are not particularly vociferous about their union sympathies, it becomes shockingly clear that workers who actively support unionization run a very high risk of losing their jobs in this age of managerial enlightenment.[2]

The idea of firing pro-union people had been on the minds of

Ethicon's local managers for a while. A mass firing had been written off as "too obvious," but the option of picking off the union organizing committee was left open as a move that could prove effective in forcing the union's hand. A worker's job had been on the block back in September 1982. In the words of the social psychologist, she was "a fat slob," a characteristic that apparently made her the focus of strategic interest. Managers had viewed her productivity as subpar, an objective reason with which to back up their decision; in addition they had seen in her the opportunity to put the union in a no-win situation.

If they fired her, they could point at her production figures and make it appear that she would have been fired months ago if not for managerial clemency. If the union made a case of her dismissal, the company could use the same reasoning and be off the hook, without missing an opportunity to criticize the union for defending poor producers. "Look at the kind of people the union defends," the social psychologist said to me as though talking to the workers, "real losers." If, on the other hand, the union did not defend its supporters, the company could also use that failure as a point of criticism. What good is a union if it will not go to bat for the people that give it strength? The message would have been heard by all teams within a week of the firing. The union would have been in a no-win situation while the company was standing on safe ground, appearing steadfast in support of employees.

This particular firing never occurred, nor was it discussed with corporate headquarters. The final decision to make firing part of the strategy was prompted by the union's reaction to two "trial balloon" dismissals early in November. Two employees were sacrificed to see what the union would do if their supporters were fired. While one worker was eventually reinstated due to weak evidence, the union's reaction was weaker than management anticipated, and the lawyers felt confident in their ability to outmaneuver the union on the legal front.

What made the firing strategy attractive was the ease with which the real criterion for the firing, pro-union sentiments, could be camouflaged with the "objective reason," for example, variations in performance levels. Although such variations are expected in any kind of work—especially in manufacturing, where workers have a difficult time maintaining a high degree of interest day after day—they were seen as reasons for firing certain workers. "Anytime we have a good objective reason and a union person is on the block, that is a good combination," the social psychologist told me. The "objective" reason used for the first clear attacks on pro-union people were related to the absentee policy, and in confidence, he admitted that the firings had given a "pretty blatant" message to pro-union people. It is doubtful whether similar behavior from anti-union people would have been so strictly punished. To make the firings appear non-discriminatory, the company used the policy on leaves of absence "really strictly," ignoring past practice in their attempt to point out inadequacies of certain union supporters.

In a second group of firings occurring in December, similarly strict standards were used to dismiss two of the most active pro-union people. The official reason for the firing was "falsifying documents." Apparently one worker had clocked in another worker who had not even been inside the plant. The facilitator had seen the second worker, Mia, come in late and go right to her machine without clocking in. He had grown suspicious, had punched up her number on the computer, and had seen the time discrepancy. After he had reported the incident and all the "proper channels" had been contacted, the two were dismissed. The fact that the worker who had been clocked in early had registered the correct arrival time on her personal time sheet had not convinced management of her honest intentions.

The "proper channels" included corporate lawyers and legal consultants, and all had given their okay, although on this issue the plant manager, B. Jackson, had already made the decision. The social psychologist reported that even if the legal specialists had not agreed, B. Jackson would have fired the workers anyway. "B. Jackson said it would be a good symbolic gesture, a good way to scare other pro-union employees. Even if we have to give their jobs back, it would be worth the hassle to fire them to see what the union would do and to see if it has a desired effect on the rest of the work force."

One of the workers fired in December 1982, O. Sanchez, talked to me at length about the event. Listening to her, and knowing what I did about the real reason she was fired, I realized how little the issue dealt with the actual production process and how much it dealt with the exercise of managerial power. O. Sanchez related the events that led to her dismissal and that of her co-worker.

GG: So they met you at the plant to tell you you were fired.

OS: Right, [they took me into] the suture conference room. What Jack had told me was he said Mia told them that I had clocked her in, and I said no. And when I said no, they got a shocked look on their face like I was going to deny it. And I thought if I denied it, then I don't think I would have been in the mess I was in. But what I did is I figured I'd go ahead and tell them the truth. I said, "No, Mia did not call me." I said, "Her daughter did." See—and that is where . . . I was going to get them, see, because Mia didn't tell them anything. She had, in fact, talked to me the night before, and she said. "I didn't say anything to them." So when I told them no, I didn't talk to Mia, that's when they had a shocked look.

So I knew something was up, but I went ahead and told them what exactly had happened. And then . . . he goes, "Well, this is falsifying records." And I went into, "well, isn't cheating falsifying records?" And he said, "Yeah but it's different, it's something different." And I said, "Well, even drugs, isn't that harsher than what I did?" And he said, "It's different." And he said, "Well, it's not up to me. It's up to B. Jackson, and you can talk to him." I told him, "What's the use in talking to him when you know I'm going to be fired?"

He said, "Well, we don't know. We don't make the final decision . . . if I were you, I'd talk to him." So I told him, "Okay, I'll call him and I'll set up a meeting with him," when I knew I wasn't going to get back in there anyway—but I went ahead and done it. And I talked to him and I went through the same thing with him. I actually broke down and cried and begged for my job back. And he said that there was no way that he could do this. That if he let me back in, this would just be opening up the door for someone else who would do the same thing. And I brought up the fact too about them having drugs in the plant and why weren't they fired for it.

Why am I fired for what I did when drugs seemed to be worse than what I did? And he said . . . he kept saying that that was a different situation, that they had a policy on drugs. And he didn't say if they had a policy on what I did, though. He just told me that . . . he goes, "We have to have trust in our people not to do that [clock others in]." He said, "if I found anyone else that did that, I'd fire them." And I said, "You'd have to fire half that plant because more than half them people do that." And he goes, "Well, if anyone ever brings it up to me, I'll fire them right on the spot."

He didn't want to believe everyone was doing it. "How come I haven't heard about it?" He said. And I said, "Jack knew about it." Because someone had clocked someone else in during a team meeting. It had come up that we were clocking each other in and out. So Jack knew about it. Whether he [B. Jackson] knew about it . . . it was up to Jack to tell him, not me. He wanted to know why I didn't go up and tell him, why I didn't tell him that everyone was clocking each other in and out. . . . He just kept telling me that there was no way, there was no way he could hire [me] back on. . . . There were other things. I don't remember everything that was said, but I actually broke down, I mean begging, and, . . . "No, there was no way." He seemed kind of cold about it. Real cold. Mia did the same thing. He told her not to come in until later on. . . . I was escorted by the guard to my locker, as if I had committed a crime.

GG: What about the drug incident you referred to?

OS: They caught someone with marijuana inside the plant, inside the production area. They weren't smoking, they just had it with them.

GG: What happened to that person?

OS: Suspended for three days. That's what I told them. I said, "I'm not begging for anything. I want a punishment, but I think being fired is going a little bit too far." That's why, yeah. This person was falsifying records, and they claimed I was falsifying records, so why should I be treated any different than these other people? . . . Jack even knew it. . . . He told me, "Yeah," I know it [clocking in and out] has been going on but I haven't caught anybody." That's what he said. B. Jackson said that he didn't know. That's when I told him that Jack told me that he knew it was going on all along, why don't you know? How would Jack know if he had not seen it done?

The two December firings produced results. As one facilitator told me, activities for which pro-union workers were fired occurred "all the time" at the plant, so anyone could be a target. While the union was arguing the issues of higher wages, equal representation, and the inadequacies of the team system, management's position became clearer and indisputably more powerful: The union can promise you anything, but only we can deliver. What is delivered, implied the message, depended entirely on workers' behavior and attitudes toward the union. Management can deliver a pleasant working environment, or it can deliver conflict; it can deliver pleasantries and a benign eight-hour day, or it can deliver a psychological campaign that will make you wilt; and, most importantly, it can deliver a paycheck comparable to most in the area, or it can deliver a pink slip.

Only one additional employee became the victim of a discriminatory firing before the election, but his dismissal gave the company more power in instilling fear in the work force. The person was not recognized as pro-union, although management saw him as a strong pro-union influence at the plant. By moving quickly on the termination, they could diminish the pro-union work force by one, and they could also present an image of impartiality in their termination procedures because this person was not recognized as pro-union. Unfortunately, they did not respond quickly enough. In a letter addressed to the plant manager, Baxter, the worker in question, wrote openly of his support for the union. Although he was eventually terminated, this action frustrated management's attempt to appear impartial in its termination procedures.

Baxter was terminated on February 28, 1983, and the plant manager, in an unprecedented move, wrote a letter to all employees explaining the reason for the termination. After carefully explaining that documents had been falsified and an attempt made to conceal the fact (something which Baxter denies to this day), B. Jackson commented on the spirit in which the letter was written and anticipated the union's reaction.

If Baxter accuses us of taking action against him for any reason other than his misconduct, that would be unfortunate. Neither poor past performance, poor relations with his supervisor nor union sympathies had anything to do with his falsification of records and cover up. Despite union sympathies, the only thing that has ever or will affect anyone's job here is whether they perform their work satisfactorily and try to improve.

The NLRB filed a complaint charging the company with discrimination and Baxter eventually received a substantial back-pay award.

As the campaign continued, the "win at all cost" attitude dominated all aspects of the plant culture. By the end of December 1982, the personnel department, its director, and the social psychologist spent most of their time on the anti-union campaign (the latter's estimate for himself was 90 percent). In addition to refining the efficiency of the screening process in identifying pro-union sentiments, staff, facilitators, secretaries, and office workers played essential roles in the short-term corporate goal of remaining nonunion, which included controlling the actions of COOL. Now more than ever, training and information was provided to help facilitators control pro-union influences in their teams.

The plant manager's overriding concern with union issues in his interactions with his subordinates had a detrimental effect on overall plant operations. Indeed, the social psychologist's team-development job became synonymous with "union-busting," and production issues were relegated to the corporate back burner. "If production suffers," he said, "we have three other plants to take up the slack for a while." At a December 29, 1982, meeting, his report was optimistic, even on the ability of facilitators to keep from asking employees direct questions about the union, which he had complained about a few weeks before. He now saw the role of facilitators in a new-design plant as a complex one. They had to be personable and friendly with workers while maintaining an authoritative, impersonal aloofness. His own training in manipulating people, as he jokingly put it, and his ability to get information without asking direct questions was by the end of December beginning to rub off on the facilitators he was trying to teach.

"You don't have to ask for information directly," he told me. "I start off asking, 'How you doing? Have you been harrassed lately?' Or something to that effect just to get them thinking union. More often than not they tell me about what is happening with the union. Then I end up by saying something like, 'Well, things could get pretty hairy around here if the union gets in.' I tell them that there are no assurances, that everything is negotiable. At least you know where the company stands."

The consensus among managers was that although interrogation was the easiest illegal strategy, it was the hardest to prove if it were done right—no unfriendly witnesses present, and veiled as an "interest in the employee." The personnel department developed a document to aid facilitators in conducting "safe" interrogations, the first draft brashly entitled, "How to make someone spill their gut—interrogation techniques." A legal training session headed by the J&J corporate industrial relations officer was scheduled for the second week in January 1983 to deal with how to make facilitators more creative in the process of gathering data about union support.

In December a new technique for controlling the influence of pro-union workers and their interactions with neutral, undecided, or shaky anti-union workers was already operating up to expectations. Facilitators were told to interrupt conversations or take part in them; to initiate conversations with employees and go with them during their ten-minute breaks; to go back to the floor with them. The method was effective enough to encourage experimentation with controls in other areas of shop-floor interaction, for example, altering the method by which employees received phone calls on the floor.

Apparently, at the beginning of the campaign frequent calls had come in for pro-union people from ACTWU headquarters outside the plant to find out what was happening on the floor. When the phone rang, whoever answered it called the person to the phone. To control access to the plant by organizers, regarded by management as well-trained professionals, one person was put in charge of taking all calls on the floor, a benefits clerk whose sympathies were, not surprisingly, anti-union. When the call was for a pro-union person, she obstructed it by saying the person could not come to the phone but that she would gladly take a message and have the person return the call. Managers figured the caller would leave a number if the call were on the level, but if it were the organizers, no number would be given and no contact made. The benefits clerk kept a tally of calls received by union people as a measure of union activity.

The procedure was effective in cutting down communications between shop activists and union organizers. I asked how the change was justified to workers. The social psychologist often stated that a good solid "objective" reason, also referred to as the "superficial" reason, had to be found for any action by management during a union campaign. In the telephone case the reason given was that with a more centralized procedure all employees would be sure to get calls that may have been missed or mishandled when no one had the specific responsibility for taking them. Now, they told workers who inquired, the phone situation was "under control."

The December creativity was extended into the new year, and the remainder of the campaign was fundamentally concerned with three tactics: increasing surveillance of pro-union activists, emphasizing the uncertainty of plant life if the union got in, and continuing to work in the "gray area" of legality. There was a certain recognition, based on knowledge of NLRB procedures, that the company could out-fox the union on the legal front but that this would not guarantee a victory. They needed to be more creative in exercising control on the shop floor. The emphasis shifted to training facilitators in the "art of industrial manipulation," with the two-pronged purpose of getting an accurate count of union supporters and dissuading others from joining them.

After the decision was made to use the psychological approach as the dominant method of controlling anti-union people, the social psychologist, with the support of the personnel department, became campaign leader. His techniques and ideas usually received the first shot at solving a problem. On one occasion, the J&J industrial relations expert suggested making a concerted effort to get a few key union people to swing over to the company's side in the belief that the rest would follow. Although the social psychologist agreed in theory, he pointed out that the chances of winning over pro-union people were slim. Workers who became strongly pro union acquired a "separate identity," and being asked questions by peers who saw them as experts on workers' rights reinforced their commitment to the union.

The trick, he said, was to keep the undecided majority, the "zeros," from ever becoming union sympathizers by finding their "button," the reason they were attracted to the union and had not already rejected it. Was it the union's support of incentive pay? Tell the high producers that incentive pay was unworkable because of the low learning curve in this new plant, union or no union. Was it the possibility of higher wages or better benefits? Tell them these things could take years of negotiations. In other words, make workers feel grateful for what they had, fearful of what they might lose, and uncertain that anything would be gained if the union got in. Thus the focus of the campaign during the last few months was to increase feelings of uncertainty and vulnerability in the work force. The resulting fear would presumably prevent undecided voters from swinging toward the union.

One of the social psychologist's main tasks was to design anti-union information for consumption by production workers during team and other plant meetings. He depended a great deal on his manipulative skills, picking and choosing and evaluating the best forum for certain information. For example, after various pro-union employees were denied entrance by J&J to the Somerville, New Jersey, plant, managers got a great deal of mileage out of communicating the idea that "only management can deliver." He did not consider this a big enough bullet to unload at team meetings and instead insisted that facilitators bring this up during "informal" conversations with pro-union people. It was "such a good screw to turn," and the effect would be weakened at a team meeting.

He instructed facilitators never to argue with pro-union people. "I can argue, so can other top management people. We don't have to see that person on the floor every day." He seldom stepped in to settle team issues, although he often felt like doing so, because it would have destroyed the elitism he tried to convey by communicating to people on his terms. Yet one of his many tasks was to help facilitators identify pro-union people and back up facilitators who were faced with strong pro-union opposition at the team level. "I'm specifically involved in the team, but the union issue is . . . a greater part of it than it was in the past, so that my role is to substantiate facilitators' impression of who is union."

He used his daily personal contacts with workers to bring up union issues—subtly, as he tried to train facilitators to do. To make a worker open up about the union without asking her to do so directly only required that facilitators make their anti-union sentiments clear, whether at team meetings or in any other communications with employees. Be open with your anti-union sentiments and information, was his message, and people will be open with their pro-union sentiments and information. He felt it didn't take much to get people talking about the union, and once they did, managers and supervisors could open up with their bits of information.

"Put a bug in their brain," he said. "Say [that] union cards are really like a blank check to the union because if you read it, the first thing it says on the back is that I allow the union, I allow the employer, the right to subtract from wages so much money for union dues or whatever. That is the first thing it says. It doesn't say, I allow my union to bargain in good faith, it doesn't say . . . you know, all the idealistic things that unions tell you. But when it comes right down to it, what is the first thing that they want the company to do? Deduct money from your wages.

"And we make that statement. And then they say, 'Yeah well, why did they do that?' And of course, once they ask us those questions we can respond. But it's a real fine art . . . it's a fine line because there is so much inherent frustration in a facilitator that it is truly hard for them . . . because it is so much easier to ask the question 'Why are you signing a union card?' And we have to go about it in such a roundabout way that it takes a while to get your answer."

One day, we were having lunch at a nearby restaurant when

two very pro-union individuals entered. He went to talk to them, remarking with a laugh as he returned to our table, "That's part of our 'take them as they come' strategy." Although he said this jokingly, it was true. He never missed an opportunity to present a worker or a group of workers with the reasons a union would not benefit them. This is what he called "having your antenna up," always being prepared to present the clearest, most effective communication regarding the union issue. The key was to "threaten workers without them knowing they are being threatened."

To pull this off, from day to day he tried to make friends with the workers. Although he was proud of the reputation he was acquiring as a "real union buster," a primary requirement was to present a friendly face, and this allowed him to be casual while identifying the worker's "button" and pushing it at the best time. He made a point of remaining accessible just in case a "loser" decided she'd had enough status deprivation and needed to confess and repent. Most workers, when the pressure became too much, would avail themselves of his function as father confessor. One woman who was on the block for a January 1983 firing made it a point to tell him that she had asked for her card back from the union. This was all it took to get her name off the blacklist. She was forgiven.

I was with him during a meeting he conducted with selected mostly pro-union employees from the channel department when an employee named Margo asked to talk with him. She first asked how the "trial today" had turned out. Since there had been no trial, she grew hopelessly confused and was forced to explain about a phone call she had received from the local NLRB agent. Apparently her name had appeared on complaints against the company about discriminatory firings. The complaints had been filed by the two workers dismissed for "falsifying documents" in December. He informed her that the NLRB had come to collect evidence that day, not to try the case.

Margo was upset because she had not known before the call from the NLRB that the complaints included her name. He told her that management had known all along. This really upset her.

Management should have warned her, she said. Someone should have warned her. He calmly told her that they assumed that if someone's name was being used on a legal document, it was being used with that person's knowledge. She angrily repeated that she hadn't known. He reassured her: "It's a dirty trick of the union." She said, "I feel like going back and suing them for using my name." He agreed: "You have the perfect right to do so." The fact that he appeared to understand her predicament encouraged her to justify her position even more.

Referring to the call from the NLRB, she said, "The woman that called me didn't tell me they were going to use my name. She said that they called me because I was unbiased. I didn't know what she meant by that, you know. I wasn't really for the union, but I wasn't really for management either. I think they're using me as a scapegoat. They need a scapegoat and they are using me as a scapegoat. I said to her that it seems to me that if the union come [sic] in here we can get away with anything. Will the union uphold things like that? Don't I have something to say about how they use my name?" He said, calmly, "You have a lot to say. They are using your name and reputation without your consent. It's just basically dirty tricks."

Margo went on telling him about the call from the woman at the NLRB. "She caught me by surprise. She asked me if the company upholds things like that other times. I said no. It's hard to say that it doesn't happen, I said, but the company don't know about it if it do. It might go on, but I don't know about it. The company don't uphold things like that. They fire people if they find them. I thought maybe I said too much to her." While she frantically tried to appease him, he stood calmly by, letting her talk, nodding when appropriate. He knew that her name had never been on the charges and that the NLRB was simply investigating the allegations in its usual systematic fashion. Her apparent concern was that being questioned during the investigation might somehow make her more vulnerable to the capricious wrath of management.

After she calmed down a bit, he told her that he was concerned about the union's use of her name and reputation without her consent and plainly said that the NLRB agent had "lied to her" about her name not being on the complaint. This satisfied Margo regarding his being sympathetic with her predicament, and she went back to work. She had been identified as pro-union (−1) by her facilitator several months before. He knew, as she did, that offences similar to that of the fired employees were everyday occurrences at the plant. He knew, as she did, the real reason for the firings. He knew, as she did, that she was simply trying to protect herself by protesting the use of her name, hoping that such a show of outrage would inspire managerial clemency, hoping that she would not be capriciously fired. From her perspective, it was all part of being powerless and pro-union in an anti-union work culture. He saw it as the fruits of intimidation, the worker's realization of the source of all power.

The two most effective ways of scaring pro-union people were, according to the social psychologist, firings and suspensions, obviously because of the loss of income or the threat of it. Third in effectiveness were consultations with "problem" employees, who would be called from their machines to the facilitator's desk. A consultation "puts the spotlight" on people, he said, adding that it served as a symbolic threat to union sympathizers. Because the person was still clocked in on productive time, the break from the machine created the additional pressure of having to make up for lost time in reaching the day's quota.

Also in January 1983, the qualifications for trainers of newly hired employees were lowered. Previously selected on the basis of merit, individuals who knew the production process well and regularly made their quotas were asked by facilitators to work at the nearby training center. The job was highly desirable. It required very little actual work, only giving a bit of advice and teaching, and it paid time and a half on the overtime scale. Unfortunately for management, those most frequently chosen had been pro-union. To address this perceived problem, the selection procedures for trainers were altered.

The social psychologist explained. "What we've done is . . . said that if you've been training for six months, you should give a chance to other people to get that experience. So preference is now being given to the younger people on the job, with less than three months experience. The pro-union people were overrepresented in the old group, although we still have a few in the new group, but not as many."

The change in requirements effectively eliminated pro-union employees from the training process. One reported her surprise when, after being told that no more training was going to be done at the center, she saw "all these anti-union people training there." Two months before the election, there were no pro-union trainers.

The multifaceted psychological campaign worked well. Even skeptics realized that ever since the team had been decided upon as the dominant shop-floor strategy to "win over" workers, the outlook for the election had changed. The company was in "the winning mode," and much of the success was attributable to the social psychologist's internal consultations. His insistence on personalizing anti-union information for workers had "hit them with what is important to them" while management still maintained the aloofness of experts. "It makes workers secure when they feel they are working for a bunch of smart cookies," he said.

Strategy for the next three months, designed in late January, kept the psychological approach in place. The communication of management's knowledge by means of the written word was intensified, which in management's view exemplified how the union situation made it necessary for management to use inflexible methods. Efforts to appear to care for employees' off-work existence were doubled. "We are trying to communicate, trying to be open," the social psychologist said. "You have to take into consideration all the facts. The other thing we decided to do was to increase our personal relations with the employees. Make a personal effort to find out what people are doing. How is the wife and kids? What their outside interests are. Not real buddy, buddy or anything. At a respectful distance."[3]

In mid-January the social psychologist commented to one of the legal consultants that part of the strategy prompted by the personnel department was to delay the elections "how ever long it took" in order to hire more anti-union people through screening of potential employees. The lawyer commented that the plant manager should be informed of that strategy because he thought they could win with the present work force and was praying for an election immediately to get the union out of town. The election did not take place until May 12, 1983, and the union, much to management's chagrin, was still not out of town.

6

Participation as Control

After months of the union's insistence that the team concept was an anti-democratic practice thinly veiling the iron rule of oligarchy, I attended a meeting in January 1983 of the channel department's task force. The channel department was a union stronghold, and the task force had been formed in October 1982, ostensibly to deal with issues that concerned all workers from the department, no matter what team they were in. The actual reason for its formation had more to do with its being a social experiment. The social psychologist felt that if channel were controlled, the threat of unionization would subside. The task force consisted mostly of union activists and sympathizers, and being in charge of it himself, he fully intended to make it an ideal team through the exercise of his manipulative skills. The few neutral people on the task force gave little input at the weekly meetings, and he was in the position of having to answer the myriad questions from union activists or somehow avoid them.

Their meeting room was adjacent to the production area and similar to all the others. We walked in before the employees and set up a tripod with a large pad of newsprint paper. After several workers arrived, he introduced some old business regarding the learning curve. This information interested some of the workers, and questions were taken up. The major topic of the meeting grew out of a question a worker asked about the relation between working on new products and one's production quota numbers. Referring to the last meeting of the compensation committee, the social psychologist said that a new policy had been formulated on precisely that issue. He asked Veronica, a worker who was a representative on the compensation committee, to correct him if he had the wrong information and went on to explain the decision.

If a worker got a new product before her "demonstration" period, all she could do was run it, regardless of the result on her numbers. If, however, a new product was introduced while a demonstration was underway, then some adjustments would be made in the expected production numbers to take into consideration the newness of the experience. After he fleshed out the details of the new policy, he turned to Veronica and asked, "Isn't that right?" Veronica replied, "I've never heard this before." He said, "It was discussed at the Monday meeting of the compensation committee." Veronica said, "I was at the Monday meeting and this was not discussed. [The plant manager] called the meeting off because not enough people showed." Silence followed.

Now, at this point the sensible thing for him to do would have been to apologize for the misinformation. He could have said he had it from someone who wanted this policy to be enacted and who, if it had taken place, expected to bring it up at the meeting. He could have asked what the people in the room thought about such an approach, considering it would address the injustice of the present system. Rather than backing down, however, he plunged right ahead, saying it was his understanding that this had been discussed at that meeting, that it was not his responsibility to run the meeting, and that he was just reporting what he had heard. Veronica had him and they both knew it. She said she had little doubt that it had been discussed somewhere, but it had not been discussed at the compensation meeting. "I'm sure management has discussed this, but we didn't hear about it. They can come in and 'vote in' an idea real easily since production people are outnumbered in there anyway."

This subject of the outnumbering of production people on the committee gave him a new direction in which to take the conversation—and he took it there. He asked her why she thought production people were outnumbered and to detail the membership of the committee, and otherwise tried to get her mind off the obvious blunder he had made. He was visibly shaken, and excused himself from the room saying he had to go look for the supervisor who was supposed to address the group on another issue. As soon as he left the room, laughter erupted. Clearly, they saw the situation as a case of outsmarting the smart ones.

At this meeting the social psychologist had shown a mixture of contempt for and fear of the workers, which explained a great deal about the managerial philosophy. My antipathy for his method increased when he laughingly told me after the meeting that he had "really blown it." He had heard the misinformation just ten minutes before the meeting from a manager who had "decided" that this was the way to deal with the problem of new products. The decision had been made, as it turned out, without consultation with the compensation committee. Such consultation was strictly *pro forma* and was not expected to alter the managerial perception of the problem. Apparently Veronica was right about management's ability to "vote in" policy decisions with little trouble. Worker participation was a formality that seldom disrupted management's "hidden agenda." The episode had shown me and the others at the task force meeting the way naked managerial power operates when there is no effective opposition.

In spite of being exposed in this way and of other instances when the arrogance of power shone brightly, most workers were made to see things from the managerial perspective, thanks to management's never missing an opportunity to paint itself, and not the workers or the union, as the victim in an unfair situation—the organizing drive. The first charges filed by the union in November 1982, for example, had been posted by management on the cafeteria bulletin board, along with a memo pointing out the vagueness of the charges, the nit-picking, and how technical the labor law, the language, and the rules became when statements between employers and employees were interpreted legally. This reasoning was used repeatedly to justify the restrictions placed on information and communications between facilitators and workers and to deny repeated requests from union activists for a debate between the union and company representatives.

Whenever possible, management made clear that communications between workers and management lost their flexibility in face of the union's campaign, a situation management claimed they abhorred but like employees had to accept until the union issue was settled. Increasingly, communications from top management to production workers were standardized, well-crafted memos read verbatim at team meetings. Often, the purpose was to gain the sympathy of workers while presenting the human face of management.

At a team meeting in late January 1983, a communication designed by "two lawyers and a Ph.D." was read. It was a response to a union leaflet. Three main points were made about the leaflet: (1) It made supervisors seem to be criminals who operate in an "un-American" fashion, which was not true. Criminal laws were different from civil laws. Labor laws were civil laws, and an indictment could only occur in criminal law. The distinction between fair labor practices and unfair labor practices was hair splitting. Supervisors did not mean to break the law. (2) The team system was not a "rat system." If a "concerned employee" were to see an illegal act, it was his responsibility to do something about it. The union wanted to present concerned individuals as "un-American," which was not fair. (3) Despite the union's position, wages were not the only expense management had. Wages at Ethicon were compatible with those in the local economy. "Why would any company prefer to pay wages higher than do comparable businesses [sic]?"

After the reading, a personal administrator attending the meeting to answer questions apologized for having to read the statement. "We read them because everyone should read the same thing. Our inflexibility increases, the deeper we get into this thing [the union campaign]. I hope we don't get to the point where this is the only way we can communicate with you. I know back a few months people asked why B. Jackson would not debate, and things like that. This addresses that question. Technicalities are incredible. Lawyers have to sort them out. Are there any questions?" There were none.

As the campaign dragged on, workers became increasingly receptive to the notion that were it not for the union, all would be normal; that without the union, stress would be reduced and life could return to normal. As far as I could tell, nothing the union said on the issue of democracy and equitable pay made a very large dent in management's domination of the work force or in the fear that company firings instilled in the majority of workers desperately needing a job.

The best facilitators developed an ability to foster a network of informants, which contributed to friction between workers on the shop floor. This was of increasing importance in the latter months of the campaign. The newest facilitator told me that one of the first things she did in her team of new employees was to set up a couple of informants, or "plants," who kept her up on matters such as when union meetings would take place and what was discussed. Workers' conversations about the union were made to appear illicit and ultimately driven underground or into the realm of whispers.

The union knew that there were no secrets from management and that union meetings were peppered with company "spies." From the earliest company tactics in the campaign, when overtime was pointedly scheduled on the same days as union meetings, to the intensity of the latest managerial tactics, in which supporters were burnt away like moths from a flame, the union knew that some of the bodies at union meetings were people who reported to management. Before one particularly important union meeting, at which someone from New Jersey came to address the workers, the social psychologist wanted an informant to go and report on the agenda, the number of people attending, and what was discussed. A friend of mine had told me of her interest in researching unions some time back, and he went so far as to ask me to send her, suggesting that I not go myself because I would certainly be recognized by the workers. I never asked her to go, but he assumed that I had, and the day after having made the suggestion, he called back and frantically asked me to "call her off." He had checked with the lawyers, and the feeling was that should it be discovered, the connection to the company would be too direct to disavow.

As the company attempted to solidify its position, union organizers and activists tried to develop some kind of solidarity among the workers. Given the amount of control management exerted eight hours a day, it wasn't easy for the union to deal effectively with the issues of substandard wages, the lack of real participation in teams, and workers' powerlessness by making house calls and holding after-hour meetings. In fact, since workers wanted to have work take up as little of their time as possible, many of these issues seemed irrelevant, and rehashing workplace inequities on a worker's own time was more of a nuisance than a consciousness-raising affair. Still, successes came in spurts for the union and in some areas more than others.

In March, to combat the control tactics of the company, the union sponsored a study trip, and five workers traveled to the Ethicon sister plant in Somerville, New Jersey. The trip was designed to prove that contrary to managerial insistence, union plants did work efficiently and with a degree of harmony that was unknown at the Albuquerque facility. In addition, the workers would see that the much bandied-about cost-of-living differences were not as great as those publicized by management, and this would make the higher wages of the New Jersey workers seem all the more attractive and feasible to the New Mexico contingent. Both management and the union were elated that Betty, an anti-union drill swager, went on the trip—the union because they were convinced that Betty would be impressed by the plant, and management because they were sure that her impressions would only increase her leadership role on the anti-union committee.

As it turned out, the union had a good laugh, but not the last one. Before the trip, the company had, in the friendliest fashion, invited any Ethicon-Albuquerque workers who were also in the

neighborhood of the Somerville installation to "drop in" to see it. During the trip, however, the J&J industrial relations department refused to let any of the visiting workers enter the plant. Despite the efforts of the manager of the ACTWU New Jersey Joint Board, J&J refused to meet with the Albuquerque workers inside the plant. The J&J industrial relations expert wrote to the manager of the board.

You have asked me to allow the Albuquerque workers to tour one of our New Jersey plants. I was disappointed to learn that you have already announced to the New Mexico employees that they would. . . . As we have stated in our relationship with your organization different pay rates and working conditions are applicable for different communities and situations which are not comparable. Accordingly we decline your request since it would only continue to encourage inappropriate and inaccurate comparisons by your organization and our employees. We do not view Albuquerque as a comparable plant with Somerville. The manner of operating is different and the comparisons you continue to seek to make are inappropriate.

Despite the company's opposition, workers from the two factories met for hours and discussed working conditions, wages, in-plant relations with management, and many other topics. The visitors also went into the community and compiled an impressive list of retail prices for frequently purchased goods, which was later compared with Albuquerque prices for the same products. Much to their surprise, they discovered that except for housing which was considerably higher, the cost of living in New Jersey was almost exactly the same as Albuquerque's. They were impressed, convinced that unionization of the Albuquerque plant would improve their quality of life, and more importantly, they came back armed with facts to back up their opinions.

Upon her return, Betty's words appeared on a union leaflet. Although she had been ambivalent and even hostile to the unionization of the Albuquerque plant before her trip, the trip had changed her mind. The attitude of the workers she had talked with was one of pride—both in the company and in their work. She felt that this type of atmosphere would be an improvement over the present situation in Albuquerque. In the leaflet and on a videotape of the Albuquerque-Somerville employee meetings, shown publicly at various union meetings thereafter, Betty confessed she felt a union was needed at her plant. Having been away from the "team" attitudes and the atmosphere of the Ethlcon philosophy, and having thought freely about the union issue, she realized that being pro-company was not antithetical to being pro-union. She signed a card and publicly announced her desire to help organize a union. Her newly found conviction was impressive, but it did not survive the company's one-on-one strategy.

One day, soon after her return, she was asked to talk with the personnel director privately. She was figuratively shoved through the "open door" and reportedly kept there for over an hour. Afterwards, Betty was reluctant to talk to fellow workers about what had occurred during that hour, but whatever it was had changed her mind. The following day a well-crafted recantation appeared on the employee bulletin board.

TO: All employees
FROM: Betty M.

As I'm sure you all know, I was one of the five employees to make the trip, to Somerville, N.J. I said in my statement that I was very anti-union when I left. I also stated upon my return that a union was in our best interest. Having had time to study things in retrospect and to do some further investigations from the opposite point of view, I believe this not to be true.

My pro-union statement was made out of emotion rather than logical reasoning. As those of you who have seen the video tape and heard the recordings know, emotions are running high at this time. Being an emotional person, I went along with the tide. I honestly feel my emotions were played upon in order to convince me to make a decision for the union.

What I observed and learned in Somerville did not change my original reasons for being against forming a union here. While in Somerville, a false sense of dissatisfaction and a great distrust of Ethicon was created. Money became out of proportion in importance to me as well as certain petty alleged violations against the company. I am and always have been satisfied with Ethicon and my working conditions. I did, though, learn many things while I was there. The cost of living is not all that much higher. I learned how the union is structured and run, and how their seniority system and incentive programs work as well as answers to many other questions I had.

I wish now to retract my statement concerning the need for a union in our plant. This decision in no way was influenced by the company or anyone else. This is not a reflection on any of the people I met in Somerville. I feel they are honest and sincere in their beliefs and I respect their opinions and I hope you will respect mine.

The social psychologist commented on the incident saying that Betty had been "made to see" that all the attention she had received in New Jersey made her react emotionally to the union issue. The union had paid her way, after all, and she, being a kind person, had repaid the favor by responding favorably to the experience. Once management presented the issue clearly, she realized that the union problem remained the same, regardless of how her particular personality characteristics had reacted to the pleasant trip.

Through this process Betty was "counseled" out of her pro-union sentiments, which had been treated as if they represented a deep-seated personality disorder, as if they were symptoms of an illness. Looking at Betty's New Jersey metamorphosis from the logic of management, by reconciling pro-union and pro-company sentiments, views which management considered irreconcilable, Betty had shown herself to be acting irrationally. She was therefore treated as if she had temporarily lost her senses; as if she had succumbed to an attitudinal sickness that needed correcting through the intervention of the personnel experts. The problem was her personality; pro-union sentiments were simply the symptoms that needed treatment.

According to company estimates, about 40 percent of the production workers signed union cards by February 1983. This was a low estimate of the actual number of cards signed, but in fact the strength of the union did decrease after having peaked in October and November. The firings, the psychological pressures, the length of the campaign, the small-group manipulations all began to take their toll. Management expected a lengthy court battle over the numerous unfair labor practice charges, but they also expected to win the election. And winning was all that mattered at that point.

"The art of social psychology, and it is an art," the social psychologist said, "is that you can plant the seed that will make people think like you think. You get to plant that seed and watch it grow. The hard part, and the part that you have to learn from experience, you can't learn it from a book or anything, is to plant the right seed in the right person. The beauty of it is that they think that it's their idea to act that way." This was how he explained his skills as a social psychologist and how they helped him control the new-design organization.

"It's like, I want you to do certain things for me. But I can't tell you 'Guillermo, do this or that.' Authority doesn't work like that. You can't tell people what to do in an authoritative way like that." Like many managers in today's "new" work environments, he expressed particular pride in being the boss without being bossy, in his ability to control "the puppet without strings." It was this particular skill of subtle control that he felt had landed him this job, and he consciously tried to hone his skill each workday. "So I plant the seed in you to make you think the idea of doing what I want you to do was yours. People have to think they are doing things because they want to, not because you make them or tell them to do it." This good-guy type of control, personal, charismatic, and designed to develop good feelings while obscuring the dynamics of power, is a major characteristic of organizations utilizing the QC and other QWL programs.

When human relations and participative techniques are introduced into a work environment, by whatever party, the stated purposes are typically (1) to democratize the workplace and (2) to increase the efficiency of the enterprise (Deutch and Albrecht 1983). Democratization of the workplace is typically de-

fined as any process "which attempts to increase employee influence in the management process, especially in decision-making" (Bernstein 1976). A more educated work force, the entrance
of women into the labor market, and the deindustrialization process with its accompanying shift from blue- to white-collar labor-
force characteristics, are presented as factors necessitating the
expansion of democracy into the work environment in order to
maintain worker satisfaction and regain the competitive edge for
American industry. Work democratization programs, allegedly
promoting various degrees of worker participation, are now a top
priority of many management and labor organizations.[1]

It is easy to see why such programs, even when only cosmetic,
are attractive to workers and managers alike. Our society tends to
adhere strongly to the so-called classical definition of a democratic society, which emphasizes the importance of participation
(Pateman 1970). This traditional view assumes that a "participatory society" is created through the contributions of a well-
informed, politically aware, and active citizenry. Structural channels, or mechanisms that allow for potential mass involvement in
the political process, must be open to the masses who are affected by hierarchical decision making in order for democracy to
exist. At Ethicon the QC structure allegedly provided the necessary channel by which workers could express approval or disapproval of the actions of both management and fellow workers,
and on this rested the managerial argument of democracy
through QC participation.

A second view of democracy, based on the belief that any citizenry fails to participate in the political process even when structural channels exist, has been more critical of accepting the mere
creation of channels of participation as the key to democracy.
Schumpeter (1942) and others maintained that the ability to form
effective forces of opposition to the ruling authority was the true
measure of democracy. Dahl (1970) noted that the general apathy
of citizens toward the political affairs of a nation was translated
at the workplace into a lack of concern for true participation in
the governing of the enterprise, and also that the converse was
true. The apathy of citizens requires some sort of democratic

structure to represent the interests of different groups equally in a bargaining process.

The traditional view of democracy is the foundation for non-union participative structures initiated by management. Proponents of the second view claim that unionism and the collective bargaining process represent the true and democratic form of participation (Clegg 1979; Dahrendorf 1959; Mandel 1973). Only by maintaining the potential for organized opposition can workers hope to countervail the power of managerial prerogatives and thus achieve meaningful democratization of the work environment. But democratization is not an end in itself, by whatever method it is attempted. The second goal of participative management, the improved efficiency of the enterprise, is the attractive result of the democratization process. By humanizing the work environment along socially approved lines, the ultimate hope of labor and management alike is that more and better products will follow.

While some contemporary studies have found an inconclusive link between employee participation and higher productivity, in the United States, supporters of this position have been few (Steinmetz and Greenridge 1976; Conte 1982; Parker 1985). The link between greater participation of workers as well as of management personnel and greater productivity rises to the level of a truism in literature representing management's view (*World Work Report* 1980; O'Toole 1981; Takeuchi 1981; Faltz 1982; Hancock 1982; Jacobs 1982; Rolland and Janson 1981; Hall 1982). The almost unanimous research conclusions in the field suggest that as participation increases, satisfaction, productivity, and efficiency also increase, although the causal links are not always clear.[2] In an extensive review of the literature evaluating participatory and self-managed firms, Jones and Svejnar (1982: 11) found "consistent support for the view that worker participation in management causes higher productivity."[3]

While the literature on participation points to the positive conditions resulting from increased worker participation in decision making on the shop floor, the literature on control emphasizes the necessity for management to maintain the maximum influence over the behavior of the workers and the plant culture.[4] This leads to the conclusion that participation must also be controlled. Tannenbaum (1968: 23) wrote:

There is no escaping the need for some system of control in organizations, including participative organizations. These organizations are not practical unless they have an effective system of control through which the potentially diverse interests and actions of members are integrated into concerted, that is, organized behavior. The relative success of participative approaches, therefore, hinges, not on reducing control, but on achieving a system of control that is more effective than that of other systems. . . . Thus, there may be relatively little order giving, as such, in the participative system, but the influence attempts that are made are effective; that is, they eventuate in control.

March and Simon (1958: 54) spelled out the benefits they perceived as enhancing control in participative programs:

Where there is participation, alternatives are suggested in a setting that permits the organizational hierarchy to control (at least in part) what is evoked. "Participative management" can be viewed as a device for permitting management to participate more fully in the making of decisions as well as a means for expanding the influence of lower echelons in the organization.

It has been said that in most allegedly participative environments, management leaves very little important decision making up to the worker and instead creates organizational structures that cleanly separate decision making from the implementation of decisions (March and Simon 1958; Dickson 1981). In an interesting piece of research on how worker participation affects managerial control, Mozina et al. (1976: 59–60) stated:

It is possible for managers to increase control they exercise . . . by sharing their decision making authority with lower levels. . . . There is a distinction between power and decision making. Decision making implies power or control only when the decisions made are carried out. Because decisions are not always carried out . . . the actual distribution of power does not always correspond to the distribution of decision making.[5]

Participation also allows for managerial co-optation of worker leadership, and by so doing, increases the control of management over the work force in general (Selznick 1953; Robbins 1983; Mandel 1973). Selznick (1953) explored how the dynamics of leadership co-optation increase management's control over the production process, implying that co-opted individuals (the workers) subsequently exert more effective influence over their peers. Moreover, through co-optation the organization's (management's) influence and control over the individual becomes greater (Witte 1980). McGregor (1960), Likert (1961), and Haire (1962), among others, successfully developed a "human resources" method of participative management that gained popularity in the 1960s and 1970s and is the direct antecedent to the participative techniques currently in vogue, which emphasize control by co-optation.

McGregor's Theory X and Theory Y dichotomy, Likert's organizational family, and Haire's work implied a control methodology based on a more active involvement of lower echelon members in the organization. The explicit goal was to utilize the capabilities and resources of people who don't ordinarily contribute to the workings of the organization so that by feeling more useful, they would identify more fully with the organization and its goals. Argyris's (1964) T-Groups led the list of managerial techniques geared to introducing the self-actualized worker into the suddenly humanized workplace. The latest contribution to the alphabet soup of participative techniques was Ouchi's Theory Z (1981), which, like its predecessors, gave managers a greater control over the attitudes and behavior of workers while giving "the impression of lessening it."

Closer to the methods of control that are utilized in the QC environment, the best-selling treatise of Peters and Waterman (1983) glorified the new humanism in American managerial ideology and admiringly pointed to the "simple control methods" of the excellent companies. Simple controls are those made possible by creating a corporate culture whose values can be internalized by employees, for example, responsibility over fellow workers. In controlling the attitudes and behavior of employees, this translates into the simplest and most effective method: peer pressure. Through institutionalizing the dominant method of controlling workers' behavior, the rule of their peers instead of the rule of law, managers can veil the hierarchical authority patterns of the firm. At Ethicon-Albuquerque the company succeeded in associating the union with "restrictions" and "inflexibility" while pointing to its own "flexible" managerial philosophy as typified by a lack of written rules, or rules of law.

Depending on how pervasive the program, peer pressure can serve as a powerful control device when combined with co-optation and the limitations imposed by management in a (pseudo)-participative environment. Management can forge powerful alliances with the co-opted leaders of the workers and thus influence the participation process though its surrogates. At Ethicon peers were supposedly encharged with the responsibility for hiring, firing, awarding raises, and otherwise controlling the work relations of the plant. That these responsibilities were illusory and that most workers were not fooled did not detract from the advantages management gained from portraying this as a highly participative experiment, an experiment in which people, not rules, governed.

With its power unrestricted by rules, management succeeded in what I call de-bureaucratizing the control mechanisms of the plant. This concept, so critical to the new-design industrial relations approach, is the direct descendant of the bureaucratic control mechanisms that have dominated the development of organizations in the twentieth century. Richard Edwards (1979: 18) considered bureaucratic control the most sophisticated form of control in advanced capitalism:

[It] rests on the principle of embedding control in the social structure or the social relations of the workplace. The defining feature of bureaucratic control is the institutionalization of hierarchical power. "Rule of Law"—the firm—replaces "rule by supervisor command" in the direction of work, the procedures for evaluating worker's performance, and the exercise of the firm's sanctions and reward; supervisors and workers alike become subject to the dictates of company policy.[6]

Yet an even greater sophistication, efficiency, and subtlety is attained by the method of de-bureaucratizing control, in which the following characteristics are explicit: (1) an increased personalization of authority in a supervisor or manager who appears to share the "working class" subjugation to the firm; (2) a decreased dependence on the Rule of Rules attributed to the institutionalization of a so-called "evolutionary managerial style," which allows for rules to be created as threats to controls arise; (3) the accepted managerial prerogative (based on the previous characteristic) of creating a preferred plant culture by defining and punishing deviance not specifically related to objective production performance; (4) the institutionalization of participation as a rigidly controlled activity of the work force designed to fulfill the psychological need of employees to express their feelings; (5) the separation of decision making from the power to implement decisions; (6) the institutionalization of peer pressure as a control mechanism by developing a mythology revolving around worker responsibility for the attitudes and behavior of peers; and (7) parallel with the foregoing characteristics, a managerial rhetoric that de-emphasizes power differences between workers and managers and emphasizes the common purpose of all and the uniqueness of the corporate culture.

Depending more on the managers' skills than on bureaucratic regulations, more on the call to voluntarism than on the appeal of authority, the trick is to make workers feel that their ideas count and their originality is valued while disguising the expansion of managerial prerogatives into the manipulative arena of pop psychology. By depending less on impersonal rules and more on personality characteristics, today's manager effectively de-bureaucratizes the control mechanism of a firm. This new type of control accompanying the new-design participative work environment is rapidly gaining currency as the foundation of industrial relations in industry.

At the new General Motors Saturn plant in Tennessee, peer control is the cornerstone of the industrial relations design. Its purpose is to solve what Braverman (1974) called "the problem of management"; that is, to control the labor process by reducing worker resistance to managerial authority.

In March 1983 the entire Ethicon experience began to make sense as an elaborate anti-democratic experiment in de-bureaucratized control with the purpose of keeping the plant non-union. I had been told at the beginning of my involvement that this was a cutting-edge plant, and had naively assumed this referred to technological innovations; but the innovations occurring at Ethicon were in the technology of human relations. Through a specifically designed, unified managerial view of the work environment, workers were encouraged to see the work experience through the eyes of managers, to realize that all were in it together as equal partners in an unequal division of labor and that it was the union's intention to disrupt this unity.

Being allowed limited participation in decisions that were usually the prerogative of managers, such as hiring and firing, workers were, in the process, encouraged to recognize and respect the myriad difficulties encountered by those in a position of power in an industrial environment. If they could be made to empathize with the problems of management, they would accept their own subordinate position with less reluctance. The effects of the team concept as the major social control mechanism reverberated throughout the entire structure of the plant. What I first saw as an innovative use of a social psychologist to develop the participative scheme was, as I learned during the campaign, a calculated deceit by management to manipulate, control, and dominate the work force. In reality, the informal relationship between facilitators and workers veiled a de-bureaucratized method of controlling attitudes and behavior.

Something about the methods of control utilized by the team system were familiar from my experiences in teaching college students. The medieval type of institutional structure at the university had given me a structural position of authority symbolized by the podium, the table, my ability to move around while lecturing, my speaking on a subject my audience knew relatively little about, and an acquired expertise that had attracted some of the students to the class. This position, however, did not guarantee obedience from students, and that was where control methodology was applicable.

Knowing that the best way to control students' desire to rebel against my authority was to appear to be as much like them as possible without losing credibility as an expert in my field. I talked their language and gained their sympathy and respect. They gave me sympathy for having spent many years reading and studying material that most of them found boring and pointless, and they gave me respect for being able to present this material in their language. The difference between teaching and managing, however, is that professors control in order to share their knowledge with students and make it accessible, thus equalizing its distribution, while managers control in order to restrict and delimit the knowledge of the worker. Indeed, managers control by using the knowledge of the labor process received from workers to foster managerial prerogatives.

In the well-documented process of de-skilling the work force, all communicated knowledge is supposed to serve the purposes of management, either by improving the efficiency of the enterprise or by encouraging workers to accept these purposes as their own. This type of control increases the subordinate group's dependence on the knowledge and expertise of the dominant group. Once this dependency is assured, as in the modern non-unionized work environment, control becomes coercion, and the purpose becomes domination. Teachers, by definition, teach. Managers manage. Thus the tasks and purposes are as different as any dictionary indicates.

Most facilitators I met at Ethicon clearly tried to appear to be working class. They dressed in the same white uniforms, the touch of supervisory difference in the hat more than overcome by the air of equality created at team meetings. Passing information from upper management down and from workers up, they, like the workers, were only doing their jobs. The nature of their jobs was more excusable when they softened the blow of authority with a joke or a pat on the back. Each was a "good old boy," as one worker said of his facilitator.[7]

A worker who in all seriousness referred to the team system as "scary" because it gave her "too much power" caught the full impact of the technique. The message that got through was: management's responsibilities are awesome, and it is the duty of workers to help make them less so. In contrast to facilitators, upper-level managers nurtured the appearance of elitism. They believed that if they became too much like their subordinates, they would lose their credibility as experts without whom the plant could not operate.

The social psychologist, especially, understood the value of keeping a respectful distance from workers and facilitators. "We can't get too chummy or we lose credibility." In order to avoid becoming too familiar, a common figure, the plant manager, visited the floor only rarely or in times of crisis, almost as though slumming it with the powerless might deprive him of his power. With every move, Ethicon attempted to perfect the art of controlling peoples' lives. Management knew how to use information, misinformation, silence, and secrecy to exert their control, all the while calmly portraying themselves as benevolent rulers of a cohesive family, team players in the team concept.

Management's success in controlling the work force through mechanisms other than rules was made clear during a team meeting the social psychologist and I attended in February 1983. The facilitator, Jason, introduced the topic of coffee breaks and what he felt were frequent abuses of the "privilege." It concerned him and other facilitators that some workers would take inordinately long coffee breaks and risk not making their quota numbers. An employee asked if long breaks were all right as long as the numbers were made, explaining that another facilitator had said it was okay at another team meeting. Jason responded, "Yes, that was what I was about to say. John said that he has a guy in his team that always makes his numbers, over 100 percent consistently. But his guy likes to take long coffee breaks and lunches. Now John said that he had no problem with this individual since his numbers are so high."

Before making any sort of recommendation for his own team, however, Jason wanted everyone to know that "we would never fire somebody for taking long breaks." The social psychologist interjected, " . . . right now." Jason said, "Yea, right now," and suggested that the team discuss the issue and formulate a solution. "Let me say something here," the social psychologist said. "Part of the team concept is that you are a responsible human being, responsible for yourself and for your team members. If you see someone else taking too long at breaks, I think it's good if you tell them that they should not. This is one of the privileges you have now. Eventually someone is going to see these people that abuse the privilege and say, Well, they are abusing the privilege, let's make a rule."

It was not until I interviewed workers after the campaign that I learned how few written rules existed at the time of this team meeting. I knew that very few booklets about regulations had been developed—no employee manual, no norms to instruct workers on how to conduct team meetings, on the tasks involved in being a team member, or on guides to behavior. All documents were eventually developed, but until they were, management made the most of the seeming flexibility by threatening to create rules. Controls were de-bureaucratized. An abundance of unwritten rules existed, however, and they were designed to veil their own existence.

It was a rule that team members interview potential employees and evaluate their capabilities and ability to fit into the team concept. It was a rule that team members evaluate each other on a wide range of issues, not all clearly related to production. It was a rule that team members discuss personal difficulties at meetings to help the facilitator decide whether and what intervention was required. It was a rule for peers to control and regulate each other. It was even a rule that workers had to belong to a team and attend team meetings. If these practices had been voluntary, the entire system of control would have crumbled. To help management control the social relations of the plant with a minimal amount of cofidied rules, the invisible hand of peer pressure was everywhere, and it did the job of the most elaborate employee manual.

This system not only allowed management to claim an unheard of amount of democracy at the workplace, but it also gave credence to management's insistent claims that the union would bring in unwieldy and restrictive work rules and make life miserable for the workers. What really concerned management was that the convenient capriciousness of uncodified rules would disappear if definitions of proper and improper behavior were written down. Rules and regulations are the great equalizers. Through bureaucratization or documentation of rules and regulations, managers control the behavior of workers and restrict their own behavior as well. Although codified rules are effective in controlling behavior, employees' attitudes are more easily influenced in an atmosphere that fosters insecurity and uncertainty about outcomes, an atmosphere in which security and certainty serve as the proverbial carrot at the end of the stick. They become rewards for those who exhibit the proper attitudes. For those who do not, there is only the stick.

When I talked to the social psychologist directly about how his skills helped the company keep the union out, he referred to the need for facilitators to become adept at the "industrial manipulation" of opinions. "I have been manipulating people [as a psychologist] for a long time. . . . That is really the skill a psychologist learns . . . to lead a patient to the point where they will think up something on their own that you want them to think up. They are the ones that have to develop it. You can't say, 'Well, the reason you feel this way is that your mother beat you when you were a child.' You have to get them to the point where they realize that the evidence shows the reason they hate women is because. . . . And they have to make that realization. . . ."

He then expounded on the similarities between social psychology, work, and therapy. "That is what I basically find intriguing, and it's basically the same process. The thing about working is that it's like a therapy. . . . [We're telling the worker] 'You will enjoy it. You will tell us everything.' " Elton Mayo expressed the same sentiments decades earlier when he said, "There is a real identity between labor unrest and nervous breakdown." This patronizing, condescending attitude toward workers turns someone who dislikes the working environment into someone who has a "problem" and has to be "treated" in order to conform and accept the legitimacy of total managerial control. The presence of pro-union sentiments among the workers is thus reduced to a symptom of an illness, the illness being an attitudinal one: the inability to accept the existing configurations of the work environment.

In cases like this, it is management's job to treat the individual symptom (pro-union sentiments) while leaving intact the cause of the problem (unequal power in the work environment). Viewed in this light, the team, the "open door," and the "open line," are all manipulative treatment devices designed to address the work-related "problem attitudes" of individual workers without addressing the sources of the problems themselves. Workers have to be led by management to the conclusion that the reason they hate work is because it is natural to hate work; it is as natural to hate work as it is to have to do it, and one must accept this as a necessary evil of life.

A facilitator who reported her disapproval of the company's manipulative strategies and how they reminded her of "KGB" tactics said, "We are being paid to keep the workers down." She knew she was part of a small minority, but in her team she emphasized to workers the importance of getting as much information as possible about the role of unions in society. She got pamphlets from the NLRB and encouraged "her people" to read them. Top management disapproved vehemently. She said management wanted to ensure the reaction of employees and thought she was not exercising enough control over employees' reactions to the union. She paraphrased what top management told her: "Don't think. We'll think for you. Just do exactly what we tell you to do and everything will be all right."

I knew from what the social psychologist had told me that the facilitator's way of doing things was considered "flaky" and unpredictable. She was angry at how top managers wanted her to treat "her people" in connection with the anti-union strategy. She said, if you do it the way she had "attempted to do, by educating . . . what you are doing is that you are gambling. You are gambling and you are being an optimist, being a humanist, believing in people." She said she had "allowed them to think for themselves," and that "doing it that other way," the company's way, the results "are guaranteed. Of course, you are dehumanizing the people you are interacting with," she said, when your attitude is "you can't trust them, they don't know what they are doing, they're dumb."

She was particularly concerned with management's illegal tactics and feared that one of her people, a nice pro-union woman, would soon be out on the street, a victim of discriminatory firing. Although she had never been asked to break the law, she knew of other managers who had not only been asked but had volunteered to do so. She had heard from one particularly anti-union supervisor that he had told the company before being hired that "if they wanted to break the union, all they would have to do" was let him "get in." Another supervisor I talked with expressed similar concerns, although not as vehemently as she. Although some expressed quite a different view, one of proud allegiance to the company and its approach, I realized that I was not the only one concerned about the tactics the company was using to keep the union out.

7

Confrontations

The legal consultant began to worry about my research and called the plant, asking for a complete description of my involvement. He considered me a "wild card" and needed to know how to play me. He suggested, according to the social psychologist, that I change my topic from "Teams in an Anti-Union Strategy" to "Decision Making in Teams" because it would make me a less credible witness if I had to testify at an NLRB hearing. "You could always say that the union issue was not the principal part of your study," the social psychologist told me. "In this way we could discuss the unmentionable topic of the union, but only as a secondary interest."

He assured me that all the information about how teams continue to work in the anti-union strategy would be available to me, but that I should write a research proposal describing my "new" research interests. I agreed to comply with an altered research proposal, but objected to redefining my research at the whim of the lawyers. I would comply but continue to research the use of teams in the anti-union strategy. Thus, in February 1983, as the lawyers worried about my research, I too began to question its purpose.

Once, while coaching me on questions I might be asked by

139

company and union lawyers during a trial, the social psychologist asked, "Are you pro-company or pro-union?" Without thinking I answered, "Pro-company." He laughed. "You can't say that. That would blow your credibility as an impartial researcher." I told him that my true response, after blundering into that knee-jerk reaction, would be, "I'm pro-worker." He still didn't like my response. He pointed out the obvious: As a social scientist gathering data, I was not pro-anything. I gathered data using tested methodology, and the data speak for themselves. "You could be a left-wing Communist and if you use the scientific method properly, your data does the talking."

My data did talk, but I didn't like what they said. I also did not like what I was saying, or seeing. In my regular visits to the plant I saw workers who were tired of it all, unwilling to look me in the eyes as I walked by their machines. Maybe they were even grateful just to work and forget about the power plays pressing in on them as relentlessly as their machines press down on the needles. To them I was not a wild card, I was a known source of stress and frustration. Among the hourly people, only the always friendly receptionist and the secretaries considered me a friend. The other workers eyed me with suspicion. It was not a good feeling. I remember wanting to tell one particularly nervous worker, paraphrasing a line from *The Elephant Man,* "I am not a manager, I am a human being."

With these realizations, and with the hope that I could make a difference, I decided to contact the union and relate what I had learned. I introduced myself to an understandably skeptical regional organizer for the ACTWU. He told me of a committee of community people that had been formed to monitor anti-union strategy at Ethicon. He was not surprised to learn that I already knew about it from the social psychologist, who, along with the personnel director, had suggested that I speak to the members of this monitoring committee to inform them of the positive aspects of Ethicon. The ACTWU organizer asked me if I would be willing to speak to the monitoring committee in an open forum. The thought scared me, but I told him I would discuss it with my wife.

My wife and I were more concerned about what I would say rather than if I would say anything. She had seen me grow increasingly more depressed about Ethicon and knew that all my good intentions to do impartial research were only confusing the ethical issues involved. I called the ACTWU organizer back and told him I would write something up. At the monitoring committee, I presented a strongly worded condemnation of company practices during the campaign. (My statement was later reprinted, with my permission, in *AFL-CIO News*, May 14, 1983.)

Things happened fast after that. I no longer had access to the plant or managers I knew, but I became more closely involved with some employees who had previously avoided me when I walked by, note pad in hand, on the shop floor. They told me a great deal about what they had been going through. I felt a certain amount of responsibility for the difficulties they related.

I was extremely ill at ease going to picnics and other social activities with workers who had considered me a union buster not so long ago. My research had helped management clarify the campaign issues, or so the social psychologist had told me. Strategy group meetings had reacted to ideas he and I had discussed during debriefing sessions. I had discovered books that appeared relevant to the company's strategy and had brought them in. The personnel director had commented on how useful two books dealing with anti-union techniques had been in strategy formation.

Initially, the company refuted my statement in its entirety, calling all my charges lies. Weeks later, the social psychologist and personnel director resigned "for personal reasons," and the company mailed a rebuttal of fourteen single-spaced pages to all employees.[1] Their reaction to my statement, not surprisingly, was to circulate inaccurate information among workers regarding my involvement with plant personnel. Reports and rumors said I had only been on the premises twice; I had invented the entire episode out of revenge; I had asked the company for a "loan" and had been refused; I had been refused a position and had fabricated the information out of desperation. One question asked was why, if I had been so concerned for the welfare of the workers, I hadn't addressed management rather than the monitoring committee.

Facilitators, under instructions, calmly attacked my personal integrity during team meetings. I had, after all, been a friend to the social psychologist and had betrayed his friendship. Some even intimated that I might have been more than a friend to him, and this made my betrayal all the more revolting, and my character all the more venomous. Workers who were influenced by my statement and asked facilitators what reason I had to lie received lectures analyzing my apparent character flaws. Undeniably, I felt a sense of having betrayed a confidence. The social psychologist and I had developed a close working relationship. He served as the perfect gatekeeper to my research information.

The company, and I'm certain most social scientists, expected this professional relationship to supercede all others. Unfortunately, in this case professionalism implied inhumanity. The data, professionally and objectively gathered, deserved my seemingly nonprofessional, value-laden human response. To say nothing would have been to condone the manipulation of people for some abstract notion of corporate prosperity. To say nothing because I valued friendship or felt thankful to the company or respected the mythical sanctity of social science research would have amounted to nothing less than placing the welfare of the workers fourth on my list of priorities.

In the four weeks between my statement and the election, on May 18, 1983, things at the plant heated up more than anyone expected. The company intensified team meetings to a level that surprised even me. For seventeen days straight, plant-wide meetings were held on the union issue. Workers related stories of two- and three-hour team meetings where the topic of discussion, and derision, was the union. Films of strike violence were shown to both shifts on company time, and the plant manager introduced each with his own earnest appeal, "Don't let this happen here." Pro-union workers were harassed more than ever, while anti-union workers enjoyed the free run of the plant during the day to campaign and pass out COOL buttons. The company slogan? "Be a Winner, Vote Company."

On house calls with union organizers and plant activists, I saw the fear that haunted many workers at work and the rage some had for me and my denunciation of the company. I don't know how many of the workers I met eventually voted for the union. If I had been a worker on the floor of that clean, respected industry, would I have had the strength and persistence to demand power? Or would I have ended up succumbing to the fear I saw in most of those I met? How well could I have held up under the subtle manipulation of Ethicon's anti-union strategy? I can't say that I would have made myself proud.

During house calls, I tried to communicate to workers the sense of confusion I felt when I began to discover the true motives of the Ethicon system. I understood their desire to believe that the system was good rather than manipulative and insidious. I told them of the sense of pride I had often felt at being allowed to do research at such a prestigious company, and how I frequently considered myself part of management as I walked the shop floor viewing workers as "problems" to be solved, and the industrial environment as an arena to control and command. In short, I had been seeing the work day from the managerial perspective. I understood the anger, disbelief, and hopelessness. "If what you say is true," one woman said, "what's the use in expecting any better." She felt that the union couldn't make a leopard change its spots.

Others wanted to believe in Ethicon because there was nothing else to believe in. In general, workers wanted to talk, hear what I had to say, argue. As I detailed my experience, pulling out documents to prove my points, a woman who could barely control her anger finally screamed, "You're a liar. You are just telling lies like all the other union people." A woman who had cried when I made my statement to the monitoring committee helped me put the role I had played in this entire episode into perspective. Until she heard me speak, she had felt as if she were crazy: "Everyone was telling me how great a place this was to work in, how lucky I was, how great the team system is. And all I felt like was crying because I felt it could be better. I thought it was all in my mind."

The day after my public declaration I received a call from a local NLRB agent who had read the story in the paper. If what I said was true, which she did not doubt, the company had committed serious unfair labor practices. We agreed to meet the next day to discuss my statement. The bits of information the NLRB had received from the company regarding its behavior during the campaign were significantly different from what I had gathered, and my sources and data were needed to prove that my version was the truth.

After a lengthy discussion, she suggested that I present an affidavit detailing what amounted to grave charges against the company. I agreed to do so, and she agreed to help. How to go about distilling the illegal practices from my 300 pages of notes did not seem an easy task, and I told her so. She suggested that I lend her my notes overnight. After getting a guarantee that no one else would read the notes, I agreed. A couple of days later I reviewed the affidavit the agent had prepared and signed it. She was particularly interested in the accuracy of the sections detailing the reasons for the firing of the four workers. Although the individuals' names did not play an important part in my notes, the descriptions of the incidents were clear enough to identify them.

Her particular interest stemmed from the fact that the NLRB had dismissed the case of discriminatory firing brought against the company by the union. I was at the plant the day the NLRB conducted the investigation into the second set of firings, and I remember the confidence of management. Neither in these cases nor in any of the other firings had the NLRB found evidence of misconduct by the company. My affidavit, she told me, could reopen the cases of all the firings. Indeed, the cases were reopened, and complaints were eventually filed against the company for discrimination in hiring and firing.

At an open meeting about a week after speaking out, I met with workers to discuss my findings. Certain they shared some of the initial skepticism expressed by the union organizers, I had to convince them that I was on the level. A leaflet had circulated at the plant advertising the meeting, which took place at the nearby Amfac Hotel, the same hotel where much of management's strategy was hatched. The secretaries of most of the managers occupied the first two rows, but I took a deep breath and went ahead to present much of the same information I had given to the monitoring committee and to workers who would listen when I visited their homes.

I emphasized the duplicity and the hidden agenda of management. I tried to get this across by making clear that the information management gave workers and the information I had gathered were not the same. Reading various documents that management had circulated for employee consumption during the campaign revealed certain inconsistencies. Employees were being directed to regard management's concern for their well-being as self-evident. Indeed, management insisted, a vote in favor of union representation was a vote against employee well-being because benefits and wages would necessarily be reduced.

Some brave employees were insisting that present benefits and wages represented the basic bargaining position and that the union contract would only increase employees' share of the pie, but management was saying the present condition was all the union had to bargain with and under no condition would Ethicon pay more than the area standard for wages. What I had frequently been told was that the union had to be kept out primarily because in the long run it would increase wages and benefits at the local plant and have repercussions throughout J&J and the industry.

In a point-counterpoint format, I continued emphasizing differences between the information management gave the employees and the data I had gathered. While the company told employees it did not break the law, I had been told explicitly that hiring legal consultants who know "all the tricks" was a great value, that they knew how to maneuver in the grey area of legality and help the company keep itself covered legally. While employees were told teams were designed to help them participate in making work-related decisions at the plant and to unify workers into cohesive groups of friends, the reality of the system was quite different and was obvious to management and most workers.

Teams developed into conflict groups and served the conscious purpose of identifying and dividing pro-union employees from those that were anti-union. Management used teams as part of an effective divide and conquer strategy. While the company said it never surveilled or watched workers, selected anti-union employees and facilitators were under explicit orders to "keep an eye" on pro-union people. The company said no one was hired for anti-union sentiments; yet the screening procedures set up practically assured the identification of pro-union sentiments at one of the various interview levels. The company said that it did not condone interrogation; yet facilitators were taught how to interrogate effectively, and management realized that it was one of the easiest charges to avoid, even if done sloppily.

The company insisted it held high respect for all employees while at the same time allowing facilitators to be overheard in the crowded lunchroom saying that these workers were "too dumb" to be educated in the ways of the real world and "not worth dealing with." The company implied in writing and conversations that the union committed acts of vandalism against employees' property. Yet I was told that the company realized this union was not composed of "goons like the Teamsters," and this realization affected the type of strategy management developed.

Similarly, the company accused the union of using fear as a tactic to divide the labor force, while I detected a primary use of fear and intimidation on the part of the company for the same purpose. If the union campaign turned out to be a social process that divided worker from worker at the plant, it was part of the managerial strategy to make this division one of conflict and distrust. There was a difference between friends disagreeing over an issue and enemies disagreeing over the same issue. It was part of management's strategy to make pro-union people the enemies of anti-union people. Dividing the work force was a tactic beneficial to management, not to the union.

I also mentioned, of course, that, unlike its public posture, management did take part in firing employees primarily for their pro-union sentiments. Most employees in the front two rows belonged to the COOL committee, which management represented as an independent pro-company, meaning anti-union, force within the plant. I pointed out what everyone knew, that upper management had worked closely with the committee, encouraging its formation from the beginning, supplying it with anti-unionist information, and guiding it as part of the overall anti-union strategy.

The workers watching me from the two front rows sat calmly waiting for their turn, and it came during the question period. One woman, a leader of the COOL committee, said that I was lying, particularly about the charges of anti-union people spying on pro-union workers. "It's your word against theirs," she said. I calmly reported that it was a bit more than simply my word. It was their words too. I then produced the tape of the telephone conversation in which the social psychologist had asked me to send a friend to attend a union meeting and report certain information back to him. This quieted many critics but converted few.

It became clear to me that the lines drawn in this union struggle had very little to do with what was right or wrong for an employer to do at work. The issue was who had the power to do more for the workers, and management had convinced most of the workers that management could do more, good and bad, than the union. Most of the workers that criticized me and my position did so because they truly felt that it was in their best interest to keep management happy by keeping the union out. For a significant few, anti-unionism was a crusade, and the union supporters represented infidels. These workers viewed all tactics of management as justifiable.

I thought of the people in the two front rows a few days later, when someone tried to break down the front door of my house, shattering the side gate and all the while screaming, "Come on out union boy, we want to talk to you." Likewise, I was certain that some of the people in that room had phoned late at night and voiced threats that made us all nervous and had called the sociology department of the university and asked whether they knew me and hung up violently when the secretary responded in the affirmative.

Such incidents clearly showed how immune a respected company like J&J is to wrath of public opinion, which expects any violence during a union campaign to come from the union, not the company, certainly not a company like J&J. I could have drawn attention to the union-busting tactics by making the company's harassment the key issue, but I decided against this because I was unwilling to become the center of the conflict. Still, the union organizer and I talked frequently of holding a press conference and detailing, in addition to management's tactics against the workers, the harassment my family and I had endured since my public statement. Although we never decided to do it, we came close, especially in the few days after my wife discovered a private detective surveilling our house.

I had driven to my office at the university that day, which meant our driveway was empty, and, by appearance, so was the house. My wife, inside with my son, noticed a car pass slowly back and forth several times, and she took down the license number. The car belonged to a local private detective, a former FBI agent. We drove past his home, located in one of the most prestigious sections of town, with the intention of demanding an explanation, but decided that would be too adventuristic. Yet, something should have been done. Our house was surveilled often for a year, and at least once an investigator posing as a government agent went through the neighborhood asking questions about me and my family. Our neighbor was asked whether I "spoke a lot about my Cuban heritage." Clearly, nothing was beneath the dignity of J&J in their attempt to disavow my statement, not even attempting to red-bait me. My family and I were forced to temporarily move out of the house on two occasions because of what we saw as real dangers posed by the J&J reaction to my statement.

The press reaction to my statement about the company's tactics was expressed in an article in the Albuquerque *Tribune* entitled "Ethicon Election Could Have Impact on Area Businesses." Anti-worker behavior is not scandalous when the principal concern of state and local governments is to bring in clean industry and keep it. The companies settling in the area did so in part because of low wages, lack of unionized traditions in the work force, and numerous economic incentives provided by taxpayers in the form of grants and municipal bonds. The article's message was clear: A union victory at Ethicon might endanger the continued industrialization of the area.

Companies like Signetics, Intel, and Sperry—Albuquerque settlers of the high-tech boom and showcases for the "benefits" of the union free environment—must have been watching the Ethicon developments carefully. They were not ready to have the issue of unionization invade the area on a massive scale. This point was made to a colleague of mine while she was doing research at one of the plants mentioned above. She inadvertently mentioned the topic of unions during an interview with a worker and when management heard of the remark, she was promptly ushered out of the plant. That crash course in area business politics made her delete any mention of unions in her interview schedule. She later did research at Ethicon while I was there and made a point of never raising the union issue in her interviews.

The union raised the problem of the company's use of teams in the anti-union campaign in communications with state and local leaders in New Mexico, and until the last pre-election moment hoped for a letter of support from the governor's office. The letter never came. Politically, the issues involved were more complex than the simple manipulation of production workers at a new area plant. Many area business people had already accused the governor of having an inordinate pro-union bias. He could not afford to alienate them for the sake of one organizing campaign, no matter how outrageous the behavior of the employer, especially if the employer was one of the new industries that was attracted to the area by government efforts in order to serve as a model for other industries moving to the Southwest.

The union had more success in drawing support from the religious and Chicano leaders. The office of the archbishop of Santa Fe issued a poignant letter to all employees emphasizing the hypocrisy of managers and politicians who self-righteously proclaimed "let Poland be Poland" but ignored violations of democratic principles during the campaign.

The church has often endorsed the idea that free trade unions and collective bargaining are a means for working people to achieve dignity and fulfillment. Pope John Paul II recently emphasized the importance of labor unions in "On Human Work." [sic]

We cannot condemn anti-union attacks in Poland while tolerating such union-busting at home. An important union election is taking place at Ethicon in Albuquerque this week. By getting a Union at this plant in Albuquerque wage earners would gain increased bargaining power, could improve their wages and job rights, and would be better able to provide for their families.

Support for those who are seeking union representation would advance the cause of workers' rights and human dignity here at home and would be consistent with the Church's teachings about the dignity of labor.

The Very Rev.
Director
Social Justice Office,
Archdioces[e] of Santa Fe

A respected former lieutenant governor realized the importance of the campaign and became involved. He sent letters and held meetings, poorly attended meetings, hoping to educate workers on the benefits of unions. At one meeting, he chided one of the secretaries who was a leader of COOL, the plant's anti-union committee: "I changed your diaper and now you're telling me I don't know you. . . . I don't know why you are thinking this way. Unions are good for Chicanos." He also sent a letter to all employees expressing support for the union drive.

I have been following your efforts to organize a Union at the Ethicon plant in Albuquerque. As the former Lieutenant Governor of New Mexico and a working person myself, I am familiar with the need for clean industry in our state. New industries bring jobs to our communities which improve the quality of life for ourselves and our families.

I strongly believe that a Union at Ethicon would have a positive impact which would benefit not only Ethicon members, but also the entire Albuquerque community. First, Union membership at Ethicon would mean higher wages. Higher wages would mean more money into Albuquerque's economy. In addition, a Union at Ethicon would help New

Mexico establish itself as a State interested in the kind of industry which provides fair wages and good working conditions.

In spite of the company's attacks, the Union has conducted itself in a responsible and honest manner throughout the organizing effort.

On May 18, 1983, you will make a most important decision. The decision you make will affect not only your own life, but will also affect all of Albuquerque and the entire State of New Mexico. I know the Amalgamated Clothing and Textile Workers Union is worthy of your support. Don't hesitate to vote for the Union on May 18th. . . .

His committed involvement did little to sway opinion. Although it might not have been too little, it certainly came too late. On the day of decision, no one doubted the outcome. The two shifts of production and maintenance workers, after all they had heard and felt during the grueling campaign lasting a year, filed into the cafeteria to cast their ballots. All they had endured had been for this moment. All they had inflicted on others had been done to sway the weak at this moment. In a moment it would all be over, and they were glad. The time for speeches was over. The high-powered legal consultant, one of many known as union busters among pro-union people, was sure the company had it in the bag, as were the anti-union workers who filed into the cafeteria, especially the clerical staff, who were not eligible to vote but had helped organize and control the COOL committee.

Those that voted for the union, at least the activists among them, felt confident of a different outcome. Although union organizers were noticeably hesitant to sound optimistic, the would-be rank and file saw the future and thought it was theirs. "It will be close," said Mike, the worker that had first contacted the union a year ago, "but we'll win. Some people aren't showing their true colors 'cause they're scared." His was the optimism of those who had overcome their fear, who had openly and democratically campaigned for union organization.

Fear was something the union claimed until the very end, that the company had created—a climate of suspicion and fear and paranoia that was a violation of both workers' rights and the democratic process. Supervisors and employees had spied on suspected union activists, the union claimed. The team system, the rat system, had been used to identify and isolate pro-union people, to create an atmosphere of institutionalized surveillance that affected workers' freedom of choice. (Management admitted to having used the union rating scale after I spoke out.)

It was because of the climate of fear that union organizers refused to be optimistic. They too were certain of the outcome. On the night before the election the union office was a flurry of activity. All had been said and done, and when they estimated their strength, they knew it was all over. "We just don't have it," the union organizer told me, "the votes just aren't there." Then, almost as an afterthought, "Maybe we were too cautious." The union cause might have been hurt by the length and intensity of the campaign, by the exhaustion, apathy, search for relief, any kind of relief, from the barrage of information and the relentless team meetings with their discussions of the union. Even though they had orchestrated the tensions and conflicts, management succeeded in making the workers blame the union. Management had been confident about their control to the very end, and to the very end the union had tried to break their stranglehold on the workers.

Two out of every three workers voted against the union. The final vote was 141 to 71. The night-shift workers I spoke with that night related the party atmosphere of the plant. So exuberant were managers over the victory that they treated anti-union leaders to the night off and invited them to pizza and champagne at a local restaurant. This prompted one organizer to remark, "Well, now we have the slogan for the next campaign. Do you want pizza and champagne, or do you want your rights?" Most pro-union people stayed at their machines, not knowing what to do other than work. Others left, sick. Some dragged into the union office in varying states of depression.

For workers harassed during months of campaigning, the defeat brought on the most damaging bit of harassment. Some said anti-union workers rubbed their noses in it, others blamed the pervasive fear of management for the lopsided loss. "They showed us they would stop at nothing to get you guys out of town," one worker said to a union organizer. Mike reported some conciliatory remarks from his facilitator. "Jack came up to me and held out his hand for me to shake. He said 'I hope now all this animosity and union talk is behind us and we can get down to work.' I said to him, Jack, I'll shake your hand because you won and you deserve to be congratulated, and I'll work as I always have worked because that's my job. But you only won this time, and the union thing will not go away, Jack, because we are the union."

The union filed charges protesting the conduct of the company and its representatives. From surveillance of employees to discriminatory firings, the charges, after the election, again thrust the legal campaign into the forefront of the battle. Lawyers from both sides exerted pressure on the NLRB to speed up or slow down the bureaucratic wheels, depending on who had the advantage. The first hearing of the charges had originally been scheduled for April 1983, three weeks before the election, but the company postponed it a few days before the scheduled date.

Of all the subsequent delays, this was the most favorable for the company. Considering the laundry my testimony would have hung out for the neighbors to see and the intensity of a hearing, in all probability numerous votes would have swung to the union side. At the very least, the sparkling J&J reputation would have been muddied by the fracas. The postponement of the hearing until after the election of May 18 saved the company from the considerable embarrassment of exposing its true colors and, more importantly, from the effect that would have had in swinging the election in favor of the union.

The hearing was postponed four times, twice by the company and twice by the union. The union's postponements were decisions reached in a "catch-22" situation. According to NLRB procedures, each time a hearing is set, only charges issued up to that date are included in the hearing. If new charges are filed, the hearing is postponed pending a decision by the regional director of the NLRB as to whether to file complaints. Twice the union had to decide whether to file additional charges on behalf of grieved employees or refuse the request and go to the hearing with the already filed complaints. The decision was not easy.

Workers came to the union with the hope that it could do something about their situation. To deny them an opportunity to tell their story was not the role the union wanted to play in the work environment. Nevertheless, the union, tired of delays, twice withdrew charges so that the hearing could be held, finally, on February 21, 1984, nearly a year after the election and nearly two years after the beginning of the campaign.

Company lawyers, seeing my testimony as the key to their future, tried everything they could to get their hands on my tapes and my 300 pages of notes. Their attempts shaded into that seemingly irresistable "gray area" of legality. In May 1983, I received what appeared to be a subpoena *duces tecum* from the NLRB. Subpoena forms are issued to all parties by the regional director once a hearing is set. The union and the company can then issue these subpoenas to key witnesses. This particular document instructed me to appear before an "Officer" at the offices of Coole, Tyner and Merwin, management lawyers in the city, on a certain date, at a specified time, and to present to this "Officer" all of my research data.

Knowing little about the legal proceedings involved, I assumed the subpoena was valid and quickly contacted my lawyer. Far from being valid, however, it verged on the illegal. NLRB subpoenas are supposed to be used only to summon witnesses to the hearing, and "discovery," or the ability of all sides to review all evidence to be presented, is not allowed. Not only had company lawyers attempted to use the process of discovery unacceptably, but they had altered the subpoena, a government document, in the hope that I would blindly follow its command.

Specifically, the word "Officer" had been substituted for the crossed-out "Administrative Law Judge," and the address of the company lawyers had been typed in where the NLRB's address should have been. In some confused fit of desperation, the high-powered legal consultants hoped I would follow their orders and meet them at 10:00 A.M. one May morning to remedy their problem of having to deal with my research as evidence. The words of the social psychologist came back like a bad smell: "The purpose of all strategy is to reduce the number of possible outcomes."

Reviewing my data beforehand would have helped them devise their legal strategy in the same way that controlling and manipulating information had operated in their anti-union strategy. The organizers felt confident that the behavior of the company had been outrageous enough to warrant nullifying the election. The union had ventured out on the uncertain legal platform by filing over 60 charges during the course of the campaign. The NLRB had responded by issuing a record number of complaints, for the western region of ACTWU, against the company. All counted, Ethicon faced over 50 unfair labor practice (ULP) complaints violating the "meaning of Section 8(a)1 and (3) of the [NLR] Act which affect commerce within the meaning of Section 2(6) and (7) of the Act." This compares favorably, if that is the right word, with the efforts of the J. P. Stevens company, notorious for its anti-union behavior in the 1970s. At one point, the unabashedly anti-union employer faced 96 ULPs, filed against its regional operations in the southeastern part of the country. Ethicon-Albuquerque, denying anti-union sentiments and operating within the confines of one facility, managed a comparable, if not respectable, showing.

It is not surprising, then, that the company tried until it succeeded to settle the complaints out of court and out of the limelight. For all its maneuvering ability, the company was mired in labor's legal system, along with the union, for a year. Like many other aspects of the labor relations process, this worked in favor of the company. Workers waiting patiently for justice were offered money. Justice was not forthcoming. Delayed and denied, justice was also controlled—by the company's manipulation of the legal process. In an attempt to settle the case immediately after the election, the company offered back pay to dismissed workers and a nominal compensation to workers who brought charges of discriminatory hiring. The union encouraged the workers to refuse the offer and demand reinstatement with back pay, something the company adamantly refused to offer.

The organizers felt certain that the company would eventually concede reinstatement and that ultimately J&J would bend over backwards to avoid the embarrassment and publicity of a public hearing. All the involved workers needed to do was hold out; resist the temptation of the cash being waved in their faces and insist upon justice. It came as a surprise, perhaps only to me, when the NLRB lobbied the workers to settle on the company's terms. According to the union lawyer, at a meeting with the suing workers and the union council, the NLRB general council informed workers that they "did not have a chance" in court and that their best bet was to settle while they could. Despite arguments by the union council that a nullification of the election and reinstatement of wronged workers was probable, the statement by the NLRB council convinced three of the four fired workers.

Had it not been for the persistence of O. Sanchez and her desire to "get back in there and tell them the truth about the company," the NLRB might have succeeded in settling the case as early as June 1983. As it was, the resistance was successful and a hearing date was set for February 21, 1984. Intense efforts by the union organizer were needed to convince the three other workers that the long delays were not the union's fault. At least one worker openly blamed the union for not agreeing to accept what for him would have been a good settlement. He had another source of income, and any back pay settlement was "gravy." In the plant, word spread that the union was again delaying the inevitable and that a good faith offer was being thrown back in management's face. The union's intransigence, not management's avoidance of the issues, became the topic of team agendas and the rumor network.

The company again offered the fired workers back pay without reinstatement, and again three wanted to settle and the fourth wanted her job back. The NLRB informed the fourth worker that they had the power to settle the three cases, separating her charge and trying it alone. Again, this infuriated the union, who saw bringing only one charge as a weak and pointless solution to the issue. O. Sanchez, after consulting with her lawyer, also decided that her case by itself was not something she was willing to pursue, and she agreed to settle. The union refused to sign the settlement, insisting that the only just solution must include reinstatement. However, when all aggrieved parties agree to settle, the NLRB has the power to put the settlement into effect without the union's approval. In February 1984, nearly a year after the election and nearly two years after the beginning of the campaign, the government ordered Ethicon to pay nearly $50,000 to eight workers—four who were fired and four more who were refused jobs allegedly because of their union sympathies. Said the union organizer of the settlement: "It's significant. But $50,000 is a small price for the company to pay for what they did to their employees." Thus ended the long siege where the only identifiable winner was the company.

8

Human Relations and Anti-Unionism

My data strongly suggest that Ethicon-Albuquerque, as a self-proclaimed enlightened employer utilizing the latest human relations approach to dealing with the work force, victimized workers who did not accept the anti-union position of the corporation. I have argued that rather than being used as a method to increase worker control over the working environment, the production team, a quality circle derivative, was used by management to increase its control over workers' attitudes and behavior during an anti-union campaign. Further, I have argued that this was done consciously and deliberately, with the realization that the team had a great potential, under the expert guidance of the social psychologist, to be an effective union-busting tool.

Some observers would view the affair as a misuse of social psychology, an abuse of the role of the personnel administrator, and/or a travesty of the usually beneficial function played by human relations in industry.

Still, others might argue, as did management, that the practices I observed or that employees related to me and to the NLRB were an aberration, the results of an overly zealous personnel

158

department not the consequences of anti-unionist policies on the part of the parent corporation or local plant managers.

My information contradicts the view that the incidents, no matter how devastating to workers, can be reduced to a series of isolated, misguided, and abnormally malicious attacks on a union and its supporters. It is my view that what occurred at Ethicon-Albuquerque was a continuation of the long tradition of using human relations in the service of anti-unionism, the result of a system of industrial relations that applies so-called liberal approaches to controlling workers (worker participation, QWL programs, personnel departments) in order to foster anti-union activities. Since the beginning of the century, social scientists, specifically psychologists and sociologists in the service of industry, have utilized their skills to help management control the labor force by expanding Taylor's logic of control into the realm of industrial relations. This control was very often exerted with the specific goal of avoiding unionization of the work force.

While literature on the current management view depicts work innovations such as those present at Ethicon as a sign of a new humanism in managerial philosophy, the fact is that management has been trying to put a human face on its authority since the beginning of the industrial period. Most of the time, this has resulted from actions of organized workers who had to wrest concessions from management that would not otherwise have been relinquished (Derber 1970; Montgomery 1979). Sometimes the mask has been donned in the spirit of prevention, in response to the threat of unionism.

Human relations techniques have often served managerial ends through the implication that organized action from workers is unnecessary in an environment where benevolent and enlightened management is the caretaker of the interests of all employees, no matter where they are located in the production process. Indeed, by emphasizing the human character of all work relations rather than their class character, human relations techniques help management control the class interests of those we usually refer to as the working class, those lowest in the hierarchy of authority in the business organization. The goal of all such techniques is to convince those lowest on this totem pole that their interests are similar to those who carved the pole.

The use of human relations techniques to convince and influence workers has reflected management's need to increase its control over the work force while maintaining the socially appropriate "liberal" attitudes toward workers and their rights. In the nineteenth and twentieth centuries, as Weinstein (1968: xii) observed, "liberalism has been the political ideology of the rising, and then dominant, business groups." Although liberalism was manifested differently as society changed, business leaders used expressions of liberalism as a means of maintaining both the status quo and their domination of the social system.

Weinstein argued (1968: xiii–xiv):

Business leaders . . . saw liberalism as a means of securing the existing social order. They succeeded because their ideology and their political economy alone was [sic] comprehensive. Radical critics of the new centralized and manipulated system of social control were disarmed and absorbed by the corporate liberals who allowed potential opponents to participate, even if not as equals, in a process of adjustment, concession, and amelioration that seemed to promise a gradual advance toward the good society for all citizens. In a formal democracy, success lay in evolving a social vision that could be shared by most articulate people outside the business community. Corporate liberalism evolved such a vision.

In the 1920s and 1930s corporate liberalism was manifested in the workplace by company unionism, personnel departments, industrial human relations, and other mechanisms intended to express management's interest in workers as individuals with their individual psychological makeup and motivations. It became the tasks of management to become more involved with workers in order to fully understand them and to develop, in line with the liberal ideal of cooperation, a nonconflictive relationship between the classes.

Yet while professing an interest in the rights and aspirations of the individual, the practices of corporate liberalism focused on controlling individuals in their function as producers. In order to make workers as predictable as machines, the "human problem" of production required the utilization of socially tolerated methods of control, and this was soon accepted as a necessary function of liberal management. The engineering of behavior and attitudes became the driving force behind the development of personnel departments, screening methods for employment, management consultant agencies, and work simplification and human relations techniques. In 1915–1916 the American Academy of Political and Social Science devoted two volumes of its *Annals* to the problem of how to manage employees. Included were the comments of Meyer Bloomfield, the Director of the Vocational Bureau of Boston and an active business leader, who wrote: "The biggest of all industrial problems is the problem of handling men" (Ewen: 1976: 13).

Although it was not until 1920 that directing the behavior of personnel began to gain currency as a separate task of management, the human problem began to affect management's approach to controlling the work process before the turn of the century. Cheap immigrant labor and the extensive mobility engendered by the Civil War had created a buyer's market for American industry, and this lasted until World War I. In this favorable environment, businesses grew, bureaucratic patterns emerged, and the by now familiar process of separating ownership from management affected the relations between managers and workers. As these and other internal changes transformed industry, controlling workers became crucial to the managerial activity.

Frederick Taylor's work in 1890 served as the foundation for the study and control of behavior in industry. The basic premise of his *Scientific Management*, as Taylor's movement was called, was the need to functionalize and standardize the production process in the modern firm, not only to increase efficiency but to reduce conflict between workers and management. The "right method" for doing work and the "right habits for the right methods" could be scientifically discovered and made obvious to both workers and managers, who would then reach an agreement regarding the validity of the methods and both parties' responsibilities for carrying them out. "What constitutes a fair day's work will be a question for scientific investigation, instead of a subject to be bargained and haggled over," wrote Taylor (1947: 142–43).

His program seemed to solve the "human problem" of production by allowing managers to calculate as part of the production formula the heretofore unpredictable human element (Taylor 1947: 29–30):

The great revolution that takes place in the mental attitude of the two parties under Scientific Management is that both sides take their eyes off the division of the surplus as the all important matter, and together turn their attention toward increasing the size of the surplus until this surplus becomes so large . . . that there is ample room for a large increase in wages for the workmen and an equally large increase in profits for the manufacturer.

"By implementing the methods of scientific management," wrote Louis Brandeis (1936: 543), "nothing is left to chance."

The formula for class cooperation rather than conflict brought Taylor and his associates over a dozen clients by 1907, companies including steel mills, railroads, foundries, and printers (Nadworny 1955). Although organized labor raised objections to the scientific management movement on the grounds that it was chiefly a scheme to get more out of workers for the same or less pay, implementation of the technique fell squarely inside management's "right to manage" prerogative, which Gompers and the American Federation of Labor (AFL) supported. As John Commons, the noted labor economist, argued, the AFL chose "distribution" rather than production as the focus of its political action. Therefore, when scientific management entered the workplace, the AFL had little choice but to endorse it as a viable method of achieving higher productivity and efficiency, provided unions were present to monitor the process.

One function of scientific management, Braverman (1974) persuasively argued, was to extract knowledge from workers and reserve that knowledge in the managerial domain, thereby controlling the work process. This "de-skilling" operation did not humanize the work environment, and in addition, it resulted in a lack of overlapping, an unnatural distinction between "thinkers," or management, and "doers," or workers (Simmons and Mares 1982; Clawson 1980). Criticisms arose almost immediately addressing the "dehumanizing" effects of scientific management. The economic analyst D. H. Robertson later summarized what had become obvious (1923: 97):

> The latest and most logical extension of the factory system—Scientific Management—aims avowedly at taking from the workman the last vestiges of responsibility for and control over his work. Everything is to be settled by the stop-watch and the instruction card: the distinction between planning and execution, the division of labor between the brain user and the muscle user, becomes complete.

This type of criticism gave practitioners of the nascent social science of psychology the opportunity to exercise their expertise. They attempted to humanize scientific management by inserting the "human factor" into the formula. Psychologists who had been trying to get a foothold in industry since the turn of the century had been mostly unsuccessful in face of the pragmatism and skepticism of management. The limited but measurable successes of scientific management opened the doors of industry to these psychologists and later to sociologists. Under the guise of social science, the study of human relations in industry began to define its purpose and its ethic: to increase the efficiency and improve the financial condition of the firm.[1]

World War I created a seller's market for labor power, and this as well as the success of the Russian Revolution directly contributed to the growth of the labor movement during and after the war. The drift into unionism continued up to 1920, spurred in part by the insistence of federal agencies that contractors participate in collective bargaining with their employees. Although the ranks of labor increased, the rapid development of company unions was also stimulated, and worker organizations controlled by management plagued the independent labor movement for many years (Baritz 1960: 43).[2] These company unions, also known as plans of representation or works councils, were described by Richard Edwards in his important work on methods of control (1979: 105):

The idea of the company union was simple: establish a formal grievance procedure within a context of rigorously defined limits. Given a channel for expression of legitimate grievances, "loyal" workmen would not be driven into the ranks of the unions. The corporation did not overlook the fact that the plans also offered extensive possibilities for propaganda, and the "American Plan" of industrial democracy was much bandied about. Yet the importance of works councils did not lie primarily in the publicity battle; company unions represented a real roadblock to independent unions.

Many major companies adopted schemes that not only offered greater control over issues of managerial interests but also identified the companies as innovative and enlightened employers. General Electric, for example, was a vanguard developer of company unions, and the company gained the benefits of enticing its workers away from independent unions. From 1918 until 1936, company unions dominated the GE work force at its major plants. International Harvester's use of company unions proved that through organizational techniques related to limited decision making, workers could be coerced into not only feeling equal to management but actually performing tasks traditionally performed by management. Their company unions were given the responsibility of hiring and firing workers, recommending wage cuts, and supporting other proposals that were in effect the anti-worker decisions of management (Edwards 1979: 108).

The war also helped social scientists gain entrance into the booming business community. The army's interest in finding people who were officer material promoted the extensive use of intelligence tests that, after the war, psychologists transformed into worker selection tests for industry. The massive testing of all army personnel, excluding officers, allowed psychologists the opportunity to develop efficient tools for measuring personnel traits and the confidence to argue persuasively that they could now measure and catalogue individual differences (Yoakum and Yerkes 1920). Industrial managers began to listen. If indeed individual differences could be effectively measured, the next step was to analyze job requirements so that an exact fit could be made between the person and the job.

The idea of personnel management as a distinct aspect of managing began to spread, and social scientists were finally looked upon as experts on the human element in industrial relations. Human relations and social science opened a brave new world of management control: "The more thoroughly management understood its workers, the less chance would there be to make those drastic errors which had nurtured unionism. If the social scientists were right, an understanding of human behavior would show how to control men" (Baritz 1960: 17). The intense interest in using social science to deal with labor gave rise to management consultant firms. The first psychological consulting firm was established in 1919 by nine psychologists, all former participants of the war effort testing programs. In 1921 James McKeen Cattell founded the Psychological Corporation, a profit-making consultant/firm that established industrial psychological consulting as a legitimate profession.

In 1920 the Bureau of Labor Statistics conducted a survey and discovered hundreds of personnel research agencies that were assisting businesses in controlling the work force. From this group, the Personnel Research Federation was formed. Through its *Journal of Personnel Research* (later *Personnel Journal*), personnel management was legitimized as an independent function of the process of management (Moore 1939: 17; Achilles 1941; Bingham 1928). The centralization of personnel departments among the managerial avant-garde slowly but significantly changed the way managers looked at workers.

The view proliferated that workers would respond with gratitude to personnel programs designed to consider their feelings and attitudes, and this translated into a variety of paternalistic systems of control. The paternalism of "welfare capitalism," initiated at such giant corporations as International Harvester, Pullman, General Electric, and U.S. Steel, was described by Richard Edwards (1979: 95):

[It] represented a sophisticated, well-financed, and widely implemented plan for controlling labor. It reflected the large capitalists' awareness of the need for positive incentives in hierarchical control in order to attract the sympathies of the workers. It promised considerable tangible benefits to those who submitted to the company's paternalism, and it especially rewarded those who over long periods refrained from union activity and remained "loyal" to the firm.

The programs included sanitary improvements of the work site, and plans for stock distribution, sickness and accident benefits, pensions, and other schemes for savings. Capitalists had hopes for such work innovations: "The interests of capital and labor will be drawn more closely and permanently together" (Edwards 1979: 94). Between 1925 and 1930 insurance plans, medical services, and luncheon facilities were the programs most frequently installed. The productivity of the average worker steadily increased, and the membership of organized labor steadily decreased every year during the 1920s. Paternalism seemed to work (National Industrial Conference Board 1931).

The variety of managerial philosophies that emerged with the evolution of personnel departments and the advances of psychological research all attempted to convince the public and the workers that managers were human and on their side. Human relations and employee representation plans designed by those knowledgeable in social scientific theories of motivation attempted to blunt worker militancy and curb unionism by implementing systematic recruitment and screening methods along with other more subtle techniques of control (Derber 1970; Montgomery 1979; Baritz 1960; Edwards 1979). In the 1920s, American management came of age and realized that the "capacity to control rested on the capacity to exclude" (Reich 1983: 53).

Rather than viewing Taylorism as a narrow time-motion study, a broader view is that Taylor opened the door for the scientific study of human behavior and its control in industry. His *Scientific Management* showed managers and capitalists that it was in their own best interest to learn as much as possible about work and workers, both for the sake of productivity and for the sake of control. Thus, although most proponents of the human relations approach point to the famous Hawthorne studies as supplying the first drops of an antidote for Taylorism, it can be said that the Hawthorne studies brought the lessons of Taylorism into the realm of social interactions, the realm of public relations on the shop floor.

The Hawthorne studies made management aware of the importance of controlling group dynamics in the operation of an efficient enterprise, but Taylor had also recognized the importance and power of small groups and the problem they posed for total managerial control. In effect, his entire system of control was designed to destroy the power of worker groups that resulted in "soldiering," or restricting production.[3] Experiments in controlling small groups were being done as early as 1918 when an engineer with an Ohio utility company reported that his use of a "team system" resulted in increased production (Benge 1920). Richard Edwards (1979: 109) reports that small groups used as "company unions" called works councils at International Harvester in 1919 were given very limited manipulative power to govern other workers. In 1920 Benge observed that by transferring low producers to different groups, management could raise the production of all groups within the factory.

Soon after the Hawthorne findings became public in the late 1920s, it became axiomatic that spontaneous natural groupings of workers emerged in all industries and companies, and while management could not prevent their formation, it could learn how to control them. To managers, the problem made explicit in the experiment in the bank wiring room at Hawthorne was that the logic of the production process as interpreted by the workers was different from the logic of management in planning that process. In modern terms, factors in a high quality of work life—low stress, feelings of kinship, and the sense of control over the work environment—were at least as important to workers as producing the highest number of high-quality goods. Management had to devise a method to make the informal groups think like management in the process of producing like workers.

Ordway Tead, an analyst of human nature and work, stated (1933: 184): "The conscious use of small groups to forward the constructive thinking of the members of a corporation about its policies and method is a possibility but newly recognized in the executive world." Precisely because the Hawthorne studies expanded the logic of Taylorism into the field of work relations, their lessons, accepted with very little analysis or criticism, cast a deep and lasting influence on the way managers view workers. The more researchers learned about the interaction of workers and the production process in the Hawthorne works, the more human relations was interpreted as the answer to newly discovered problems of managerial control. Accordingly, work designers have since attempted to develop structures to deal more effectively with the human problem.

In 1929 the industrial research division was formed at Hawthorne with the directive to interview employees about how best to achieve the managerial goals of higher productivity and efficiency. Elaborate questionnaires were developed, and a well-trained staff began the laborious process of interviewing thousands of workers. In spite of attempts to direct the interviews according to the topics on the questionnaires, workers insisted on talking about seemingly unrelated issues—subjects that were of interest to themselves, not to management. After an initial reaction of annoyance, researchers and interviewers realized that the interview experience itself was serving a positive function.

Researchers decided to continue, but with nondirective interviews, a format that fostered confidence, because a worker could talk to a manager or representative one-on-one, and also fostered an emotional release and a feeling of recognition (Haire 1954). As a result of the interviews and management's interest in their opinions, employees began to talk about improved conditions at the plant, and even of a seeming improvement in wages. They were happier and more contented with their lot, even though nothing had in fact changed.[4] Again, through listening to employees, managers came to realize how little they knew about the social dimensions of industry and, thanks to Hawthorne, to realize the potential for industrial human relations. Happy workers had fewer grievances and accepted the working conditions as part of the job, and some managers suspected they even produced more. Managers were convinced that workers were grateful for any attention paid to them and that this gratitude would be expressed in their accepting the conditions of work with less resistance.

The specific result of these findings was the establishment at the plant of a "personnel counseling" service whose task was to change people's thinking in such a way as to make them happier with their jobs. As Baritz (1960: 105) stated, counselors dealt with "attitudes to problems, not with the problems themselves."

The counselor was not to be limited by a problem- or efficiency-oriented approach; he was just to listen to the employee talk. Among his duties, according to an official publication of the Western Electric Company . . . was to watch constantly for signs of unrest and to try to assuage the tension by discussion before the unrest became active.

Listening to workers, which helped drain off grievances that might find other channels, such as unionism, cost management relatively little.

From 1936 to 1955, 22 percent of the counseling contacts at Hawthorne were instigated by the employees, 73 percent by counselors with the consent of the employees, and 3 percent by supervisors (Baritz 1960: 104). Not surprisingly, Hawthorne successfully resisted organizing efforts from several national unions during this period and instead established an independent company union, the Communication Equipment Workers. Personnel departments learned how to adjust people to situations rather than situations to people, and human relations techniques achieved respectability as a method of managerial control.

The conclusions of Elton Mayo, well-known reviewer of the Hawthorne experiments, significantly influenced the continued development of the human relations approach to industrial problems. His ideas are still frequently heard in our age of managerial humanism. Managerial practices and organization before the discoveries at Hawthorne had engendered conflict, and conflict in industry, according to Mayo and his group, was unnecessary, a sign of malfunction and organizational illness. Management's job was to create a cooperative atmosphere in the workplace by (Mayo 1945: 20) "introducing in its organization an explicit skill of diagnosing human situations. . . . By means of this skill management should commit itself to the continuous process of studying human situations—both individual and group—and should run its human affairs in terms of what it is continually learning about its own organization."

Mayo believed that management could overcome much of the alienation of industrial workers and that the small group in the factory could help replace the lost intimacy of preindustrial society and increase the sense of community between management and workers. Managers were entrusted with organizing for cooperation rather than for conflict, and control of the small group was the key to this ideal work environment. Mayo mentioned unions explicitly only twice (Baritz 1960: 113), pointing out their function as bureaucratic forces that resist change and their organization to create conflict rather than cooperation. Although he never said unions were unnecessary, this idea is implicit in his insistence that it is up to management to create the ideal working environment. His solution for the key problem of the day, the conflict between labor and management, ignored organized labor.

Regarding what the Hawthorne experiments showed Mayo, Reinhard Bendix, a noted analyst of work and authority in America, noted (Bendix and Fisher 1949: 316): "Cooperation in the Mayo perspective is a relationship involving happy unorganized (ununionized) workers who unthinkingly and enthusiastically comply with the wishes of management toward the achievement and maintenance of its economic objectives." Mayo and his followers did not analyze the manipulative and contradictory aspects of control implicit in the Hawthorne studies. For example, when management realized that groups such as the one discovered in the bank wiring room could achieve enough power to rival managerial prerogatives, it resorted to psychological methods of control in the form of individual counseling. In addition, regardless of the studies' emphasis on groups, management recognized that being one-on-one with workers was the best way to utilize the structural power of managers and their agents to reduce worker resistance in the workplace.

It was troublesome to management that whenever workers organized, even in small groups, without its direct supervision, they responded by defining and protecting interests not necessarily in tune with management's purposes and goals. By isolating workers from each other under the guidance of a manager, however, he could be transformed back into a boss. The human relations approach started from the conviction developed by psychologists that individuals had to be dealt with individually. It returned to that position after the Hawthorne studies had unveiled the power of the spontaneous unplanned and unmanaged informal group.

Thus, early twentieth-century experiments in worker control resulted in benefits for management. First, individual workers, isolated from their peers and positioned in a solitary stance against management, were rewarded when their "loyalty" to company policies was manifested through returns on investments, that is, through increasing their productivity (under Taylorism) or remaining nonunion or under the regime of company unions and welfare capitalism. Secondly, management was in a position to attempt to convince workers that their interests were shared by management, that conflict was an individual problem to be solved individually and not through organized action, and that managers, more than mere representatives of capital, were also human and shared the shop floor concerns of workers. By rewarding certain behavior, the experiments had a common purpose: to undercut the worker militancy created by alienating and oppressive conditions on the job in this particular historical period. These attempts were ultimately failures due to the gains of organized labor during the 1930s, yet they did not disappear.

As the horrors of the depression and the Congress of Industrial Organizations (CIO) descended on management during the 1930s, industrial personnel work expanded to countervail the appeals of unionization. By 1935 over one-third of the corporations in the United States had established centralized personnel departments. This proportion was higher as the size of an industry increased, indicating that the more workers a corporation had, the more elaborate was the control structure. Proctor and Gamble, a leader in control through human relations, realized that personnel departments were no longer a luxury: "Enlightened industrial relations are a matter of sound business and not of paternalism and welfare" (*Business Week* 1936: 22).

The effects of the Hawthorne findings continued to dominate personnel work. The small group gained a reputation as the ultimate weapon against unionization. This was a consequence of the view of most social scientists and personnel developers that workers who joined unions were stupid, had deep-seated emotional difficulties, lacked recreational or aesthetic interests, were afraid of responsibility, and were irrationally class conscious. A worker joined a union because of the authoritarian character of the union's organization and the psychological benefits of its authoritarianism. An unsympathetic management consultant wrote (McMurry 1944: 15):

[The union] may tell him what to do. He no longer has to think for himself. . . . Once he has been relieved of personal responsibility for his actions, he is free to commit aggressions which his conscience would ordinarily hold in check. When this is the case, his conscience will trouble him little, no matter how brutal and anti-social his behavior.

Unions, then, satisfied only the emotional and social needs of workers, and the small groups, organized and controlled by management, could be used to satisfy the same set of needs. To T. North Whitehead, one of the many Harvard researchers at Hawthorne, unions were only social clubs designed to meet psychological and social needs and merely provided for self-expression and the consideration not found at work. To divert workers from seeking solace in unions, said Whitehead (1936: 80), informal groups had to be developed under the guidance of management. The informal type of organization of workers in the bank wiring room had to be combined with the direct type of management orientation of workers in relay assembly, and management had to "assist working groups to build and then maintain their own social integration and to have these sentiments and customs oriented towards the policies of the firm."

In the decade before World War II, personnel techniques became increasingly more sophisticated, relying heavily on screening tests and attitude surveys to curtail the threats of unionism. Employee training programs surfaced in a big way when the massive organizing drives of the CIO made management realize the need for establishing greater control over workers. In general, the increased activity of the labor movement contributed greatly to changes in the nature of authority in the industrial environment. Emphasis on leadership and persuasion supplanted the crude demand for discipline and obedience, and the dynamics of supervision relied more on understanding human behavior and ostensibly less on raw power. Although the age of human relations did not officially arise as a managerial philosophy until the problems of controlling an expanding work force surfaced during World War II, the labor radicalism of the 1930s made management realize the need for sophistication in control.[5]

The amount of literature on motivation and morale increased. Absenteeism, tardiness, even sickness were seen as problems that management had to control, and the literature signaled the "alienated worker" as the source of the problem. An alienated worker already employed could be dealt with by using human relations techniques. As an industrial consultant observed (McMurry 1944: 13–14):

At least half of the grievances of the average employee can be relieved merely by giving him an opportunity to "talk them out." It may not even be necessary to take any action on them. All that they require is a patient and courteous hearing, supplemented, when necessary, by an explanation of why nothing can be done. . . . It is not always necessary to yield to a worker's request in order to satisfy them.

Even in the heavily unionized core industries, management introduced structures intended to create a caring atmosphere in the plants, and during World War II over 5,000 labor-management committees were operating. Entering the decade of the 1950s these had dropped to only a few (Deutch and Albrecht 1983). To avoid dealing with troublemakers during this time, personality tests designed to cull political radicals and pro-union liberals and to identify passive workers were used more widely. Reportedly, screening for men who were dominated by their wives identified workers who would do what the company told them to do (Knowles 1955: 59). Clearly employers' methods of controlling the work environment were becoming increasingly sophisticated.[6]

Both during and after the war, the idea that supervisors could do their own counseling began to catch on. It was, after all, the process of listening to the worker that created a change in attitude, not necessarily the qualities of the person doing the listening. Supervisors had to become experts in human relations, as C. Wright Mills wrote (1959: 90):

It is in keeping with the managerial demiurge and the changed nature of the foreman's role that he is led into the ways of manipulation . . . to develop discipline and loyalty among the workers by using his own personality as the main tool of persuasion.

Counseling departments began to disappear, and new training methods for supervisors surfaced in their place, with industrial consultants emphasizing the role of leadership and communication. Role playing became a favorite device in supervisor training, first at Harwood Manufacturing, a well-known anti-union firm, and also at other top corporations, including Proctor and Gamble and Johnson & Johnson (Baritz 1960). In the 1950s human relations became an interdisciplinary profession combining psychology and sociology as it addressed the business community's concerns with motivation and small-group dynamics. Business leaders accepted as a truism that the most significant industrial problems were problems of human relations.

Even the ever-present quest for a better machine took second place to the human factors of production. Said *Business Week* (1953: 52), "No matter how fancy the equipment, output takes a wallop unless the worker gets a kick out of his job."

With the acceptance of human engineering (Taylorism with humanism) as a major component of managing for higher productivity, came the necessity to change counterproductive attitudes among the workers. Motivation research advanced to a new phase, drawing heavily from the successes of advertising. Since the Hawthorne studies had unveiled the power of small groups, consultants had emphasized the need to control them for the benefit of management, which was increasingly encouraged to support friendly and informal associations among workers (Scott 1946).[7] Those that did not took the chance that workers would turn to unionism for a solution to their problems. One personnel consultant reported that in 1944, when he advised a company to divide its 25,000 employees into small groups, the company ignored his advice, and "the CIO got them" (Pickard 1944: 236).[8]

Labor relations consultants expanded their influence during and after the war. Nathan Shefferman, an acknowledged and successful union buster (Hutchinson 1970: 179), had founded Labor Relations Associates in Chicago in 1939 with working capital from his employer, Sears and Roebuck, who provided most of his early business. By 1954 he had offices in New York and Detroit and was providing services nationwide to over 400 individuals or organizations. In seven years his firm earned $2.5 million, and his success was largely attibuted to his using the lessons of Hawthorne to help employers avoid unionization. He conducted so-called morale surveys for employers to help assess employees' attitudes toward unionism. He set up on-site employee committees in which he orchestrated anti-employer criticism to uncover pro-union employees. He established "anti-union" committees in shops undergoing union organizing attempts.

By the mid-1950s, social research for industry had become a lucrative business that effectively veiled the function of managerial power at the workplace. Baritz wrote (1960: 209):

Through motivation studies, through counseling, through selection devices calculated to hire only certain types of people, through attitudinal
surveys, communication, role playing, and all the rest in the bag of
schemes, social scientists slowly moved towards a science of behavior. A
new slick approach to the problem of control. Authority gave way to
manipulation, and workers could no longer be sure they were being
exploited.

Participation programs for workers did not develop as a major
trend in the United States until its productive superiority was
first challenged in around 1964 by foreign competition. Before
this time, the workplace was one of the last accepted bastions of
authoritarian leadership in an otherwise supposedly democratic
system. Workers had a better chance of affecting the diet of Soviet
cows through democratic elections of individuals with specified
trade policies than of creating an impact on their work environment. This limitation of democracy in the economic realm together with the alienating character of much industrial labor created a work force that in the view of management and scholars
did not think it had a stake in the products it produced. American workers were alienated. They were, in Mills's phrasing, un-
cheerful and unwilling, and they did not participate in the decisions that affected them most directly—those related to the shop
floor.

During the 1960s, the democratization of the workplace became an ideological banner for many New Left groups. Perhaps
their position was best articulated by the small but influential
Students for a Democratic Society (Newfield 1966: 83, 91–92):

Work should involve incentives worthier than money or survival. It
should be educative, not stultifying; creative, not mechanical; self-di-
rected, not manipulated; . . . the economic experience is so personally
decisive that the individual must share in its full determination; . . . the
economy itself is of such social importance that its major resources and
means of production should be open to democratic participation and
subject to democratic social regulation.

The vision of participatory democracy prevalent in the 1960s
implied a restructuring of American society that was antithetical

to the capitalist mode of production. Nevertheless, personnel departments and human relations experts throughout the country realized that the primary issue management would have to face in the near future was the part individual workers would play in determining the economic experience. It was up to work-innovation specialists to design work environments that combined the pragmatic concerns of management with the necessities of the capitalist system and with the humanizing factors that concerned a more educated work force. Once again partnership plans of various kinds received intense attention.

Although cooperative plans between business and labor date from the turn of the century (Das 1964), nothing parallels the recent surge in programs dealing with the quality of work life in American industry. International meetings on the subject of worker participation have been in vogue for over a decade. Work-reform experiments presented in the government report *Work in America* chronicled the need to align worker aspirations with the work experience. Work-innovation programs began to appear in unionized industries undergoing economic difficulties. Labor-management cooperation increased as international economic conditions negatively affected domestic production.

In unionized shops QWL programs developed, not always without criticism, within the collective bargaining process. In nonunionized shops, QWL programs allowed management to try the preventive approach through worker participation in labor relations. In a time of economic downturn and organizational innovations, QWL programs found their niche in nonunionized shops (Walton 1979). It is precisely this entrenchment and the apparent historic relationship between anti-unionism and human relations that should concern us regarding the true nature of present participatory schemes.

In developing a typology of management-initiated worker participation programs in industry, Poole (1975) asserted that it was of the utmost importance to identify the initiators of participative programs because they often signaled which groups held dominant power in the daily operations of the enterprise. More importantly, the programs tended to communicate the interests and values of the initiating party, and he concluded that manage-

ment often offered "pseudo-participation" schemes that imped-
ed rather than aided workers' attempts to truly influence their
work environment.[9] In nonunionized environments, managerial
initiation of participation programs is the rule, and we can expect these programs to be nonthreatening to management's
"right to manage" and in many cases to be geared exclusively to
increasing productivity and improving quality rather than to promoting meaningful participation.

Participation to some degree in industrial decision making
might make workers more satisfied with their work, more in-
clined to identify with managerial goals, and more willing to contribute voluntarily to the efficient running of the enterprise, but
most managers remain reluctant to relinquish any real power.
Participation is often granted only where no important decisions
are made, from the point of view of managerial interests (Hirszowics 1981: 233, 236), thus reducing the large majority of these
programs into nothing more than elaborate experiments in social control. Companies develop participation schemes to grant a
"feeling" of involvement and a "sense" of control to their workers. (Levitan and Johnson 1982). Without contractual agreement
between workers and management as legal entities, management
will not give up its authoritarian control of "its" enterprise. The
most that can be hoped for is a benevolent dictatorship at the
workplace.[10]

In its attempts to reform the labor law that made the Ethicon
fiasco possible, labor has not been very successful. In fact, labor's ability to work constructively within the present legal system has deteriorated rapidly in the last decade. The Reagan
NLRB came under attack for being an "anti" labor relations board
because of the ideological bent of its members and its record
backlog and predominantly pro-business decisions. The attitude
of the board has undoubtedly left many infringements of labor
law unreported because unions have increasingly refused to deal
with the board in filing charges of misconduct by employers.

Many unions have ventured into civil law to address grievances, and the number of legal actions against employers has

increased for mental duress, sexual discrimination, and even violations of right-to-work legislation, which prohibits discrimination against union members. Creativity becomes necessary when the legal system that protects rights does not operate successfully. Perhaps the best indication of just how strongly business forces oppose labor was the failure of the Labor Law Reform Bill of 1978, a relatively mild piece of legislation introduced in the summer of 1977. The business lobby waged a unified and obsessive campaign to defeat this bill and after its passage in the U.S. House of Representatives spent an estimated $5 million in grass-roots lobbying. Exerting its control over the legislative process, the business lobby prevailed, and the bill died in committee in the Senate.

The thrust of the bill was to streamline NLRB procedures to facilitate more rapid handling of petitions and charges, to apply stricter sanctions to employers who break existing labor law, and to provide "equal time" for unions to "address employees on company time and property prior to a representation election." With these three main objectives, the bill did nothing more than extend some of the rights and procedures we expect from civil law into labor law. Because the efficiency and equality of treatment it stressed are patently in harmony with our democratic ideology, the bill threatened a deterioration of managerial control over the work force. If the bill had passed, with its provisions for equal time for unions on the site of the election and increased punishment for illegal behavior, companies such as Ethicon would be less successful at refusing employee requests for union-management debates and more likely to lose campaigns fought with intimidation and misinformation.

Even if considered "mild," the bill's passage would have reshaped shop-floor labor relations during organizing campaigns. While surprising, the defeat was not unprecedented. Labor has been relatively ineffective in passing what has been termed "special interest" legislation. Attempts have always generated strong opposition from the powerful business lobby. Considerably more success has been evident in labor-supported social legislation, which does not pose a frontal threat to the interests of the business community even though it enhances labor's ability to join with other groups. It is necessary to appeal to a broad base and reevaluate labor law and how it applies to management-initiated QC-QWL programs.[11]

There is a sense of malfunction in the Ethicon case, where work innovations were used to bust an organizing attempt, and in the fact that these work innovations are spreading to encompass an increasingly larger portion of the American work force. Some significant literature has already appeared suggesting that there is something wrong with a labor law that permits the type of control QCs afford management.[12] If participative programs in general and quality circles in particular serve as such potent tools of exerting managerial control over the behavior and attitudes of workers in a nonunionized environment, do they violate specific sections of existing labor law? Specifically, how do the employer restrictions in Article 8(a)2 of the National Labor Relations Act (NLRA) apply to management controlled quality circles? Specifically in the case of Ethicon, to what extent do the ostensible "managerial" powers of production workers—for example, to hire, fire, discipline, and assist in promotion—affect the designation of "appropriate unit" during an election?

Let's take each point separately. The NLRA presented certain safeguards, somewhat weakened by the Taft-Hartley Amendment, inhibiting the potential for employers to exert undue control over the formation of employee organizations at a work site. Section 8(a)2 forbids domination and assistance by an employer of a labor organization. The understanding is that only an independent organization can represent the interests of workers if they are to have equality in confrontations with management. Two questions, then, arise: Are quality circles labor organizations according to the NLRA definition of the term? And if they are, what constitutes illegal domination and control by management?

In deciding what constitutes a labor organization, the NLRB refers to Section 2(5) of the NLRA:

[A labor organization is an organization] of any kind, or any agency or employee representation committee or plan, in which employees participate and which exists for the purpose, in whole or part, of dealing with employers concerning grievances, labor disputes, wages, rates of pay, hours of employment or conditions of work.

An organization does not have to label itself a union to be considered a labor organization under this broad definition. In specific cases, however, the NLRB looks at three primary criteria to determine if a labor organization exists.

First, the NLRB looks for certain structural components of the organization. Does its structure allow its members substantial participation in the affairs of the organization? It is not necessary for the organization to have an elaborate administration consisting of bylaws, officers, and dues. This is a broad criterion that gains its interpretation from specific situations. Secondly, the NLRB reviews the subject matter discussed at organizational meetings and who participates in the discussions. Does the organization allow interchanges between management and employees, or their representatives, on the topics referred to in Section 2(5), grievances, wages, labor disputes, rates of pay, hours of work, and conditions of employment? If this is the case, a labor organization might exist.

Thirdly, does the organization exist "in whole or part" for the purpose of dealing with the employer? What constitutes "dealing with" has been interpreted by both the NLRB and the U.S. Supreme Court as not being restricted to bargaining. Other less formal exchanges between management and employees qualify, including counseling, advising, making suggestions or recommendations, and simply asking questions.[13] These three criteria are met rather easily by any participative program in a nonunion environment that uses the group approach to organizing workers. In fact, much of the rationale for participative management rests on the principle of opening the channels of communication between management and workers on issues such as grievances and other aspects of working conditions.

Certainly at Ethicon workers were reminded that the QC already provided all that the union could offer in terms of communication between managers and workers, and no topic was out of bounds for discussion at team meetings. The facilitator heard workers' suggestions regarding all aspects of work conditions and relayed their concerns to upper management. Indeed, a facilitator once told me of the routine bargaining that used to occur at team meetings over specific work conditions and how this practice had to be curtailed during the campaign. The QC served as an "innovative" labor organization, an alternative to unionization.[14]

While the intent of the law is to prevent an employer from establishing a "company union," the type of managerial involvement in Ethicon quality circles resembled the company union structure of the 1920s and 1930s. They too offered management the appearance of encouraging participation while maintaining absolute control. They too offered the opportunity to control participation and by so doing to avoid dealing with independent labor organizations. The specific question in establishing managerial domination of a labor organization is how much an employer can cooperate with an employee organization before it is considered domination or interference. The NLRB has emphasized that it will strictly interpret the NLRA by finding violations even when the evidence points to potential control.

The more the employer or the supervisors are involved in the regular operations of an employee committee or of labor organizations, the more likely that a violation will be found.[15] While there is a growing body of court-made law that permits greater cooperation between employees and employers, the possibility of using cooperative programs in the service of anti-unionism is evident. Brown (1986: 316) wrote: "The board and the courts should be cautious that such cooperative approaches are not used as anti-union devices by sophisticated employers." Schmidman and Keller (1984: 778) issued a warning that fits the Ethicon case:

Except in blatant cases, antiunion animus is difficult to prove. Managers are increasingly sophisticated and subtle in their strategies to keep unions out. The publicly stated goals of employee participation plans are often mere gloss and state only a portion of the intended goals. No informed manager will openly reveal that an important goal of an employee participation plan is to weaken existing unions or to keep employees from unionizing. Cases involving less direct evidence or motive are often found not to violate the Act.

It appears arguable that quality circles as used at Ethicon provide direct evidence of the anti-union use of such programs.

On the determination of "appropriate unit" and quality circles, a couple of points should be mentioned. The Taft-Hartley introduction of the appropriate-unit clause is generally interpreted as an attempt to weaken the threat posed by the CIO's insistence, and successes, in organizing "one big union" at each work site. The new regulation effectively fragmented the industrial labor force. The less cohesive the labor force, the easier it is to control. The ostensible reason given for the segmentation (the "superficial reason," as the social psychologist would have said) was that certain workers have more job-related interests in common. Typically this is interpreted according to duties detailed in work descriptions. Workers directly involved in the production process, for example, have different interests from white collar workers associated with production. Thus secretaries and even quality-control personnel are routinely excluded from "appropriate units" composed of assembly-line workers.

The knife of the appropriate-unit clause also cuts along the seams of power. Supervisors, although operating in the same production area as workers, represent the interests and possess the powers of managers and are not to be represented in the same unit. A supervisor, according to the NLRA, is anyone entrusted with the authority to effectively recommend hiring and firing of employees. The intent of the law here was to separate individuals not only according to interests but also according to power.[16] Equality in the union hall depends on equality on the shop floor. The power to control the activity of workers in the process of production could coerce compliance from the powerless, even outside of the confines of the plant. Simply put, no one needs to be in the same union with someone who can fire you tomorrow.

At Ethicon the NLRB had no problem in identifying the appropriate organizational unit. All production workers, together with mechanics, comprised one block of interests at the plant, while quality-assurance personnel, supervisors, and white-collar workers comprised a different unspecified block of interests. Yet, as we have seen, production workers were told that they had power over the hiring, firing, wage-setting and disciplinary processes of the plant. Many of the tasks traditionally reserved for foremen or supervisors were entrusted to workers, and no matter how ultimate the power of management, the workers believed in their authority over each other. Such powers, granted as part of company policy, seemed to cast a reasonable amount of doubt on the appropriateness of the designated appropriate unit. It is understandable that the NLRB did not want to deal squarely with the issue. It is less clear how such a failure can help resolve the issue.

When workers are given authority over their peers while performing the same work, management has succeeded in fragmenting the labor force even more. The power to hire and fire, even if merely rhetoric, remains an effective measure for preventing workers from recognizing their common interests while identifying with the interests of management. In this way, quality circles veil not only the true nature of power, but also the true nature of powerlessness.

Epilogue

Working in a self-styled democracy can be a peculiar business. On the one hand, the existence of free labor unions is one of the accepted contours of the United States political landscape. Unions are free to solicit support from employees during an organizing campaign. If recognized by a majority of the work force, unions are free to bargain collectively with employers to determine their members' working conditions. On the other hand, employers are also free to wage bitter anti-union battles to ward off having to deal with an organized work force and its demands. In years past, this other hand sometimes wielded a club heavy enough to crush even the most ardent unionist's skull. In this day and age, the other hand is wrapped in the velvet glove of human relations.

Although the state does flex its brute muscle every once in a while in a predictable anti-labor direction (witness the Phelps-Dodge Strike from 1983 to 1985), most anti-union battles are now waged inside the heads of workers. The trick is to get inside the skull without crushing it. The trick is to let the employees fight the union while management upholds the democratic process, asserts the importance of maintaining American superiority in the world economic system, praises the integrity of the American worker. The trick, in short, is to veil the true nature of both power and control in the workplace.

A type of national corporatism has evolved that allows skilled work-design experts to orchestrate priorities and extract loyalties from workers. The company comes first; it offers jobs and rebuilds the economy. The image of the country, as represented by the national government, comes second; it offers corporations the exclusive right to rebuild the economy. Church and family surface when the government wishes to use them as symbols of what made and makes America great. Even the concept of individualism is shuffled off to the side both on the shop floor and at the national level. We are to "pull together" and regain our place militarily and economically. We, the workers, are to tighten our belts and work for the higher patriotism of renewing America's world leadership.

That this goal might be unreachable or anachronistic in the present and future world economy is seldom mentioned. That workers might simply be working for the boss, that the boss is simply working for money and cares about America's image only as it affects the "bottom line" are motivations that are never mentioned. Nor is it mentioned that the true purposes of the new managerial humanism are maintaining and increasing managerial power. These purposes remain veiled with ambiguous references to worker involvement and participation. Work relations in industry are designed and operated for the purpose of allowing the groups with power to maintain maximum control over various elements of the labor process.

We respond favorably to the type of smoke screen that emphasizes the human commonalities between workers and managers. We humans all have strikingly similar concerns about the well-being of ourselves and our loved ones. Most of us work to secure this well-being. Work-design experts can forge a strong sense of kinship and belonging by carefully emphasizing what we all have in common, the desire to survive. The realization that even our superiors face similar problems bonds us to them at an emotional level that discards class as an artificial barrier. At work, where inequality stares us in the face like a hypnotist, we grasp at promises that will make us equal, even for a moment, to our peers and to our bosses. We truly want to believe and perceive that we are all in this together, but such a perception would be largely illusory.

In addition, the idea of equality at the workplace is noticeably presented as an equality based on impotence. At Ethicon workers were encouraged to view supervisors as being helpless in the face of the commands of the higher-level managers for whom they were working; to see upper managers as working for the "company," and having to meet the company's demands for certain standards of performance, measured by costs and profit margins. The company, in turn, was working in and for local and national economic environments that had their own rules and regulations and that did not tolerate failure. The message was: We are all in this together because we are all equally impotent.

It benefits those with superior power to encourage the belief and perception that we are all equally subservient to unresponsive ultimate forces. The hierarchy of the workplace is then transformed from a structure derived from a division of interests into a structure merely responding to a necessary division of labor. If we are all in this together, we each have our duty to perform. The techniques of positive labor relations based on the human-relations approach to worker control encourage this unitary vision of the problem of work. Quality circles encourage the workers' perception that they belong to one big team, individuals doing their jobs for their own benefit and for the benefit of society.

This view tries to overlook the issue of who controls and has the power over whom, which is what separates workers from managers and the manipulated from the manipulators. If workers accept this chain of impotence they forsake their ability to facilitate change. Making demands of the shop floor supervisor or of the plant manager becomes analogous to killing the messenger. Workers thus accept the work environment as a result of the interplay of forces beyond their control. They accept their role as workers, and perform their duties and responsibilities for a higher good, a nobler goal.

The new humanism in management is, on the whole, a creation of business schools and personnel departments as they re-act to the age-old problems of controlling the labor force in an age of "new patriotism"—an age when America's might is being challenged on all fronts, and when the free enterprise system, unfettered, is being called upon to restore America's position as world leader. In the ideal (managerial) workplace workers would be unconcerned about power sharing with management because management, allegedly, is under attack and therefore needs all its power, including that provided by the workers, to fight off the attackers.

For the time being, mastering Japanese managerial techniques offers hope for American industry and diverts attention from the deep-seated sources of our economic decline. When our economic "system" accuses management of failing, management points the finger at the workers. Who do the workers blame? Based on lessons from the Japanese and from the history of industrial relations in the United States, managers are finding that the power vested in them by the capitalist system can be used to make workers blame each other and themselves. The success of this strategy depends on managerial ability to maintain control over all major decisions concerning workers.

What I found out at Ethicon was not only about work, but about how work is controlled; not only about the workers' hopes, fears, segmented daily routines and duties, but how through management's control of these hopes, fears, and routines, the workers themselves are controlled; not only about managers' view of work, but about their view of workers as problems to be solved. As part of their jobs, managers, consultants, and personnel directors in our society portray the power of new management as being democratic, enlightened, and benevolent. They portray workers as being patriotic and passive producers who, through their (newly acquired) intelligence and freedom, recognize their responsibility to serve and obey under the well intended superiority of management. When power sharing is not a genuine concern, however, the result of work innovations can be manipulation, intimidation, and co-optation, rather than democracy. It is time to announce that the emperor has no clothes.

The words of workers and organizers who refused to serve and obey came to mind as I synthesized the lessons of Ethicon. After the campaign, when the supposedly stable status quo had been restored, a worker who had been on the organizing committee was fired, as were various other union supporters, and she later related the circumstances that led to her firing. It became obvious to both of us that if she had fought for her job the way she had fought for her union, she would still be working at Ethicon, but she had grown tired of working for the company and all it entailed, the harassment, the manipulation. Artificial hassles had been piled on top of very real production hassles by "enlightened management." The campaign taught her how far management would go to avoid unionization, how much management "hates unions," and how much she, in turn, could hate management.

She had held up to the pressure this time by the skin of her teeth, she said. Next time, if there was a next time at another job, she would not be a militant organizer. For her own sake whenever possible, she would avoid frontal attacks by management. She hoped to work in an environment where a union already existed: "Having no power is no fun." If there were no union, and her employer proved to be as anti-union as Ethicon, however, she would not lead the battle. The union could count on her vote—she was sure now more than ever of the need for unions— yet she did not want to suffer again as she had suffered at Ethicon. "I am pro-union," she said, "but I am not a martyr."

Her responses were exactly what management wanted. The fear implanted in her would take a long time to dissipate. She would go out into the community, find another job, continue her associations. She would talk about her experiences at Ethicon to her friends and family as if relating a bad dream. They would sense her fear and she would deny it, claiming it was all over. But it wouldn't be all over because next time she would be fearful of the power of management. This type of humanized manipulation and control does not stop at the plant gate. Their effects, like an invisible pollutant, are carried into the community by victimized workers. Ethicon management had thus rendered a valuable service to the area's business community. Perhaps in recognition of this, the plant manager was elected president of the Greater Albuquerque Chamber of Commerce.

A certain inevitability develops about the relationship between managers and workers, so that the more workers expect to be used by managers as one would use a machine, the more this abuse becomes a "natural" aspect of work, and similarly, the more managers deny workers their rights, the more this denial will blend in as a natural condition of working. Managerial practices gain currency in geographic areas, and expectations about work are shaped and defined in the minds of the area's inhabitants. Rare was the Ethicon worker I talked with who did not relate some comment by a relative regarding how lucky they were to be working in such a nice place and how it would be against the worker's interest to put a job at Ethicon on the line for the sake of a union or a principle. Without ever having set foot inside the building, friends and relatives felt authorized, based on the J&J reputation, to praise the company and its work. The manipulation to which managers were willing to subject workers was seen to be of secondary importance, part of what working in a clean, attractive new plant was all about. Manipulation came to be accepted as the price an employee had to pay to work in a landscaped portion of the desert.

A veteran organizer of the National Union of Hospital and Health Care Employees-1199, who was closely in touch with the Ethicon campaign, remarked: "If nothing else, going through a union campaign will teach you how much employers can scare employees." At Ethicon to control meant to instill fear, but at another level fear was also a structural component of the relationship between worker and manager. Management's problem became how to intimidate without letting workers know they were being intimidated, how to institutionalize fear as a method of control. This was done by making workers fearful of the union and what it could not do for them, fearful of management and what it could do to them, and fearful of what they could do to each other at team meetings and on the shop floor.

Management "managed" to convince workers that power, like

some kind of magic potion, could anoint the chosen and abandon the condemned. Yet, management did not dole out powers indiscriminately. Only the power to punish could be safely granted to the chosen ones. Other powers were guarded by the elaborate new-design mythology. Ironically, those willing to be lulled by the new-design melody, to forget their interests long enough to help management maintain absolute control of all its powers, were the chosen ones. The condemned, awake and acting in accordance with their own interests, were those who challenged management's exclusive right to those powers. Only management stood to gain from fanning the flames of fear.

Workers at Ethicon were asked to accept as logical and good a system of social control based on peer pressure and intimidation. They were asked to accept as just a system of monetary rewards in the form of raises based on peer evaluations that pitted worker against worker and that made it a requirement for workers to "pay back" management for the time it took to learn to behave like efficient, well-oiled machines, as if management were doing them a favor.

No matter how ethical an employer, the firm's authoritarian manner of controlling a worker's life is challenged only by relentless democratic forces, such as health and safety restrictions, equal employment regulations, and, in many cases, unions. Few workers realize that the right we most frequently associate with democracy, the right to freedom of speech, is not guaranteed in the nonorganized private sector of our country. It was this right, among others, that some workers at Ethicon wanted to secure though a free election, and it was this right that was most dramatically and efficiently denied by management.

In spite of the large number of women and Hispanic workers at the plant, it would be a mistake to blame the defeat of the union on the passivity of women or on some interpretation of "traditional Hispanic values." The type of fear that the company inspired cuts through boundaries of sex and ethnicity. (The links between ethnicity, sex, and union activism are explored in a chapter by Lamphere and myself in Bookman and Morgan 1988). In understanding the effectiveness of the traditional and innovative approaches to union busting at Ethicon, the key factors are the economic vulnerability of the work force and the company's success in establishing clear boundaries of acceptable attitudes and behavior.

Utilizing a variety of forums, from team meetings to mass meetings, from impersonal group discussions to one-on-one sessions, managers made it clear that working at Ethicon implied having a particular set of personality attributes. A lack of these attributes implied personal deficiency (being a "loser") and also raised the possibility of termination. As the personnel administrator put it in his memo on combatting counterproductive activity, if employees cannot "commit to upholding . . . common sense rules . . . they would be better off pursuing other employment."

One woman worker addressed her response to fear and its effect on co-workers:

Some people react different to scare tactics. Me, I stand up and fight. That's the way I am. If someone threatens me, especially if I am boxed in a corner, I come out fighting. Some people don't. They give in to the threat. And I think that's what a majority of the people did do. They were afraid, afraid of losing their jobs, afraid of the humiliation you were put through . . . and you were humiliated. All these things added up and they just didn't want to go through with it. So they went to the side they thought would win.

Workers at Ethicon were frequently asked to forgive the apparent blunders of management. Managers told "their" people that this was a new company, a new experiment, that mistakes would be made, and made again, and that the workers had to forgive. The community was given the same message. A new plant in a new, traditionally nonindustrial environment was taking many chances and learning many new lessons, and the community that accepted the benefits driving from the new plant had to forgive the mistakes. This type of message confused the issue.

Ethicon was not a new company, and J&J was not a new employer. The company had a long tradition of working in all kinds of community environments. It had not stumbled upon Albuquerque in the dark while searching for a new plant. The corporate planning process had targeted the area for its overabundance of cheap labor and its nonunionized industrial environment. Ethicon-Albuquerque was a piece in the corporate chess board, but it was not a pawn. It was substantially more important than that. The workers were the pawns. How long the community and the workers would continue to give Ethicon-Albuquerque the benefit of the doubt was not certain.

A woman hired after the campaign was over told me of her hiring interview by the new personnel administrator (the social psychologist's former secretary). The woman was shown newspaper clippings about the campaign, told of the "union vandalism" that occurred, and otherwise warned of the terrible circumstances resulting from a "third party's" attempt to alter the existing and excellent working conditions. Once hired, she and other new employees attended a meeting with the plant manager where the union issue was again brought to her attention. It was a strange experience, she told me. The plant manager spoke about the union in a strange way. On the one hand, he stated that it was an individual's free choice to make, to be for or against the union. But then he also made clear that the choice to be for the union was not a wise one, that those who had made that choice before at this and other plants had regretted it. It should not be a decision made hastily, he made the audience understand, for the consequences were not trivial.

"We listened," she said, "and just nodded." Anti-unionism remained as much a part of the Ethicon philosophy as ever. The same worker recounted various experiences with her peers. "Everyone is brainwashed around here. People think that the company is doing them this great favor by giving them a job. I'm grateful, yeah, but I know that without us, the company couldn't make any sutures. It's not noble of them to hire me, it's necessary." This was a worker who knew her job, who did it well, and who knew her power. This was a worker who would one day fight for a union.

The observations detailed in this study have implied that the de-bureaucratized methods of control made possible by QWL programs such as QCs are very effective and pose a substantial threat to serious efforts to democratize the work environment. In effect, the study argues against the view that considers participation a sufficient condition for democracy. While workers at Ethicon did participate in enforcing the rules and regulations of the plant, they had no say in designing the rules. Their participation was allowed only in areas that did not threaten managerial control. They participated in the work process much as slaves participated in slavery—as captives of an economic and social structure beyond their control. Indeed, by eliminating the potential for opposition, participation was utilized as a form of control.

Although I have explored these manipulative and coercive aspects of QCs in a nonunionized environment, this study suggests certain policy guidelines for unions and union organizers. First, and of particular importance to unionist supporters of QWL programs, is the observation that QWL groups such as the QC develop their own dynamics once they are activated. As small-group theory suggests, the work group designs its own layers of stratification, supports its internally derived criteria for excellence, renders its distinct judgments over attitudes and behavior, and develops its own leaders and followers.

Unionists involved in QWL programs must be aware of these dynamics because policies and arguments developed by the complex organization of the union might be reinterpreted by the distinctly different dynamics of the small group. In this process, the problems identified and the solutions designed at the level of the complex organization might not strike responsive chords at the small-group level. The work group might not agree with decisions and strategies derived from more bureaucratized levels of the organization. No matter how strong or large the union, the small group stands as a potential barrier to solutions designed by union bureaucrats.

This means that unions will be forced to reach more than ever into the rank and file for leaders and supporters. The QWL program demands that workers be educated regarding the importance of unions in the attainment of true quality of work life. Not to do so ensures that managers duly trained in control and schooled in viewing QWL-QCs as the most significant managerial phenomenon of the 1980s will attempt to imprint their vision of work and work relations on workers. In this vision, unions often represent, at best, archaic and ineffective methods of satisfying worker self-interest and at worst, the primary cause of all problems in American industry.

On the bright side is the observation that the small-group environment could be used to favor organization efforts by the union. Organizers discovered during the postelection analysis of the voting patterns at the Ethicon plant that in QCs where at least two union sympathizers were verbal in their support, the union "won" the QC. Apparently by shattering the image encouraged by the company that union people are losers and deviants, organizers were able to gather the support of workers. It is significant that a team in which the initial contacts were made by the union immediately became a union stronghold and remained one until the end of the campaign, even after its meetings were suspended.

This result in teams with verbal pro-union support might be a function of the leadership patterns that develop in small groups. Organizers facing similar campaigns would do well to review this small group dynamics literature and apply the findings. For example, the extensive research on the elements of tasks and social and emotional leadership in small groups might help organizers identify key people in QCs and target them for house calls and other communications. It is essential that organizers develop an accurate view of each team member and his or her role in the group.

One clear implication of the QC experience at Ethicon is that organizing a QC plant should be done by targeting key individuals of each team and swaying them to the union side. Since most of those who vote for the union are not verbal in their support, it is important to enlist certain personality types in promoting the union line. This is common knowledge for most organizers but gathers new importance in campaigns that utilize QCs. The strategy here should be to identify the leaders of the small group rather than of the department or plant. Organize each individual QC, and you'll organize the plant.

Ironically, QCs offer the organizers an opportunity to "demystify" the very illusion QCs intend to foster: that the supervisor is just one of the "gang." By directing the attention of workers to the difference between the supervisor and themselves, organizers can use the proximity of members in the small-group meeting to lay bare class differences such as income, social activities, and aspirations and thus disarm one of the most effective functions of the small-group environment. Supervisory and non-supervisory employee groups can be exposed as being radically different. As supervisors try to convince workers that all are in the same boat, union organizers should point out which group beats the drum and which rows to the beat.

Organizers should find out immediately who is running the QC program. The training of the QC designer will tell a great deal about the dynamics, or at least the ideal dynamics, of the group. The expectations of a social psychologist about the performance of a QC and its members will differ from those of an industrial engineer, for example. Similarly, organizers should predict managers' use of the functions and dynamics of the QC as a method of control. For example, they should make it known as soon as possible that management will try to isolate QCs from each other during the campaign by creating intergroup conflict and by pitting pro-union against anti-union workers within each QC.

When conflict is encouraged among workers or between QCs, pro-union supporters should be trained to clarify the sources of conflict by always discussing the issues, not the people or groups involved. It is important to prevent management from attributing conflict situations to the union because this will encourage neutral people to turn away from the union simply to avoid conflict. In addition, organizers should make an analysis of each QC to see whether they are all working smoothly and to see how the supervisor handles the union issue and whether the workers like the supervisor. When the supervisor engenders conflict or is unable to control the topic of unionization in the QC, it becomes an ideal milieu because pro-union leaders can emerge as the stabilizing force in the group.

Finally, no organizer should ever oppose the QC program on principle. Doing so places the mantle of innovation on managers and supervisors while the union is once again depicted as an organizational dinosaur. Organizers should point out, however, the difference between decision making, pseudo decision making, and implementation of decisions. They should encourage employees to make self-interested changes through the quality circle. This will unveil the limited power allowed by management and the different interests involved in making true improvements in the quality of work life. From the perspective of worker power, the QC program at Ethicon was a failure because it did not offer the workers a voice—only an echo of management.

The union estimate of the costs of the campaign at Ethicon from May 1982 to May 1983, which included consultant expenses and lost production time due to anti-union meetings, put total company expenditures at a little under $1 million, a small bite off the $3-5 million a year in projected saving in wages, benefits, and bureaucratic expenditures by keeping the union out. The annual July pay raise for employees turned out to be $.30, rather than the $1.00 that was "promised" prior to the election. The union spent approximately $100,000 on salaries and costs in the organizing campaign. In addition was the expense of keeping some of the most effective organizers in the West bogged down for a year. Yet, to those involved, there was nothing tragic about the loss. They saw it as a first step in a frequently necessary process of education. "The workers didn't want it. They believed in management and all its promises. Management is right when it tells them only it can deliver. But they don't say that they won't unless they are forced to deliver by a union."

Elections often have to be held several times before workers recognize and accept the responsibility for controlling their own interests. The first step was taken. The union and the employees could go on to work toward the next challenge to managerial omnipotence at Ethicon-Albuquerque. Being optimistic comes from the conviction that occurrences such as what happened at Ethicon cannot be repeated indefinitely without repercussions. At some point the thin veneer of benevolence disintegrates and exposes a manipulative system of control operated by individuals not worthy of respect or allegiance. While fear definitely controls, it doesn't control indefinitely. Eventually, the fearful refuse to be fearful, and they resent those whose arrogant power kept them silent for so long. The union's strongest allies in subsequent organizing drives at Ethicon-Albuquerque are the experiences of this campaign. The union's strongest hope is that workers will remember them.

Notes

1. The best presentation of programs related to quality circles (QC) and quality of work life (QWL) in unionized industry is Mike Parker's *Inside the Circle* (1985). Although critical of present practices, Parker does not rule out these programs, if labor were to set the priority and design models for union implementation and control.

2. In addition, I was graciously granted access to data from numerous interviews conducted by another researcher at Ethicon during the campaign. Although her information about the work culture at the plant had nothing to do with anti-union strategy, the union issue surfaced frequently in her interviews. She frequently turned off her tape recorder, having been specifically advised by management not to discuss unions, but she received enough information to state in a paper presented at a professional conference: "There is some evidence that aspects of the high-involvement design are geared towards keeping the union out of the plant." Her independent research proved a valuable confirmation of my analysis (Lamphere 1982, 1984).

3. Strictly speaking, this is a study of how management went about making the attempt to control the work force in order to keep the company nonunion; it is not a study of how effective or successful management was. Because nearly 50 percent of the work force signed union membership cards (the usual measure of willingness to vote for the

199

union) and ultimately only 33 percent voted in favor of the union, it can be argued that the company was very effective in controlling the work force. I argue that fear, manipulation of small-group dynamics, and various sorts of managerial tactics decreased support for the union. Nevertheless, I cannot prove that the union would have won the election in the absence of these unethical and malicious tactics, nor is that the intent of this study.

CHAPTER 1

1. Other definitions have followed this general line with some authors specifying the size of group (six to sixteen) and others drawing criteria for participation, mostly emphasizing their voluntary aspect. Implicit in the Ouchi definition, and explicit in others, is the need for the group to be composed of workers from the same production unit. This allows for focused discussion on issues that are of immediate concern to all participants. Dewar's definition was typical (1980: 2): "a group of workers from the same area who usually meet for an hour each week to discuss their problems, investigate causes, recommend solutions, and take corrective actions when authority is in their purview."

2. According to Peter and Waterman (1983) in their popular presentation of current American managerial ideology, most of the "excellent" companies have been experimenting with QCs. This is not what makes them excellent, the authors are quick to add, but it does testify to their "bias for action" and innovation.

3. In recent years, QWL and QC have come to be nearly synonymous concepts. According to a foremost expert in QWL programs (Deutch 1984, personal correspondence), however, QWL refers to a broader set of work innovations that do not restrict themselves to the small group format of the QC. While most QWL programs include some sort of QC involvement, they supposedly deal with aspects of the worker's job other than participation in problem solving and decision making. Yet QCs are considered to be QWL innovations, especially in nonunionized workplaces, where they have been hailed as the most advanced type of QWL design. QWL and QC programs have spread rapidly in unionized industries. The first QWL contractual agreement, reached in 1973 between the United Auto Workers and General Motors, included small-group components. By 1981 one-fifth of all organized workers were covered by a contract that acknowledged the importance of an institutionalized QWL program (Burck 1981). This book considers QCs in this wider sense as QWL innovations.

4. See Parker (1985) for studies questioning the production efficiency of QCs in industry in the United States.

5. One study in the latter category measured democratization by measuring the involvement of employees in making suggestions. The study cited an increase of 50 percent in participation through suggestions by QC members as opposed to a decrease of 2 percent by nonmembers at a General Dynamics plant (Hunt 1981). This type of study has supported the criticism that considers QCs "glorified suggestion boxes" (Krishum 1983).

6. Although he now favors the development of QC and QWL programs in unionized industries, Thomas Donahue, AFL-CIO secretary treasurer, faced the problem directly a few years back when he stated: "At best the quality of worklife group concept poses a problem to the labor movement because of the potential that exists for management to penetrate and influence small, informal work groups to a degree, and on a scale . . . never dreamed of" (Donahue 1982b).

7. Given all this, we might expect a great deal of analysis of the role of quality circles in nonunionized environments. This is not the case. Mostly, studies of QCs and other QWL techniques have been done in unionized environments. The only contemporary study of the broad topic of participation (Witte 1980) discussed (briefly) small-group dynamics in a nonunionized plant. No study has dealt with the use of QCs as union-busting tools during an anti-union campaign.

CHAPTER 2

1. This drop is less attributable to the J&J image of being a "good" company than to the questionable expansion decisions made, which, according to some analysts, is taking the company dangerously away from its "knitting."

2. Although operations in the United States account for over one-half of J&J's total profit, rates of profit have been higher in foreign regions. In Europe, with 44 facilities, and in the rest of the western hemisphere, with 33, the operating profits as a percentage of identifiable assets surpassed those of the United States. The last two plant expansions have been in the Far East, one in Taipai by J&J Taiwan, Ltd., and another in Singapore by J&J Pte. Ltd. (from J&J's *1983 Annual Report*).

3. In 1959 the enigmatic General threatened to delist the company from the New York Stock Exchange rather than issue a proxy statement. He finally relented, but the tradition of maintaining a closed-door policy on its corporate affairs remains (Jensen 1971).

4. The San Angelo Ethicon plant, for example, achieved unionization by means of a union card check demanded by the Textile Workers Union and accepted as valid by management.

5. The purpose and results are stated in the *1981 Annual Report*:
The heart of it was getting small groups of workers together to see if they could suggest better ways of identifying and solving problems. There was skepticism on the part of both management and workers but the "quality circles," as they are popularly known, began to convene. Most were workers who did the same kind of work; others were groups from different departments whose work was connected.

The Special Care teams meet twice a month and continually present recommendations to management. As a result, new materials, new parts, new procedures, and new designs have been, and continue to be adopted. There have been other efforts to boost productivity but management credits the Special Care teams with much of the improvement. Most importantly, the high quality of the dialysis machine was reflected in virtually no customer complaints in two years. Other positive benefits abound: costs reduced by 20 percent despite inflation; an almost perfect safety record; absenteeism down by 75 percent and worker turnover down 60 percent.

CHAPTER 3

1. Pro-union workers said the benefits and functions of discussion changed as the union campaign progressed from being a way to identify pro-union employees to suppression of pro-union discussions in order to isolate these employees.

2. The innovative control design of Ethicon-Albuquerque is reflective of the J&J corporate structure, which has long had the reputation for being a lean, decentralized bureaucracy. The managers running its 200 plants enjoy an autonomy unheard of among industrial corporations. According to *Business Week* (1984), J&J's corporate headquarters staff is a "scant 750. And only one management layer separates division presidents from the 14-member executive Committee to whom they report." While other corporations labor to eliminate costly bureaucracies and increase control over operations, J&J is already there.

The decentralized system is part of the J&J tradition in management handed down from the General and the chief executive officer, who sees management efficiency as the key to the company's future (*The Sunday Star-Ledger* 1982: 9): "The only limitation to the company's growth will be that ability to manage. I don't know if we'll be able to do that by 1985 or 1990." Experiments in participative management through quality circles at J&J companies must be analyzed as part of the larger picture of corporate obsessions, as they attempt to increase control, and the efficiency of management to achieve corporate growth.

3. I expanded this practice to include taping official discussions with the social psychologist and other managers and relied on the tapes to check my notes and develop my analysis.

4. The extensive lack of scientific validity throughout the studies was noted by Alex Carey (1967). He pointed out that much of the increased productivity attributed to the effect of human relations had really resulted because rate busters, who had to support their families, were introduced into the work groups. Indeed, he finds no evidence of increased productivity resulting from "friendly supervision." Carey points out that "nearly all authors of textbooks who have drawn material from the Hawthorne studies have failed to recognize the vast discrepancy between evidence and conclusions in those studies, have frequently misdescribed the actual observations and occurrences in a way that brings the evidence into line with the conclusions, and have done this even when such authors based their whole outlook and orientation on the conclusions reached by the Hawthorne investigators." These and other significant critiques of the Hawthorne studies have had little influence on the managerial interpretation of events and the subsequent human relations school of ideas that bases worker control on this traditional interpretation.

5. The tendency for this facilitator to orchestrate his team meetings did not go unnoticed. A member of his team later stated: "I think he tried to create conflict. There really were some hard core (anti-union) people in our team. This is only a guess. But I think he got those people aside and said, 'This is what I want you to do—bring up such and such an issue. When I'm talking about something, cut in.' I can't say for sure, but that is what I suspect, because two or three of them were right on cue. They would chime up. And bring up personal experiences—really gung ho. These people had to be put up."

CHAPTER 4

1. For an excellent discussion of the concepts of exit and voice and their relationship to unionism see Freman and Medoff's *What Do Unions Do?* (1984).

CHAPTER 5

1. Desperation manifested itself in strange ways during strategy sessions. Each Friday, the eight top managers met, and the social psychologist, who was not only team developer but also one of the few managers seen daily on the production floor, reported on the status of facilitator control. At one of these meetings of the gang of nine, which were the main forum for communications between the various levels of management, someone raised the issue of references to union vandalism as a way of creating suspicion among employees. Although management had been making such references since August 1982, the social psychologist felt they had not been effective because, as he put it, "this union is not that way." Nevertheless, one manager suggested hiring security personnel to hide inside the cars of anti-union people and wait for "union-goons" to come around. The social psychologist raised the voice of moderation, insisting that this would be a waste of time and resources. He was outvoted eight to one, but as the wheels began to turn to carry out this tactic, the corporate lawyers came to town and shot down the idea by agreeing with him. This increased his prestige among his peers, and saved the company from some embarrassing moments as well.

2. They write: "The studies of illegal company opposition show that employer discrimination against union activists, particularly firing, . . . has a great impact on the success rate of unions, though the magnitude of the impact varies. Two studies estimate a drop in union success in the area of 7–10 points . . . while two others estimate declines in union success by 14–25 points. Only in the rare case where a fired worker is ordered reinstated by the NLRB and actually returns to his job before the election does breaking the law backfire."

3. At least one bit of evidence signals that corporate headquarters felt some apprehension over the psychological manipulation going on during this time. A flurry of ULPs filed by the union in January caused J&J's industrial relations expert to remark, according to a source: "What are you doing down there, screwing over the workers?" For the social psychologist, this type of reaction typified a lack of confidence in local managers. By comparison, the legal consultant's reaction was more to the liking of managers; he undermined the importance of the charges, calling them "chicken shit" and difficult to prove. These charges referred predominantly to interrogation and surveillance, the easiest offenses to commit and the hardest to prove, and thus the most frequently committed. The lawyers knew this, as did management. "We are never going to

admit to surveilling our employees. Never," said the social psychologist. As long as all facilitators held this line, the company was safe.

CHAPTER 6

1. Worker participation was evaluated in numerous studies by measuring the amount of control workers exercised over different aspects of the work process (Child 1973). Control was evaluated by measuring the degree of influence workers wielded in enterprise decision making. Poole (1975) identified two levels at which workers could exert power on the formal patterns of decision making within a firm: (1) In on-the-job decision making, workers were viewed as having some right to organize their activities in the production process within certain discretionary limits, the limits being set by the production technology that controlled their work activity. (2) In the work group or work team decisions could cover production questions, especially when group activities were involved in the actual production process. However, at this level a number of further possible decision-making areas could involve the workers actively. As a rule, however, management has sought to determine these areas unilaterally and to define them as its "prerogatives," for example, in hiring and firing, starting and stopping times, the distribution of wages, hours of work, and overtime.

2. On the ambiguity of causal links see Coch and French (1959) and Das (1964). In a comprehensive study of participation experiments in industry, Blumberg (1968: 123) marveled at the level of agreement on the results of participation: "There is hardly a study in the entire literature which fails to demonstrate that satisfaction in work is enhanced or that other generally acknowledged beneficial consequences accrue from a genuine increase in workers' decision-making power. Such consistency in findings . . . is rare in social research."

3. For example, Bowers and Seashore (1976: 203) measured leadership styles among managers and discovered that various performance variables in firms are negatively affected by traditional, nonparticipative structures. Regarding business growth, for example, they wrote: "Business growth is high when the agent force does not hold a classical business ideology; when regional managers, by accepting the opinions and ideas of their agents, encourage professional development; and when managers reduce rivalries among agents by encouraging their interaction. . . . This paradigm presents a picture of growth through cooperative professionalism."

4. Discussions of the methods of control in literature from the view of management has addressed the question (Tosi 1983: 271): "How is the behavior of individuals and groups influenced so as to ensure that members act in ways to minimize problems and maximize their compliance with organization norms, policies, and goals?" The concepts of leadership qualifications, formalization, employee selection, socialization into specific work cultures, the reward system, job descriptions, and technology are all components of the control structure of a firm. The new-design plant utilizes the additional focus on human relations in an attempt to direct and control work relations between supervisory and nonsupervisory personnel as well as between nonsupervisory workers.

5. Echoing the observations of Tannenbaum (1968), they wrote: [Worker] participation can often bring about a system of control much more substantial and effective than that in a traditional industrial bureaucracy." They proposed that "successful managers foster an atmosphere of support so that members working in the organization feel a sense of personal worth and importance." The result "is more, not less control than is usually found in organizations," control meaning managerial domination of interactions resulting in higher productivity, and predictable profits.

6. According to Edwards (1979: 18), a true system of control must coordinate three elements of the relations of production within the firm: (1) the direction of work, (2) evaluation of product and worker, and (3) discipline of the work force. He also spoke of three types of control mechanisms, each corresponding to a specific era of capitalist development. Simple controls are characterized by face-to-face interactions between the owner-entrepeneur and the worker. They developed during the early periods of capitalism and they continue today in parts of the secondary market sector of our economy. As firms increased in size, they were supplemented by a hierarchical command structure that increased the power of the supervisor while keeping the worker subservient to management.

Technical controls are regulated by the operations of the technological processes of production. Although Edward's argument was elaborate, for our purpose we can simplify it without distorting it by saying that machines and engineering logic rather than the firm's head control employees' behavior. The last stand made by this type of control was at Lordstown in 1972, when a worker revolt signaled that technical controls by themselves would no longer be sufficient to control the work force and the additional mechanisms of bureaucratic control would be required. Bureaucratic controls are dominated by the submissiveness of the individual personality to the "rules by rules," and policies and manuals detail the parameters for behavior. Predictability is increased by following the written word. Bureaucratic controls are the dominant form of behavior control in the core industries, the large firms operating in the economy today.

7. Asked by a colleague to describe what she liked about working at Ethicon, one worker responded by directly addressing the issue of the "friendly management" (Lamphere and Grenier 1988: p. to come): "Feeling important . . . and how it associates with other people. . . . I like everything about the job. The management people; they are so nice, they are just so down-to-earth people. They are never really your bosses as much as your friends. They have never taken that superior attitude over us. Never. They have an open door policy. Any time we want to, we can go up and talk to them."

CHAPTER 7

1. The personnel director took a similar position at a large bank in New Mexico almost immediately after leaving Ethicon. The social psychologist reportedly got employment as a management consultant.

CHAPTER 8

1. The concrete industrial applications of the system, despite humanizing efforts, almost always meant the use of time and motion studies to devise wage-incentive systems. By 1940 the system was sufficiently appealing to entice over 90 percent of American industry into adopting the wage-incentive aspects of scientific management (Horning 1940).

2. While before the war no more than three million belonged to the ranks of organized labor, membership doubled after the war, mostly swelling the ranks of the AFL, which, unlike the Socialists and Wobblies, favored the war effort.

3. He recognized two types of soldiering: the natural form, which derives from the instict of men to take it easy, and the much more insidious systematic form, which grows out of workers' associations with other workers with the deliberate object of keeping employers ignorant of how fast work can be done. See Simmons and Mares (1983) for a good review of Taylor's approach to industrial relations.

4. Fritz Roethlisberger, a researcher in charge of interviewing, com-

mented as a social scientist about these results. He observed that such aspects of work as wages, hours, and working conditions, were not "things in themselves" (Roethlisberger and Dickson 1939: 374–75):

They must be interpreted as carriers of social values. . . . To understand the meaning of any employee's complaints or grievances, it is necessary to take account of his position or status in the company. This position is determined by the social organization of the company: that system of practices and beliefs by means of which the human values of the organization are expressed, and the symbols around which they are organized—efficiency, service, etc. In these terms, it is then possible to understand the effects upon the individual of . . . the events, objects, and features of his environment, such as hours of work, wages, etc.

5. The introduction in 1935 of the Wagner Act, also known as the National Labor Relations Act (NLRA), made it more difficult for employers to deal with workers on an individual basis, especially during union organizing campaigns. This, in turn, increased the need to formalize relations with employees through regular personnel work.

6. With the influx of women into the work force during the war years, the use of subtle control mechanisms increased. Counseling was found to be particularly effective for the female work force, and its use spread.

7. The most significant development in labor-management relations during this time was the Scanlon Plan. This power- and profit-sharing program initiated by unions did not support small-group manipulation; rather it promoted equal knowledge of a firm's economic conditions on the part of workers and managers. Its basic premise was that labor should profit from labor savings and the company should profit from a better use of its assets, that is, greater sales, lower unit costs. See Frederick Lesieur, *The Scanlon Plan*, for a good review of its successes and failures.

8. Participation was combined with small-group dynamics at Atlantic Richfield based on the realization that members tended to accept the decisions of their group. Group pressures were correctly assessed as being so relentless that regardless of personal convictions, conformity to a group decision was virtually guaranteed. Similarly, Cessna Aircraft advised that the "group leader's job is to mold the human weaknesses of his men and women in the proper direction." Alfred J. Marrow, president of the Harwood Manufacturing Company and a Ph.D. in psychology, said (Baritz 1960: 187) that leaders in his company "must be prepared to channel discussion so that the group decision springs from the persons in the group and is agreed to unanimously by them."

Lewis Corey (1950), a professor of political economy at Antioch College, said that the Harwood system of participation was "vicious" and that the effect of dividing workers into small groups or "teams" was to "fragmentize the labor force and make managerial control of it easier." He said: "The objectives of this usage of 'group dynamics' are to get the workers to accept what management wants them to accept but to make them feel they made or helped to make the decision." He went on to say that the system was at best "paternalistic and at worst despotic."

9. Poole (1975: 48) presented a typology of forms of participation initiated by management:

Direct participation: (1) piecemeal attempts by management to raise productivity and efficiency while reducing conflict and increasing workers' satisfaction on the basis of work-group participation, "total participation" exercises; (2) joint consultation in primary working groups; (3) job rotation, job enlargement, job enrichment; (4) suggestion schemes, employee shareholding and other profit-sharing schemes, co-partnership, "commonwealth" ventures.

Indirect participation: (1) joint consultative committee; (2) specific committees covering productivity, welfare, and safety; the administration of various trust funds; and so on; (3) productivity bargaining.

10. A basic question raised by Blumberg (1968: 129) regarding worker participation deserves restating. It addresses the issue of control facing both management and workers today: "To what extent does private ownership and control of modern industry place sharp limits upon the amount of participation that is structurally possible? Given the demonstrated beneficial effects of participation, to what degree is its application inherently limited by the framework of private ownership?"

11. See Freeman and Medoff (1984) for a thorough analysis of the political successes and failures of labor.

12. Brown (1986), Schmidman and Keller (1984), Hogler (1984). Fulmer and Coleman (1984) argue the opposite position.

13. These three factors arose out of the *NLRB v. Cabot Carbon Co.* decision (1959), in which a committee set up by the employer to deal with grievances, labor disputes, wages, rates of pay, and conditions of work was considered a "labor organization."

14. I witnessed an interesting form of bargaining between two teams led by the same facilitator. Team 1 presented a proposal to Team 2 asking for a change in the usual procedures for evaluating peers for their six-month raises. Team 1 wanted to give the raise to anyone who was "improving," even if the worker had not attained the production requirements prescribed by the learning curve. Team 2 did not agree. As

one worker put it: "Either you make your numbers or you don't. Improving only counts in horseshoes and hand grenades." Team 2 reminded the facilitator that they were autonomous and that Team 1 had no right to make decisions for them.

The facilitator presented himself as neutral in the conflict. He wanted the teams to make the decision. "This is the type of decision I would like both teams to make," he said. "Consistency is needed but not at the expense of the self-determination of the group." He then asked Team 2 to select three representatives to meet with the representatives of Team 1 to hammer out an agreement. He would set up the meeting with the other team. The matter was settled a few weeks later. The production requirements for six-month raises were maintained.

When I told the social psychologist about the process, he accused the facilitator of acting improperly. The decision, whatever it was, should have been made unilaterally by the facilitator after consulting with the teams. At no point should he have lost control over the vital decisions of team operations. Various training sessions had already reminded facilitators to make decisions without asking for the approval of the team.

15. Employers providing facilities and other compensations to employee organizations have been found guilty of unlawful "assistance and support." Other employers have been found guilty of domination by setting up employee committees, by designating committee members, or by controlling the agenda. See Brown (1986) for a good review of existing practices.

16. According to the NLRA, the term "supervisor" is defined as "any individual having authority, in the interest of the employer, to hire . . . discharge . . . or effectively to recommend such action." The term "employer" includes "any person acting as an agent of an employer, directly or indirectly."

Bibliography

Achilles, P. S. 1941. Commemorative address on the twentieth anniversary of The Psychological Corporation. *Journal of Applied Psychology* 25: 609–18.

AFL-CIO. 1981. Positive Labor Relations. Draft photocopy.

AFL-CIO News. 1983. The union buster's shadowy world. No. 160. Reprint of December 1982 and January 1983 articles.

———. 1981. GE slapped for subtle anti-union tactics. 26: 8.

Allied Industrial Worker. 1981. Study cites threat of anti-union consultants. 25:7.

American Center for the Quality of Worklife. 1981. Quality Circles. Washington, D.C.

American Productivity Center. 1980. Quality circles tighten purchasing, reduce defects—case study 9, Waten Associates, Inc. Houston.

———. 1981. Modified quality circles produce savings, create cooperative atmosphere—case study 17, Tektronix, Inc. Houston.

———. 1982. Quality circles expand to involve 1,000 blue and white collar staff—case study 22, Northrup Corporation. Houston.

Argyris, C. 1964. Integrating the Individual and the Organization. New York: Wiley.

Aspin, L. 1966. A study of reinstatement under the National Labor Relations Act. Ph.D. dissertation. Cambridge: Massachusetts Institute of Technology.

Babbit, R. C. 1981. One company's approach to quality circles. *Quality Progress.* October: 28–29.

Backer, H. J., and H. Q. Overgaard. 1982. Japanese quality circles: a managerial response to the productivity problem. *Management International Review* 22: 13–19.

Bailey, K. E. 1984. Union busting in the public sector. Paper presented at Southern Belt Labor Studies Conference, University of Texas, Arlington, March 30.

Baird, J. 1981. Quality circles may substantially improve hospital employees' morale. *Modern Healthcare* 11: 70–74.

Balfour, C., ed. 1973. Participation in Industry. London: Croom Helm.

Baritz, L. 1960. The Servants of Power: A History of the Use of Social Science in American Industry. Middletown, Conn.: Wesleyan University Press.

Bartlett, E. D. 1927. A test to gauge business knowledge. *Personnel Journal* 6(3): 199.

Bendix, R. 1956. Work and Authority in Industry. Berkeley: University of California Press.

Bendix, R., and L. H. Fisher. 1949. The perspectives of Elton Mayo. *Review of Economics and Statistics* 31(4): 312–21.

Bendix, R., and M. S. Lipsett, eds. 1967. Class, Status and Power. London: Routledge & Kegan Paul.

Benge, E. J. 1920. Grouping workers to get best results. *Factory* 24(8): 1332–33.

Bernstein, J. 1980. Union busting: from benign neglect to malignant growth. University of California—Davis Law Review. Fall: 11.

Bernstein, P. 1976. Workplace Democratization: Its Internal Dynamics. Ohio: Kent State University Press.

Bingham, W. V. 1928. The personnel research federation in 1928. *Personnel Journal* 7(4): 300.

Blauner, R. 1964. Alienation and Freedom. University of Chicago Press.

Bloomfield, M. 1915. The new profession of handling men. *Annals of the American Academy of Political and Social Sciences* 61: 121–26.

Bluestone, I. 1981. The union and the quality of worklife process. Paper for Work in American Institute, Inc. Photocopy.

Blumberg, P. 1968. Industrial Democracy: The Sociology of Participation. London: Constable.

Bly, S. E. 1980. Japanese Management Systems: A Comparison with U.S. Management Systems and the Application to U.S. Industry. Ph.D. dissertation. Little Rock: University of Arkansas.

Bottomore, T. B., and M. Rubel, eds. 1964. Karl Marx: Selected Writings in Sociology and Social Philosophy. New York: McGraw-Hill.

Bowers, D. G., and S. E. Seashore. 1976. Predicting organizational effectiveness with a four-factor theory of leadership. In Participative Management. Concepts, Theory and Implementation, edited by E. Williams. Atlanta: Georgia State University School of Business Administration Publishing Services.

Brandeis, L. 1936. Letters. New York: Doubleday.

Braverman, H. 1974. Labor and Monopoly Capital: The Degradation of Work in the Twentieth Century. New York: Monthly Review Press.

Brody, E. W. 1982. Japan's quality control circles fall flat for American hospital industry. Modern Healthcare 12: 96.

Broussard, K., and H. Langford. 1984. Quality circles get around but will they circle health care? Lafayette: University of Southwestern Louisiana. Paper draft copy.

Brown, R. C. 1986. Labor law issues facing multinational and Japanese companies operating in the U.S. and U.S. companies using Japanese-style labor relations: Agenda items under the "new labor relations." University of Hawaii Law Review 8 (Summer): 261–337.

Bryant, S., and J. Kearns. 1981. The quality circle program of the Norfolk Naval shipyard. Manufacturing Productivity Frontiers. September: 34.

Burck, C. G. 1981. What's in it for the unions? Fortune 104(4): 88–92.

Burns, J. E. 1982. Honeywell quality circle boom part of growing American trend. Industrial Management 24: 12–14.

Business Week. 1936. How Proctor and Gamble do it. July 4: 31–34.

——. 1953. Psychologists at Work. September 19: 52.

——. 1979. The anti-union grievance ploy. February 12: 117.

——. 1984. Changing a corporate culture. May 4: 130–38.

——. 1981. The new industrial relations. May 11: 85–98.

Calhoon, R. P., and C. A. Kirkpatrick. 1956. Influencing Employee Behavior. New York: McGraw-Hill.

Carey, A. 1967. The Hawthorne Studies: a radical criticism. American Sociological Review 32: 3; 403–16.

Child, J., ed. 1973. Man and Organization. London: Allen and Unwin.

Clawson, D. 1980. Bureaucracy and the Labor Process: The Transformation of U.S. Industry, 1860–1920. New York: Monthly Review Press.

Clegg, H. A. 1960. A New Approach to Industrial Democracy. Oxford, England: Blackwell.

Clegg, S. 1977. Power, organization theory, Marx and critique. In Critical Issues in Organizations, edited by S. Clegg and D. Dunkerley. London: Routledge & Kegan Paul.

————. 1979. The Theory of Power and Organization. London: Routledge & Kegan Paul.

Clegg, S., and D. Dunkerley. 1980. Organization, Class and Control. London: Routledge & Kegan Paul.

Coch, L., and J. R. French. 1959. Overcoming resistance to change. In Group Dynamics, edited by D. Cartwright and A. Zonder. London: Tavistock.

Cole, R. 1979a. Quality control circles in Japan: their value to the U.S. Paper presented at Quality of Working Life and Productivity Conference, New York, May 9.

————. 1979b. Made in Japan—quality control circles. Across the Board 16(11): 73–78.

————. 1979c. Work, Mobility and Participation: A Comparative Study of American and Japanese Industry. Berkeley: University of California Press.

————. 1980a. Some principles concerning union involvement in quality circles and other employee involvement programs. Paper presented at Employee Participation Workshop, March. Detroit: Solidarity House. Photocopy.

————. 1980b. Learning from the Japanese: prospects and pitfalls. Management Review. September: 22–42.

————. 1981. QC warning voiced by U.S. expert on Japanese circles. World Work Report 6: 49–51.

Conte, M. 1982. Participation and performance in U.S. labor-managed firms. In Participatory and Self-Managed Firms: Evaluating Economic Performance, edited by D. Jones and J. Svejnar. Mass.: Lexington Books.

Corey, L. 1950. Human relations minus unionism. Labor and Nation 6(2): 50.

Courtright, W. E. 1981. Hughes circles: an update. The Quality Circle Journal 4(3): 30–34.

Crawford, A. 1982. Jersey's power and sometimes light. The (Moorestown) Sunday Record. April 18, Section E.

Cummings, L. 1980. Improving Human Resource Effectiveness. Berea, Ohio: ASPA (American Society of Personnel Administrators) Foundation.

Curtin, E. R. 1970. White Collar Unionization. New York: National Industrial Conference Board.

Cushing, D. 1980. Should you train to keep unions out. Training 17: 61–65.

Dahl, R. A. 1957. The concept of power. *Behavioral Science* 2: 201–18.

———. 1961. Who Governs? Democracy and Power in an American City. New Haven, Conn.: Yale University Press.

———. 1970. After the Revolution? Authority in a Good Society. New Haven, Conn.. Yale University Press.

Dahrendorf, R. 1959. Class and Class Conflict in Industrial Society. Conn.: Stanford University Press.

Dailey, J. J., and R. L. Kageres. 1980. A primer on quality circles. *Supervisory Management* 27: 40–43.

Das, N. G. 1964. Experiments in Industrial Democracy. New York: Asia Publishing House.

DeMaria, A. T. 1980. How Management Wins Union Organizing Campaigns. New York: Executive Enterprises Publication Co.

Deming, W. E. 1967. "What happened in Japan?" *Industrial Quality Control* 24(2): 91.

Derber, M. 1970. The American Idea of Industrial Democracy, 1865–1965. Urbana: University of Illinois Press.

Deutsch, S., and S. Albrecht. 1983. Worker participation in the United States: efforts to democratize industry and the economy. *Labour and Society* 8(3): 243–69.

Dewar, D. L. 1979. Quality Circles: Answers to 100 Frequently Asked Questions. Red Bluff, Calif.: Dewar and Associates.

———. 1980. The Quality Circle Guide to Participation Management. Englewood Cliffs, N.J.: Prentice-Hall.

Dewar, D. L., and J. P. Beardsley. 1977. Quality Circles. Mento, Calif.: International Association of Quality Circles.

Dickens, W. F. 1980. Union Representation Elections: Campaign and Vote. Ph.D. dissertation. Cambridge: Massachusetts Institute of Technology.

Dickson, J. W. 1981. Participation as a means of organizational control. *Journal of Management Studies* 8(2): 158–65.

Dollars and Sense. 1983. Union busting today: rats teach old dogs new tricks. 85: 8–9; 18.

Donahue, T. R. 1982a. Labor looks at quality of worklife programs. Paper presented at Labor Research Center, University of Massachusetts, Amherst January 7. Photocopy.

———. 1982b. Analysis Section. Bureau of National Affairs *Daily Labor Report* 96: 1–3.

Dunsire, A. 1978. Control in a Bureaucracy. New York: St. Martin's Press.

Edwards, R. 1979. Contested Terrain: The Transformation of the Workplace in the Twentieth Century. New York: Basic Books.

Eisenstadt, S. N. 1959. Bureaucracy, bureaucratization and debureaucratization. *Administrative Science Quarterly* 9: 6–37.

Electrical World. 1918. Team System is thought to be best labor solution. 72(7): 298.

Ellenberger, J. N. 1982. Japanese management: myth or reality? *AFL-CIO American Federationist.* April–June: 3–12.

Employee Gazette. 1983. Mind the quality, feel the effect. 91 (June): 220.

Ephlin, D. 1982. In *Bureau of National Affairs Daily Labor Report* (analysis section) 95: 1–3.

Ewen, S. 1976. Captains of Consciousness: Advertising and the Social Roots of the Consumer Culture. New York: McGraw-Hill.

Faltz, R. G. 1982. QWLs effect on productivity. *Personnel Administration* 27: 20.

Fox, A. 1971. A Sociology of Work in Industry. London: Collier-Macmillan.

Freeman, R., and J. Medoff 1984. What Do Unions Do? New York: Basic Books.

Fulmer, W. E., and J. Coleman. 1984. Do quality-of-work-life programs violate Section 8(a)(2)? *Labor Law Journal* 35(11): 675–84.

Gibney, F. 1982. Miracle by Design: The Real Reasons Behind Japan's Economic Success. New York: Times Books.

Glaberman, M. 1981. Is it quality or is it control in the quality control circles? *Labor Notes.* August 26: 9–10.

Gottchalk, E. C. 1980. U.S. firms worried by productivity lag, copy Japan in seeking employee advice. *Wall Street Journal,* February 21: 48.

Greenberg, R. S. 1981. Quality circles grow, stirring union worries. *Wall Street Journal,* September 22: 1.

Grenier, G. J. 1983. Twisting quality circles to bust unions. *AFL-CIO News.* May 14: 4–8.

———. 1984. Quality circles in an anti-union strategy. Paper presented at Southern Belt Labor Studies Conference, University of Texas, Arlington, March 30.

———. 1985. Quality circles and union busting. Presentation to Industrial Relations Research Association monthly forum, Denver, Colo., March 26.

Guest, R. H. 1979. Quality of worklife—learning from Tarrytown. *Harvard Business Review* 57(4): 76–87.

Haire, M. 1954. Group dynamics in the industrial situation. In Industrial Conflict, edited by Kornhauser et al. New York: Wiley.

―――. 1962. The concept of power and the concept of man. In Social Science Approaches to Business Behavior, edited by G. Strother. Homewood, Ill.: Dorsey Press.

Haire, M., E. Ghiselli, and L. Porter. 1966. Management Thinking. New York: Wiley.

Hall, J. 1982. Managing for greater productivity. *Advertising Management* 47: 20–28.

Hancock, W. M. 1982. Quality, productivity, and workplace design. *Journal of Contemporary Business* 11: 107–14.

Hansen, W. 1981. True confession: my life in a quality circle. *Labor Notes.* August 26: 8–10.

Hayes, R. H. 1981. Why Japanese factories work. *Harvard Business Review* 59(4): 57–66.

Herwig, M. 1985. Academic fingers quality circles as runaround. *Colorado Labor Advocate* 63(11): 3.

Hirszowics, Maria. 1981. Industrial Sociology: An Introduction. Oxford, England: Martin Robertson.

Hogler, R. 1984. Employee involvement programs and *NLRB v. Scott & Fetzer Co.:* The developing interpretation of Section 8(a)(2). *Labor Law Journal* 35(1): 21–27.

Homans, R. 1983. Labor struggles. *New Mexico Business Journal.* December: 16–20.

Horning, E. S. 1940. Some problems in wage incentive administration. Conference Board Reports, Studies in Personnel Policy (*CBR, SPP*) 19: 17.

Hoyt, D. 1984. Quality circles: short term fad or long term trend? Paper presented at Southern Belt Labor Studies Conference, University of Texas, Arlington, March 30. Photocopy.

Hunt, B. 1981. Measuring results in a quality circle pilot test. *The Quality Circle Journal* 4(3): 18–23.

Hutchins, D. 1983. Quality circles in context. *Industrial and Commercial Training* 15: 80–82.

Hutchinson, J. 1970. The Imperfect Union. New York: Dutton.

IBEW [International Brotherhood of Electrical Workers] *Journal.* 1980. Unionized construction workers are more productive. 79: 4–5.

Ingle, S. 1982a. Quality Circles Master Guide: Increasing Productivity with People Power. Englewood Cliffs, N.J.: Prentice-Hall.

―――. 1982b. How to avoid QC failure in your company. *Training and Development Journal* 36: 54–59.

Jacobs, A. D. 1982. Productivity improvements—beyond quality circles or how I.E.'s can work smarter, not harder. *Industrial Management* 24: 3–5.

Jensen, M. C. 1971. J&J spans life cycle. *New York Times*. July 25: 1, 4.

Johnson, R., and W. Ouchi. 1974. Made in America (under Japanese management). *Harvard Business Review* 52(5): 22–31.

Johnson, R. W. 1947. Or Forfeit Freedom. Garden City, N.Y.: Doubleday.

Jones, D., and J. Svejnar, eds. 1982. Participatory and Self-Managed Firms: Evaluating Economic Performance. Mass.: Lexington Books.

Jones, W. G. 1983. Quality's vicious circle. *Management Today*. March: 96–98.

Juran, J. M. 1967. The QC circle phenomenon. *Industrial Quality Control* 23(7): 329–36.

———. 1978. Japanese and western quality: a contrast in methods and results. *Management Review* 67(11): 27–48.

Kamata, S. 1983. Japan in the Passing Lane: An Insider's Account of Life in a Japanese Auto Factory. New York: Pantheon Books.

Kanter, R. M. 1982. Dilemmas of managing participation. *Organizational Dynamics* 11: 5–27.

Karpel, J., R. Spencer, T. Schamberger, and W. Klein. 1983. Record ring: moving toward solutions—a quality control circle in a medical record department. *American Medical Record Association Journal* 54: 15–20.

Klein, H. 1982. Productivity seminars grow but draw fire. *The Wall Street Journal*. June 17: 27, 31.

Klein, S. M., and K. W. Rose. 1982. Formal policies and procedures can forestall unionization. *Personnel Journal* 61: 595–601.

Knowles, W. H. 1955. Personnel Management. New York: Wiley.

Kochan, T., H. C. Katz, and N. R. Mower. 1984. Worker Participation and American Unions: Threat or Opportunity. Working Paper. Boston: Alfred P. Sloan School of Management.

Konyha, W. 1980. The union buster's shell game; now you see us, now you don't. *Carpenter* 100: 40–41.

Konz, S. 1981. Quality circles: an annotated bibliography. *Quality Progress*. April: 30–35.

Krishum, K. 1983. Worker participation at Ethicon. Paper prepared for union involved in case study. Confidential photocopy.

Lagerfeld, S. 1981a. The pop psychologist as union buster. *American Federationist* 88: 6–12.

———. 1981b. To break a union. *Harpers*. May: 18.

Lamphere, L. 1982. Bringing the family to work: women's culture in an apparel factory. Paper presented at meeting of American Anthropological Association, Denver, December 6.

Lamphere, L., and G. Grenier. 1988. "Women, Unions, and 'Participative Management': Organizing in the Sunbelt." In Women and the Politics of Empowerment, edited by Ann Bookman and Sandra Morgen. Philadelphia: Temple University Press.

Landsberger, H. 1958. Hawthorne Revisited. Ithaca, N.Y.: Cornell University Press.

Lawler, J. 1981. Labor-management consultants in union organizing campaigns. Paper presented at 34th annual meeting of Industrial Relations Research Association, Washington, D.C., 1983.

Lesieur, F. 1958. The Scanlon plan: A frontier in labor-management cooperation. Cambridge: Technology Press, Massachusetts Institute of Technology.

Levitan, S., and C. Johnson. 1982. A view of labor management cooperation. John Herling's Labor Letter 32(43): 1–4 (Washington, D.C.).

Likert, R. 1961. New Patterns of Management. New York: McGraw-Hill.

Lipset, S. M., M. A. Trow, and J. Coleman. 1962. Union Democracy. New York: Anchor Books.

List, C. E. 1982. How to make quality circles work for your organization. Personnel Journal 61: 652.

Lloyd, B. 1982. Does more input from employees mean higher mill efficiency and a better product? Daily New Record. August 2: 4–6.

Lynch, D. 1981. Circling up Japanese style. American Way. April: 34–41.

Macarov, D. 1981. Humanizing the workplace as squaring the circle. International Journal of Manpower 2: 6–14.

Magnum, M. 1981. Quality circles. Personnel Journal 60: 424.

Makin, C. 1983. Ranking corporate reputation. Fortune 107(1): 34–39.

Management Review. 1981. Quality circle survey shows significant change in participants' attitude. 70(8): 29.

———. 1982. Research Spotlight. 71(9): 56–58.

Mandel, E. 1973. Workers' control and workers' councils. International 2: 1–17.

Manz, C. C., and H. P. Sims. 1982. The potential for "groupthink" in autonomous work groups. Human Relations 35: 773–84.

March, J. G. 1955. An introduction to the theory and measurement of influence. American Political Science Review 49: 431–51.

March, J. G., and H. A. Simon. 1958. Organizations. New York: Wiley.

Maser, M. 1982. Mount Sinai invests in quality circles. Health Services Manager 15: 12–13.

Maser, M., and E. Randall. 1981. Implementation at Mount Sinai Medical Center of Greater Miami. The Quality Circle Journal 4(3): 16–19.

Mayo, E. 1933. The Human Problems of an Industrial Civilization. New York: Wiley.

———. 1945. The Social Problems of an Industrial Civilization. Cambridge, Mass.: Harvard University Press.

McGregor, D. 1960. The Human Side of Enterprise. New York: McGraw-Hill.

McMurry, R. N. 1944. Handling Personality Adjustments in Industry. New York: Wiley.

McNeil Consumer Products Company. 1981. Problems, perspectives, and strategies in creating a "new design" organization: Round Rock, Texas. (Booklet.) Minneapolis: McNeil.

Melossi, D. 1980. Strategies of social control in capitalism: a comment on recent work. *Contemporary Crisis* 4(4): 381–402.

Metz, E. J. 1980. Caution: quality circles ahead. *Training and Development*. August: 71–85.

Mills, C. W. 1956. White Collar. New York: Oxford University Press.

———. 1959. The Sociological Imagination. London: Oxford University Press.

Mills, T. 1975. Human resources—why the new concern? *Harvard Business Review* 53: 120–34.

Miner, J. B. 1975. The Challenge of Managing. Philadelphia: Saunders.

Mitchell, D. 1979. Control Without Bureaucracy. London: McGraw-Hill.

Moch, M., and A. Huff. 1983. Power enactment through language and ritual. *Journal of Business Research* 11: 293–316.

Montgomery, D. 1979. Worker's Control in America. New York: Oxford University Press.

Moore, H. 1939. Psychology of Business and Industry. New York: Wiley.

Mozina, S., J. Jerovsek, A. Tannenbaum, and R. Likert. 1976. Testing a management style. In Participative Management: Concepts, Theory and Implementation, edited by E. Williams. Atlanta: Georgia State University School of Business Administration Publishing Services.

Munchus, G. 1983. Employer-employee based quality circles in Japan: Human resources policy implications for American firms. *The Academy of Management Review* 8(2): 255–61.

Murphy, D. F. 1981. Discriminatory dismissal of union adherents during organizing campaigns. *Industrial Relations Law Journal* 4: 61–89.

Nadworny, M. J. 1955. Scientific Management and the Unions, 1900–1932. Cambridge, Mass.: Harvard University Press.

National Industrial Conference Board. 1931. Industrial Relations. New York.

————. 1936. What Employers Are Doing for Employees. New York.

Newfield, J. 1966. A Prophetic Minority. New York: New American Library.

New Mexico Employment Security Department. 1984. New Mexico and Albuquerque Area Hours and Earnings Estimate. February.

O'Neill, H. 1982. Quality circles: let's try to make it work. *Industrial and Commercial Training* 14: 279–85.

O'Toole, J. 1981. Making America Work: Productivity and Responsibility. New York: Continuum.

Ouchi, W. 1977. The relationship between organizational structure and organizational control. *Administrative Science Quarterly* 22: 95–114.

————. 1981. Theory Z. New York: Avon.

Ouchi, W., and M. A. Maquire. 1975. Organization control: two functions. *Administrative Science Quarterly* 20: 559–69.

Parker, M. 1985. Inside the Circle: A Union Guide to QWL. Boston: Southend Press.

Parker, M., and D. Hansen. 1983. The circle game. *The Progressive*. January: 32–35.

Parrish, J. 1985. U.S. labor relations in revolution. *The Journal of The Institute for Socioeconomic Studies* 9(4): 23–36.

Pascale, R., and A. Athos. 1981. The Art of Japanese Management: Applications for American Executives. New York: Simon & Schuster.

Pateman, C. 1970. Participation and Democratic Theory. London: Oxford University Press.

Pennock, G. A. 1930. Industrial research at Hawthorne. *Personnel Journal* 8(5): 296–313.

Perry, N. 1984. America's most admired corporations. *Fortune*. January 9: 50–62.

Peters, T., and R. H. Waterman. 1983. In Search of Excellence: Lessons from America's Best-Run Companies. New York: Warner Books.

Pickard, C. O. 1944. Small group plan. *Personnel Journal* 23(6): 236.

Pinyan, C. 1984. In these circles workers can affect quality. *Rocky Mountain News*. August 14: 21.

Plous, F. K. 1981. The quality circle concept: growing by leaps and bounds. *World Work Report* 6: 27–37.

Poole, M. 1975. Workers' Participation in Industry. London: Routledge & Kegan Paul.

Productivity Digest. 1982a. Let's hear it from a quality circle. January 1.

————. 1982b. Quality circles at Pneumafil. May 5.

Ramsay, H. 1977. Cycles of control: worker participation in sociological and historical perspective. *Sociology* 11(3): 27–57.

Rehder, R. R. 1979. Japanese management: an American challenge. *Human Resources Management* 18: 21–27.

Reich, R. B. 1983. The Next American Frontier. New York: Times Books.

Rendall, E., and M. Maser. 1980. Using quality circles in the health services. *Training* 4(6): 12–14.

Ridgeway, C. L. 1982. Status in groups: the importance of motivation. *American Sociological Review* 57(1): 76–88.

Roach, J. M. 1973. Worker Participation: New Voices in Management. New York: The Conference Board.

Robbins, S. P. 1983. Theory Z organization from a power-control perspective. *California Management Review* 25(2): 67–75.

Robertson, D. H. 1923. The Control of Industry. New York: Harcourt, Brace.

Roethlisberger, F. J. 1942. Management and Morale. Cambridge, Mass.: Harvard University Press.

Roethlisberger, F. J., and W. J. Dickson. 1939. Management and the Worker. Cambridge, Mass.: Harvard University Press.

Rolland, I., and R. Janson. 1981. Total involvement as a productivity strategy. *California Management Review* 24: 40–48.

Rowland, A. D. 1984. Combining quality control circles and work simplification. *Training and Development Journal.* January: 90–91.

Salaman, G., and K. Thompson, eds. 1980. Control and Ideology in Organizations. London: Open University Press.

Sasaki, N., and D. Hutchins, eds. 1984. The Japanese Approach to Product Quality: Its Applicability to the West. New York: Pergamon Press.

Schmidman, J., and K. Keller, 1984. Employee participation plans as Section 8(a)(2) violations. *Labor Law Journal* 35(12): 772–80.

Schumpeter, J. 1942. Capitalism, Socialism, and Democracy. New York: Harper & Row.

Schwartz, H., and J. Jacobs. 1979. Qualitative Sociology: A Method to the Madness. New York: Free Press.

Scott, J. 1946. Team work. *Modern Management* 6(4): 59–69.

Scott, W. G. 1962. Human Relations in Management: A Behavioral Science Approach. Homewood, Ill.: Irwin.

Selznick, P. 1953. TVA and the Grass Roots. Berkeley: University of California Press.

Shelby, L., and R. A. Werner. 1981. Quality circles forge a link between labor and management. *Defense Management Journal* 17(2): 40–45.

Shepard, J. 1971. Automation and Alienation: A Study of Office and Factory Workers. Cambridge: Massachusetts Institute of Technology Press.

Simmons, J., and W. Mares. 1983. Working Together. New York: Random House.

Small Business. 1980. Productivity teams. 5: 21–25.

———. 1980. QC circles: a productivity tool. 5: 20.

Soyka, D. 1981. Honeywell pioneers in quality circle movement. World Work Report 61: 65–67.

Statistical and Tactical Information Report. 1984. Organizer survey. April: 1–6.

Steinmetz, L., and C. D. Greenridge. 1976. Realities that shape managerial style: participative philosophy won't always work. In Participative Management: Concepts, Theory and Implementation, edited by E. Williams. Atlanta: School of Business Administration Publishing Services.

Storey, J. 1983. Managerial Prerogative and the Question of Control. London: Routledge & Kegan Paul.

Sunday (Newark, N.J.) Star-Ledger. 1982. J&J's planners looking to new opportunities. August 29: 5, 9.

Takeuchi, H. 1981. Productivity: learning from the Japanese. California Management Review 23(4): 5–19.

Tannenbaum, A. S. 1956. Control structure and union functions. American Journal of Sociology 61(2): 127–40.

———. 1968. Control in organizations. In Control in Organizations, edited by A. S. Tannenbaum. New York: McGraw-Hill.

———, ed. 1968. Control in Organizations. New York: McGraw-Hill.

Tannenbaum, A. S., and R. L. Kohn. 1957. Organizational control structure. Human Relations 10(2): 127–40.

Taylor, F. W. 1947. Scientific Management. New York: Harper & Row.

Tead, O. 1933. Human Nature and Management. New York: Wiley.

Thompson, P. C. 1982. Quality Circles: How to Make them Work in America. New York: AMACOM.

Tosi, H. 1983. The organizational control structure. Journal of Business Research 11: 271–79.

Training. 1982. People building is essence of QC way. 19: 12.

Training/HRD. 1980. Honeywell imports quality circles as long-term management strategy. August: 91–92; 94.

U.S. Department of Health, Education and Welfare. 1973. Work in America. Cambridge: Massachusetts Institute of Technology Press.

U.S. General Accounting Office, Human Resource Development. 1982. Concerns Regarding Impact of Employee Charges Against Employees for Unfair Labor Practices. Washington, D.C.: GAO.

United Way of Greater Albuquerque. 1981. Human Services Needs Assessment: Special Analysis. Planning and Allocation Division.

Vogel, E. F. 1979. Japan as Number One: Lessons for America. Cambridge, Mass.: Harvard University Press.

Wall Street Journal. 1984. Labor Report. November 20: 1.

Walton, R. E. 1979. Work innovations in the United States. Harvard Business Review 57(4): 88–98.

Watts, Glenn. 1982. In Bureau of National Affairs Daily Labor Report, analysis section, no. 96: 1–3.

Weber, M. 1947. The Theory of Social and Economic Organizations. Fairlawn, N.J.: Oxford.

———. 1961. Three types of legitimate rule. In Complex Organizations: A Sociological Reader, edited by A. Etzioni. New York: Holt, Rinehart and Winston.

Weinstein, J. 1968. The Corporate Ideal in the Liberal State, 1900–1918. Boston: Beacon Press.

Werther, W. B. 1982. Quality circles: key executive issues. Journal of Contemporary Business 11(2): 17–26.

Whitehead, T. N. 1936. Leadership in a Free Society. Cambridge, Mass.: Harvard University Press.

———. 1938. The Industrial Worker. Cambridge, Mass.: Harvard University Press.

Witte, J. F. 1980. Democracy, Authority and Alienation in Work: Workers' Participation in an American Corporation. University of Chicago Press.

Wood, R., F. Hull, and K. Azumi. 1983. Evaluating QCs—the American application. California Management Review 26(1): 37–53.

World Wide. 1982. New design manufacturing at Round Rock. 17(1). Somerville, N.J.: J&J.

World Work Report. 1980. U.S. Chamber of Commerce finds workers want to raise productivity; seek recognition, decision-making role. 5: 73.

———. 1981. Quality circles boost productivity in North Carolina state offices. 6: 65.

Wright, E. O. 1976. Class boundaries in advanced capitalist societies. New Left Review 98: 3–41.

———. 1978. Class, Crisis and The State. London: New Left Books.

Wright, E. O., C. Costello, D. Hacken, and J. Sprague. 1982. The American class structure. American Sociological Review 47: 709–26.

Wright, P. J. 1979. On a Clear Day You Can See General Motors. Grosse Point, Mich.: Wright.

Yager, E. 1979. Examining the quality control circle. *Personnel Journal* 58: 682.–703.

———. 1980. Quality circles: a tool for the 80s. *Training and Development* 34: 60–62.

Yoakum, C., and R. M. Yerkes, eds. 1920. Army Mental Tests. New York: War Department Documents.

Zucker, S. (and the *Business Week* team). 1982. The Reindustrialization of America. New York: McGraw-Hill.

Zimbalist, A., ed. 1979. Case Studies on the Labor Process. New York: Monthly Review Press.

Zwedling, D. 1980. Workplace Democracy. New York: Harper & Row.

Index

AFL-CIO, 162
Albuquerque *Tribune*, 148
"Alienated worker," 173
Amalgamated Clothing and Textile Workers Union (ACTWU), xvii, 107, 122, 140; and Ethicon campaign, 61–68, 79–80; and Johnson & Johnson, 67–69
American Academy of Political and Social Science, 161
Answers to union questions booklet, 68
Anti-union campaign, 149; cost of, 197; employee reaction to, 191
Anti-union committee, 175. *See also* Committee Opposing Organized Labor
Anti-union meetings, 66, 82, 83, 142
Anti-union strategy, 60; design of, 99; and employee evaluations, 83; and employee experiences, 93–96; and employee reactions, 147; and employee screening, 69; facilitator training in, 106; and fear, 78, 111–13, 151; and firings, 100–6; and informa-

tion control, 106–8; and psychological strategy, 106–8, 124–25, 136–37; and proactive strategy, 58–60; and social psychologist, 98–99, 106, 136–37; and status deprivation, 100–101; and team meetings, 74–78; and pitting worker against worker, 88–97. *See also* Committee Opposing Organized Labor, Management Consultants, Quality circles, Teams
Anti-union workers, 58–60, 74–78; in Committee Opposing Organized Labor, 88–90
Anti-unionism, 14–22; and Hawthorne experiments, 167–71; and human relations, 13, 158–84; and Johnson & Johnson, 36–38; and Tayolorism, 161–62, 166–67. *See also* Small groups
Appropriate unit determination, 183
Archbishop of Santa Fe, office of, 149

Back pay, xvii, 155
Bloomfield, M., 161
Braverman, H., 131, 162